*Agape,*
*Moral Meaning*
*And*
*Pastoral Counselling*

# *Agape, Moral Meaning And Pastoral Counselling*

## *Simon J. Robinson*

Aureus

First Published 2001

©2001 Simon J. Robinson

Front cover: 'The Presence' ©Laurence Pusey

ISBN 1 899750 09 6

Printed in Great Britain.

A catalogue record for this book is available from the British Library.

Aureus Publishing Limited, 24 Mafeking Road, Cardiff, CF23 5DQ, UK.
Tel: (029) 2045 5200 Fax: (029) 2045 5200
Int. tel: +44 29 2045 5200 Int. fax: +44 29 2045 5200
E-mail:   sales@aureus.co.uk
          meuryn.hughes@aureus.co.uk
Web site: www.aureus.co.uk

# Contents

# *Preface*

I began to think about this book in a sabbatical spent in New College, Edinburgh. There are few better places to think and to be challenged, and few better mentors than Duncan Forrester who gave me the space. I thank him and David Lyall for their support.

Yet even that space was nothing as that given to me by my family for that three months. My wife Angie, daughter Sarah, and son Jamie all gave me permission to be absent. Doubtless they will say that being absent is nothing new. I thank them for a tolerance I do not deserve, and promise to love them better.

Whilst in Edinburgh I was privileged to experience another space, created by the profound hospitality of my uncle and aunt in law Douglas and June McKinnon, who I stayed with in Larbert. I thank them for their friendship.

As I write I have heard of the death of Douglas. Douglas McKinnon was a rare breed. He was a high achiever, head of the Scottish Mutual, but a man who kept his feet firmly on the ground. He worked with the big picture but was acutely aware of the small details, and especially the small personal details. A man of learning he was also a man of popular culture, even to supporting Glasgow Rangers. He exuded warmth, humour, spirit and challenge, in many ways summing up the agape I have tried to write about.

I dedicate this book to him and to his memory.

Leeds, 23 January 2001

# Introduction

'Counselling is dedicated to increasing the autonomy of the individual and providing the environment in which individuals can find their own answers to their own questions. The Christian religion on the other is based on the idea that it possesses truth and knowledge which is revealed to it by God. The Christian Church professes to know what is right behaviour in a significant number of situations, notably in the area of sexual behaviour. Since this area is one which impinges upon virtually all human beings, and certainly many of those who seek counselling, I do not understand how a pastoral counsellor can be encouraging autonomy in a client when he or she knows the 'right answer' to a dilemma being presented to him or her. How, for example can a Catholic priest 'counsel' on the matter of abortion? Encourage, support, instruct, yes: counsel, no. How can an evangelical church worker counsel on the matter of sexual relations outside marriage? How can a Church of England clergyman counsel on the matter of homosexual relations?' (Julia Buckroyd, Review of David Lyall, Counselling in the Pastoral and Spiritual Context, *Journal of the British Association of Counselling*, Nov. 96, Vol 7, No. 4).

Julia Buckroyd sums up the gulf that many practitioners in and outside the church see as existing between counsellor and pastor. Firstly, the main aim of counselling is said to be the increase of autonomy of the individual. She does not attempt to define what this self rule might mean, but it clearly for her involves learning, and hence the *increase* of autonomy, and enabling the individual to take responsibility for her own situation and life meaning. This would seem to broadly espouse the Rogerian view of counselling and learning which seeks to enable the person to make their own decisions.

Secondly, over against this autonomy is the institution of the church which, it is argued, is concerned with moral norms derived in some way from the underlying life meaning and community narrative. Such norms do not seek to take away the autonomy of the individual but they do assert a moral truth which applies to all and which thus in some way determines what the moral end of any situation or problem should be. In general terms the pastor knows the moral parameters, especially in such areas as abortion or homosexuality, even if there may be some leeway when the casuistry is worked through. Therefore, argues Buckroyd, the church cannot be concerned primarily with the autonomy of the individual and should stick to moral guidance.

The debate in these terms rapidly becomes polarised and begins to operate on two levels. Firstly, how is the term autonomy to be defined in pastoral care? As the debate is charted it will become apparent that there are many different meanings of autonomy and freedom being used, including *negative freedom* (freedom *from*), *positive freedom* (freedom as enabling the person do something, freedom *to*), and *moral freedom* (freedom to make moral decisions- often associated with the development of virtues). It is important for these to be clarified and to see how they fit into a broad Christian Ethic.

The second area of debate concerns moral meaning and how it is communicated. Is morality primarily a set of rules, or is it about detailing and assessing consequences, or is it largely about moral character and Christian community, or is it about liberation from different oppressive forces? What we believe ethics to be greatly influences how we see moral meaning being dealt with in the counselling process.

All this takes place in the context of the broader debate about post-modernity. This questions whether the 'grand narratives' which underpinned a common view of moral meaning in the past have any meaning now. For many this also questions the possibility of having any agreed set of moral principles, even within the church. This debate highlights another critical tension, that between content and process. Some would argue that it is important to share a common meaning, others argue that the important thing is how any moral meaning is reached. At both extremes of this debate lies fear- fear of a contentless, relativistic morality, and fear of a content dominated approach will take no account of human dynamics.

In the first chapter of this book the recent history of the debate about ethics and pastoral care and counselling will be reviewed, examining different ways of balancing the demands of autonomy and moral meaning. I will conclude that tensions within the debate cannot be simply resolved, but rather have to be held together.

Chapters two and three argue that the only effective way of holding together freedom and moral meaning, process and content, is through the concept and experience of *agape*.

In these chapters I will firstly examine the nature of agape, with a stress on *faithfulness, veracity, vocation, mutuality*, and *forgiveness*. Agape provides the bridge which enables interpersonal relationships, giving power to the other and enabling the perception of and reflection upon the truth of her situation, including her relationships with herself and others. This holds together several different views of freedom. The process also involves an underlying spirituality which is not simply an understanding of life meaning - mediated often through symbolic understanding - but also a way of knowing, being aware of the other and the self. This forms the basis of care.

Secondly, I argue that agape provides the basis for Christian Ethics. It is the irreducible moral attitude, but also informs substantive moral principles, strengthens the specific moral rules and enables different principles to be held in tension. The focus of this moral meaning is the process of reflection and learning which not only enables the proper concern for principles but also enables creative transformation of the person and of the situation as a whole. It is important to note that agape is essentially embodied, and that an understanding of agape comes as much through the experience of that agape as through any reflection on concepts or practice. Such an awareness of embodied agape involves a testing of its congruence over a period of time.

The second part of the book examines the agapeic counselling process. In chapter four I begin by examining the moral world of the counsellee. Many of the writers in this area implicitly or explicitly assume that there is no moral engagement there before the counsellor might or might not raise the moral agenda. I will argue that the moral agenda is engaged from the word go in the way in which a dialogue is set up at various levels between the counsellor's unconditional ethic of agape and the conditionality of the counsellee's moral world.

Chapters five and six work through the counselling process and the way in which agape enables the freedom of the client to develop and also contributes to the moral meaning of the relationship and by extension to the wider moral experience of the counsellee and her social network. They conclude that the dynamic of agape in counselling is fundamentally about challenge and transformation, and that this precludes moral directiveness.

Chapter seven tests the conclusion of chapter six on cases which seem to demand ethical direction from the counsellor and examines the implications of this for the church and church discipline. Chapter eight examines counselling in its socio-political context and works through questions of love and justice.

I conclude that church has little to fear from the development of such agapeic freedom. On the contrary, it provides an approach to Christian Ethics which enables a critical awareness of the church's narratives and moral principles and the development of moral meaning in and through practice, without losing the distinctiveness of the gospel or any sense of continuity. In a postmodern era this provides a view of morality which can develop real confidence, and yet involve a dialogic openness to other traditions. This also provides congruence between the public and pastoral face of the church.

This is a book which focuses on practice, and which demands that theology and ethics be viewed in the light of that practice. Throughout, unless context demands it, I have used the female gender in referring to counsellee and counsellor. This is purely in the interest of inclusive language.

# I

## The Debate

### History

Pastoral care in its Judeo Christian history was always firmly rooted in broader religious and ethical commitments. In ancient Judaism care was practised in the context of a corporate and communal sense of responsibility. Within this there were different elements of care ranging from the advice and instruction of the sages to the prophetic concern for justice and righteousness that extends to all members of the community and beyond. Later the scribes developed the functions of systematising and re-coding the Mishnah (oral law), and of advising members of the synagogue about how the law applied in their lives. All this was in the context of a covenant theology, and God's care for the people of Israel.

The caring ministry of Jesus took place within the framework of the Jewish law and, far from sidelining the religious and ethical insights, he sought to reinforce the inner meaning of this law over against any ritual requirements (Schrage 1988, 40-62).

It would however be wrong to say that ethics and care came together as a seamless web, not least because there was continual debate over moral and religious meaning. Walter Brueggemann notes the very different ethical and religious narratives in the Old Testament of the Torah, Kingship, Prophets, Wisdom, and the Cult (Brueggemann 1997). Jesus himself was at the centre of debate which continuously questioned how the ethical/ ritual rules related to practice. Wayne Meeks reminds us that the most striking aspect of the ethos of the early church was its multiplicity:

'Christians responded in different ways to the peculiar ecology of culture in which each group found itself and to the peculiar pressures and opportunities that each had experienced. Christians disagreed amongst themselves on such fundamental questions as how one ought to treat one's own body, whether marriage and the raising of children were good or evil, whether the powers of government were instruments of God or the devil' (Meeks 1993, 213).

Nonetheless, we can say that the debate took place within the context of a shared religious framework, where all participants acknowledged some form of transcendent spiritual reality. Hence, as McNeill writes of the early church reflected in the Epistles, the task of the shepherd was 'to create an atmosphere in which the intimate exchange of spiritual help, the mutual guidance of souls, would be a normal feature of Christian behaviour' (McNeill 1977, 85). Thus whilst there may have been different ethical narratives at least the broad connections between spirituality, care and morality remained intact.

In broad terms five major factors can be said to be responsible for the severing of those connections: The Reformation; the Enlightenment; the emergence of a pluralistic culture; the growth of dynamic psychology; and the increase in professional care and the related growth in therapies.

*The Reformation.* This has been held responsible for many things not least the rise of capitalism. Martin Luther's Protestant individualism also made a clear break with the penitential system which had effectively kept ethics and pastoral care together since Gregory the Great. Ethical decision making was now increasingly a matter for the prayer life of the individual and the mutual examination of the faithful.

*The Enlightenment.* Whilst assessments of this time (late 17th century - 18th century) differ there is no doubt that the work of philosophers reinforced the individualism of the Reformation with a great concern for the autonomy of the rational decision maker.

Immanuel Kant sums up this concern for freedom as follows:

'Enlightenment is man's emergence from its self imposed nonage. Nonage is the inability to use ones own understanding without another's guidance... *Sapere aude* "Have the courage to use your own understanding" is therefore the motto of the enlightenment' (quoted in Gay 1973, 384).

*Post modernity.* Whilst there remains debate as to what this era might involve, there is no doubt that the second half of the twentieth century has seen an increase in both ethical pluralism and liberalism, leading to the questioning of any overall moral map. Pluralism recognises that there are in fact many different ethical narratives in any culture - something highlighted by modern media. In the light of that the former grand narratives - not least those underlying the Judeo-Christian view of ethics - have lost any privileged position.

Liberalism, with its stress on the right to hold the individual's belief and values, also stands out against the grand narratives asserting their power. This carries with it a sense that no values can be challenged unless the consequence of holding those value leads to the diminishment of another's freedom. This has two consequences. Firstly, the publicness of morality tends to recede. Values and related beliefs become private and are not to be examined or challenged. Secondly, ethical discourse tends to centre on individual rights.

*Dynamic psychology.* Sigmund Freud and his followers opened up a new world of unconscious drives, instincts and conflicts. They argued that many values were based not upon rational reflection but upon other unconscious agendas, many of which were the result of parental oppression and which would in turn lead to oppressive behaviour. Ethical ideas and injunctions were thus often seen as destructive to the ego, increasing suffering rather than promoting healing. The thrust of this was to influence pastoral care away from simple moral guidance into self exploration and self discovery.

*Professional Care.* With the rise of the psychological healing professions came the stress on technique, scientific skills and knowledge. Hartman, for instance, argued that psychoanalytic theory was essentially a practical science, 'a kind of technology', and as such was neutral to all questions of morality (see Strunk 1990). This is very much allied to the medical model of health which sees psychotherapy and counselling as forms of healing, or talking cures.

After the second world war two factors took these developments further. Firstly, there was 'the coming of the counsellors'. Paul Halmos focused on the rise of several professions, including counsellors, psychologists and social workers, who, he argued, took over the pastoral care role formerly occupied by the clergy (Halmos 1964). They were motivated by a form of love which was informed by the unconfessed hope in 'a kind of humanistic Kingdom of God' (Campbell 1984, 8). However, such a hope did not involve advice or direction in counselling. On the contrary it led the counsellor to give power to the client to take responsibility for handling the many antinomies which emerge in the counselling process.

Secondly, Carl Rogers built on many of these elements in developing the concept of non-directive counselling. Like Freud, Rogers was concerned about the negative effect of moral injunctions upon the development of the person. The aim of counselling was to enable the client to free herself from the imposed conditional standards which were 'conditions of worth'.

Counselling then was not about the transmission of values or guidance but rather the space to discover one's own values. The source of any value system would then be the individual herself, as she reflected on her experience and clarified for herself the important values and principles in her life. Hence, for Rogers it was important that the whole process was non-directive, with the counsellor providing simply acceptance and positive regard, empathy and congruence (Rogers 1942).

Unlike Freud, this approach did not demand a major theoretical underpinning, or the skills of analysis. Also, unlike Freud, Rogers had a far more positive view of human nature. Given the essential trustworthiness of human nature, client centred therapy would lead the counsellee somewhere along the way to being a fully functioning person, summed up as, 'the individual who has experienced optimal psychological growth - a person functioning freely in all the fullness of his organismic potentialities; a person who is dependable in being realistic, self enhancing, socialised, and appropriate in his behaviour; a creative person, whose specific formings of behaviour are not easily predictable; a person who is ever changing, ever developing, always discovering himself and the newness in himself in each succeeding moment of time' (Rogers 1983, 295). Needless to say no such person actually exists. It is rather a theoretical model which demonstrates what counselling is aiming for.

Such a concern for moral neutrality and non-directiveness was taken up by many pastoral care writers. Tom Oden, for example, analyses concepts such as empathy and acceptance in theological terms. Empathy, for example, reflects the prior truth that God himself has entered into the human experience through the Incarnation. The unconditional acceptance of the client reflects the covenant relationship of God with humanity (Oden 1966).

Seward Hiltner argued that counselling should be 'eductive' in nature (Hiltner 1958). The pastoral counsellor should bring a non judgmental, client centred approach to the relationship and through empathic reflection enable the counsellee to bring forth or educe her own approaches and initiatives. This same approach was to enable the counsellee to reflect on and develop her own values and value systems, to act as the framework within which difficulties would be addressed.

None of this is to say that Hiltner broke away from a theological framework. He used the method of correlation as set out by Paul Tillich, which broadly involved identifying problems from experience and then demonstrating how the Christian response could answer them. This often became a dialogic process with experience raising questions of the theology.

Howard Clinebell continued this tradition but modified it, noting that the counsellor may well have to stress different approaches, from supportive, to more directive, to reality testing, depending upon the situation (Clinebell 1966).

## The Trouble with Counselling

Faced by the increased professionalisation of the counselling function and the increase in plurality the churches have been severely challenged. There is a concern to make clear the difference between the secular and the religious counsellor; a concern to not lose focus of the importance of moral meaning; and a concern not to uncritically swallow the secular counselling approach.

Hence, the critique of counselling and its moral neutrality is both of the counselling culture *per se* and of the application of that culture to pastoral care, and can be seen under three heads: value neutrality; counselling as therapy; communication of value.

### Value Neutrality

Firstly, it is hard to see how the counselling process can be seen as value neutral when in fact the very definitions and classification of mental health and illness are so filled with moral assumptions. The Diagnostic and Statistical Manual (US,1987), for instance, ambitiously attempts to classify a full range of psycho-social functioning, leading to the conclusions that all abnormalities are in some way illnesses. However, whilst the dementias and psychoses can be easily categorised as illness, it is less easy to see substance abuse, psycho sexual disorder, problems of impulse control, such as stealing gambling or firesetting as forms of sickness. Their definition depends upon questions of responsibility and the effects upon others, as well as relationships to the law. The so called personality disorders also involve strong moral overtones. Some, such as obsessive-compulsive disorders seem to deprive the patient and others of certain freedoms, pleasures and effectiveness. Others, such as histrionic or antisocial disorders are viewed as disorders precisely because they radically affect others.

Richard Erikson concludes:

'The point is that the attempts to describe human behaviours in non evaluative terms break down. Clinicians can and do make moral judgements, formally and informally, clinical euphemisms notwithstanding. The question is why clinicians are so committed to portraying themselves as morally neutral' (Erikson 1994, 83).

Similarly in psychology the work of Lawrence Kohlberg sets out stages of moral development which are clearly linked to the maturation of the person. The stages are hierarchical, sequential and invariant - the person has to progress through each in order. Though Kohlberg does not intend to be judgmental about any of the stages it is clear that the development of moral autonomy and moral responsibility are seen as part of the what it is to be a healthy and mature person (Kohlberg 1984).

Don Browning amplifies this, arguing that moral and life meaning is a critical part of the development of the person and thus the counsellee. Hence, 'To minimize value confusion, to clarify the objects and values worthy of peoples loyalty, is to contribute to their emotional and mental well being' (Browning 1976, 99).

An absence of worked out life meaning and moral relationships is precisely what leads to many peoples unhappiness: 'Without a fund of normative, religiocultural meanings and symbols, the general confusion about the nature of good in living will itself be enough to cause untold personal difficulties, muddled lives, overt illnesses and emotional conflicts' (Browning 1976, 98).

Browning also argues that it is precisely the church which we would expect to have a concern for these elements of moral meaning, over against any narrow therapeutic aims. Hence, he develops the idea of pastoral care, and by extension pastoral counselling, which will facilitate a mode of enquiry which enables the church member to work through the moral meaning in their life. The person becomes the ethicist in her own life - searching for the norms, and working out her own moral decisions.

Quite apart from the concern of the church with values, others argue that its is simply not possible to be value neutral in the counselling process. The concern to respect the dignity and autonomy of the patient simply obscures the fact that the therapist has a belief system and that related expectations are subtly communicated through interpretations, feedback, selective attention, body language and tone of voice. As Erickson argues,

'Therapists cannot not influence patients. The question is (a) whether therapists are clear in their own minds about the belief systems they are conveying and how their belief systems relate to competing value systems and (b) whether therapists are direct or indirect in communicating their sets of values (Erikson 1994, 84. See also Halmos 1964).

Some therapists argue that this is to concentrate too much on the cognitive side of any therapeutic relationship, and that the real focus of therapy is feelings. Dealing with feelings has to be value free, not least because of the danger of judgementalism. However, even reference to feelings involves values. The counsellor may view feelings as appropriate or inappropriate, positive or negative, and with that there is a judgement about those feelings and the values which they reflect.

## The therapeutic model of counselling

The most recent attacks on counselling, from a religious perspective, have come from Gordon Graham and Alan Billings. Both are careful to note that they are not arguing against the practitioners of counselling as such but against the concept of 'psychological healing' (Graham 1990; Billings 1992).

Firstly, they argue that it is not certain what the theoretical basis of that healing is or whether such theories are practically testable. There is a bewildering array of different theoretical schools ranging from Gestalt, with its emphasis upon the here and now, to primal therapy with the emphasis on birth trauma, to transactional analysis with its focus on ego states and the life scripts chosen by the counsellee. Some seek to have the counsellor or therapist making interpretations, others demand that the client frames her own. Some focus on the person and others look to relate to the wider grouping - as in family therapy.

Without a clear theoretical underpinning, it is very hard to see just what healing in counselling and psychotherapy can mean. Indeed Graham argues for the 'debilitating flexibility' of the therapeutic model of counselling. He uses the example of a paper delivered to the Family Welfare Association conference on Family Therapy. The paper suggests that if a significant member of the family is absent 'then a caseworker may be assigned his place, and then we have found that families tend to engage in family therapy more readily' (Graham 1990, 34). It is not clear how such a major modification of the therapy approach can be sanctioned, without losing the whole point of a therapy which should, by definition, involve all the functioning members of the family and so speak to all.

Over against such variety stand the claims to the healing techniques of counselling. Just as the doctor cures through the use of medicine and different techniques, so the counsellor 'cures' through talking. The aim of counselling 'is not the rational resolution of difficulties through conversation, but the use of talk to effect a cure by the elucidating of underlying causes and, through their exposure, the relief of symptoms' (Graham 1990, 38).

However, for something to be a technique there is need to define it, to say what it consists of, apply it and know when it is being applied, and know when success has been achieved. Counselling theories fail to do any of this in a rigorous way.

When attempts are made to begin to define what is common to all the theories, these come down largely to techniques of listening, reflective response which re-present to the client what has been heard, giving responsibility to the client for decision making, avoiding any judgementalism or moralism when problematic behaviour is revealed by the client.

However, it is not clear that this list of listening skills can be referred to as techniques and certainly not as specialised professional technique. These are rather general life skills. Alan Billings goes further and suggests that these are life skills which cannot be taught (Billings 1992).

Secondly, counselling as therapeutic healing has all the problems of the medical model of health. This model focuses on the reduction of suffering, emphasising the technical solution of medical problems, and thus sees the professional as expert, the patient as passive recipient of treatment, leading to a power imbalance and to the exclusion of the wider community contribution to healing (Pattison 1989, 22).

Counselling as healing is always in danger of treating clients heteronomously - as means to an end, not ends in themselves. The psychotherapist has great power, not least because she makes interpretations of the client's presentations. Such interpretations can themselves be a means of coercion - causing the client to see things in her way. The focus on searching for an underlying cause to the client's problem can also lead to scientism, treating her as a case, and of excluding her from the whole process.

Ironically then, the very process which claims to respect the autonomy of the client becomes coercive. There is some argument for a degree of coercion in some forms of psychosis, but most emotional problems or neurotic conditions are not of this kind, demanding help not 'therapy'. In all this the therapeutic model tends to individualise the therapy. The cure is found in and through the work with the expert. Counselling as therapy can in fact be seen as the imposition of a grand narrative of illness and cure - disempowering the other.

Thirdly, Graham and Billings return to the non-directive approach and note the constant confusion between the two ideas of non-directiveness and psychological healing, arguing that they are contradictory. The idea of healing assumes that there is an end which is set down and valued. It makes assumptions about healthy responses, relationships and behaviour, as clearly seen, for instance, in the case of anorexia. Such assumptions inform the aims of counselling and psychotherapy, argues Billings. Faced by a couple whose marriage is breaking up, the aim of the counsellor will be affected by assumptions she has about marriage. If marriage is seen as a contract there will be less concern for an attempt at reconciliation than if it is seen as a sacrament (Billings 1992, 6). It is at this point that we are faced with the idea of non-directiveness, which demands that the person should simply be allowed to work their own path whatever the end point. Such an approach has precisely no assumption about appropriate behaviour and no sense of what might be a cure. Hence, the two approaches are contradictory.

## Communication of Values

A further set of arguments examines what values are, or should be, as part of the counselling process. Far from being value-free the counselling relationship turns out to be a battle ground for competing narratives, whether the therapist knows it or not.

The basis of so called non-directiveness is respect for the autonomy of the counsellee. However, simply enabling the counsellee to reflect upon the values is not so much enabling the development of values and principles, but rather introducing what Billings refers to as permissive values - you are allowed to believe what you like. Gilbert Meilander notes this with value clarification as a whole, arguing that clarification simply enables the person to reinforce her own values, whatever they are (Meilander 1984). There is no basis for values development or change, something that would demand challenge or guidance.

Billings goes further, arguing that this in general leads to an unreflective acceptance of the prevailing utilitarian ethic held in a liberal society, something which the counsellor consciously or unconsciously colludes in. This in itself is based upon some form of individualism which sees individuals as the primary reality, with society as a second order, derived construct. R. Hogan suggests that the major schools of psychology, including Rogers, Freud and Kohlberg, reflect particular views of individualism including romantic (the idea that the individual has all she needs to find fulfilment), and egoistic (self fulfilment as the main aim of life) (R. Hogan 1974). Whatever, the difference in emphasis, he argues, all are individualistic and ego-centric.

None of these points directly argue against the individualist philosophy *per se*. They do question whether therapists or counsellors realise that they consciously or unconsciously represent or promote value systems - often based upon the value of the individual, and often dismissing the claims of other more communitarian philosophies as repressive. Kenneth Leech takes this further, introducing another possible competing value narrative. He argues that one of the consequences of not questioning the underlying value assumptions is falling back on to a model of counselling as enabling conformity. This is a model of helping the client to adjust, something to do with returning to norms, and a concern for inner equilibrium. All this tends to uncritically accept the norms of society, often set by those in power, and by extension the very structures and attitudes which may have contributed to the distress of the client in the first place.

Here the church is in danger of not simply propping up to the prevailing moral views but of a different kind of coercion and collusion - offering a spiritual narcotic to deaden the pain. Hence, Leech challenges the church:

'It seems that Christian theology needs to ask questions about the politics of therapy and counselling. What are therapy and counselling doing about the problems confronting human society? Are they simply helping people to be well adjusted in a society whose fundamental values and interests remain unquestioned?' (Leech 1981, 80).

Peter Selby argues, therefore, that there should be a social dimension to pastoral care and counselling, that it should be politically aware, and be prepared to locate relationships in their political environment, not least where they are in networks of oppression and injustice (Selby 1983, 100).

Gordon Graham, from his perspective, argues for the direct communication of the Christian narrative in the counselling relationship. He argues that the idea of non-directiveness is actually 'incompatible with the Christian Gospel'. The aim of Christian counselling is the call to charity. This involves encouraging a concern for others. A part of that message is to do with eschatalogical hope. Final judgement will depend upon the decision which any person takes, and whether they are really open to the call of love. This is not something that the Christian pastoral care worker can keep back.

'Since Christians believe that an eternal destiny awaits us they must believe that every individual has a major interest in that destiny. If therefore there is a right or wrong about behaviour, and upon it our fate for all eternity will turn, anyone genuinely concerned for our interest will not be able to hide it from us' (Graham 1990, 65).

Re-expressed in terms of the post modern debate, it could be argued that faced by many other competing narratives the Christian rightly should aim to challenge them and to set out the Christian narrative as an alternative. It is important to note the sense in which this is not necessarily an imposition of values. Simply to raise the value questions and the different perspective in the context of the counselling relationship is actually respecting the autonomy of the client to decide for herself between different ethical narratives.

Graham anticipates the objection that the church is not free from post modern ethical pluralism, something which undermines any attempt to introduce particular Christian values. To begin with, the fact of disagreement within the church does not of itself denote a lack of generally accepted values. There is often disagreement in law or the sciences, but still a clear body of practice which all respect and work within. Graham then develops this into a form of middle axiom thinking, the view that there are certain major principles whose meaning is agreed upon and accepted by the majority - such as equality or freedom. These should be used as part of a larger decision making process in which the church could help different parties to focus on middle level principles and then more detailed work would take place on the application of such principles. Graham distinguishes between beliefs about values and beliefs about conduct. Most disagreements, he argues, take place at the level of conduct not values, leaving values as a whole intact. Hence, there is little to support the idea of a genuine narrative division in the churches. Graham illustrates this with the Christian view of marriage. He fully accepts that there are no simple resolutions to be had to marriage difficulties. Some Christians argue that the covenant of marriage means no dissolution. Others argue that to stay in a marriage which is in reality over would make a mockery of the purpose of marriage. Either way they agree on the ideal of marriage as a life long commitment and fidelity to one member of the opposite sex, and any disagreement only makes sense in the light of that ideal.

## Guilt and repentance

A great deal of this debate comes to a head in the question of guilt. The therapeutic approach to counselling tends to see guilt as a uniformly bad thing as that which in many contexts actually causes the problems for the person. However, as Erikson notes there is an important distinction to be made between healthy guilt and the guilt which is neurotic (Erikson 1994. See also Fowler 1996, Hoffman 1974). Healthy guilt can be as important as the experience of physical pain. It enables the person to see a problem and leads in itself to change.

Erikson argues that psychotherapists deal poorly with guilt, often treating all guilt as misdirected, and he suggests that it is not hard to find the reasons:

'Given the assumption that one's highest duty is to oneself it is hard to see how a patient can be expected to apologise and make amends except as an instrumental act designed to enhance ones position. Furthermore, many therapists help patients explain away their responsibility. Moral failures are reframed as misunderstandings, communication problems and mistakes. Parents or environmental circumstances may be invoked to explain the behaviour. The super ego (Freud) and the ideal self (Rogers) is regarded with ambivalence and mistrust... Patients are taught to avoid using the word "should" in addressing themselves or others, using instead "I want" or "I feel" ' (Erikson 1994, 86).

In all this the patient is encouraged to accept the fallibility of the person without the responsibility demanded of any relationship. The Christian perspective cannot be happy with either the Rogerian or Freudian view of guilt. Freud, leaves little hope for the person, trapped between the unconscious drives and the repressive superego. Rogers optimistic view of man excludes the full reality of sin, and thus an element of human experience that cannot be remedied alone. It is precisely an awareness of such sin which enables the person to feel healthy guilt and reach out to others, embarking on radical change. Awareness of sin thus introduces the possibility of change and of hope, something that we will return to in more detail in subsequent chapters.

## Practice

None of the arguments above deny the need to respect the autonomy of the counsellee. On the contrary, autonomy is an essential element in the very definition of morality (Noyce 1989, 21ff.). Hence, the burden of any developments has been on how the balance between personal autonomy and the development of moral meaning can be enabled. Browning argues that this is the crucial question for all Christian counselling.

The concerns raised in the arguments above have led to a number of different attempts to work out the balance in practice. These have focused broadly on two areas - ethical methodology (Browning and Poling) and the skills of confrontation (Underwood and Hoffman).

## Ethical methodology

Don Browning is concerned to enable the counsellee to become her own Christian ethicist. Ethical meaning is apparent in some way in all aspects of the counselling process and the counsellee has to be enabled to deal with this herself. Browning's response to this is to develop a methodology of ethical reflection and decision-making that will enable the person to practice ethics (Browning 1976).

The aim of this process is to move away from a knee jerk response to problems and to begin to articulate the norms which should be aimed at in the light of the Christian community. The process begins with the identification of the problem. Secondly, the situation is focused on, with the different interpretations (a hermeneutical process). Thirdly, a critical analysis and comparison is undertaken, using five levels of practical moral reasoning (see below). Finally, an appropriate strategy of action is formulated and a decision taken.

The five levels of practical moral reasoning involve:

## Metaphorical level

This is a basic level of life meaning, involving the metaphors and symbols which underlie and shape beliefs, values and actions. For the Christian these commonly involve three views of God, as creator, governor and redeemer. In turn these undergird a material world which is good, a world of moral order, and the possibility of change and renewal. Browning notes that this level does not directly inform what is right or wrong, but it does shape the understanding of what is possible and so radically affects life values.

## Obligational level

This level explores the principles which ground obligation. Browning suggests, for example, that the basic Christian principle is impartiality, equal care for others. Grounded in the Golden Rule, this is one of many such principles which can be reflected on.

## Tendency / need level

This explores which tendencies or needs we are morally justified in satisfying. The principles identified in the level above have to be applied in the light of human needs. Data on such needs is gathered from personal experience, intuition, and from the social sciences.

## Contextual / predictive

The previous levels are all quite general, looking to determine the basis of value and the nature and end of humanity. This next level moves to the actual context of the problems, asking the question, 'What is the immediate context of our action and the various factors which condition it?' Having assessed the psychological, social and cultural factors which make up the situation this can be critically compared to the previous level.

## Rules / Roles level

This considers the ways of implementing the aims in the given context, asking the question, 'What specific roles, rules and processes of communication should we follow to accomplish our moral ends?'

This process is termed the 'revised correctional approach', building on the work of Paul Tillich, who aimed to correlate questions raised from experience with response based on theology. It should be worked through in the order given, and Browning argues that theologians might be involved at the different levels - with systemic theologians concerned for the first, ethicists for the second and so on. This is a dynamic approach in the manner of a critical conversation. Such a conversation acknowledges the contribution of all involved and of discourse beyond theology, all of which can take place in the context of the Christian community. If the dialogue is genuine then conflict may emerge, something which may need to be handled over a long term.

In all this the method acknowledges that there are a number of different ways of engaging and interpreting human experience and the Christian tradition. Hence, the importance of correlating the interpretations of the Christian narrative with the questions and answers raised by the interpretations of experience and other disciplines. Similar attempts have been made to develop moral reflection methodology. James Poling, for instance, sets out the following framework as a basis for ethical reflection:

1. Decisions;
2. Rules- middle axioms;
3. Norms- intuition and purpose;
4. Social analysis of Oppression and Power;
5. Community story and vision:
    a. Anthropology. What kind of persons?
    b. Ecclesiology, What kind of community?
    c. Doctrine of God, What kind of God?

This is a very flexible method with counselling moving back and forth between the different levels.

In this approach Poling stresses the importance of the middle axioms, which he defines as rules based on ethical systems which provide concrete guidelines for behaviour. This provides an area of broad agreement and rests itself on an ethical system, made up of story, metaphor, social context, and norms which are discovered through reflection on purpose. The middle axiom level then goes on to the levels of decisions: actual choice in concrete situations.

Poling sees this framework as enabling many different approaches to ethics to be brought together in practice:

- The ethics of intuition - of revelation and conscience;
- The ethics of purpose - focusing on consequences;
- The ethic of Character - Ethics is not so much about discerning the right and the wrong, as about how the person and community grow. Character emerges from the vision and narrative of the community;
- The ethic of liberation. Ethics as identifying the oppressive powers and achieving liberation from them (Poling 1984).

## Ethical confrontation

Ralph Underwood argues that both empathy and confrontation are an essential part of respect for a person (Underwood 1985). Empathy demonstrates care and concern, whilst confrontation reflects a concern for the truth of the client's story. Such confrontation is largely non-judgmental and reflective, reflecting back to the counsellee different aspects of her situation and enabling her to perceive the truth. Reflective confrontation, raising issues of perception of data as well as value perception, is not of itself moralistic but rather, in the context of acceptance, enables the counsellee to reflect more effectively. As Stephen Pattison notes,

'It allows the enlargement of peoples' self understanding, prevents self idealisation, affirms sociality and communality, helps people to be more objective in their analysis of themselves and their situation, turns them away from self reliance, expands the horizon of the pastoral encounter spiritually and morally, and can help people to realise that judgement is a means of grace when it is sensitively and appropriately administered' (Pattison 1993, 50).

John Hoffman also argues for confrontation in the context of genuine care. He acknowledges the importance of Freud and Rogers in detailing the difficulties of counselling people who have internalised a non rational guilt. Moreover, he supports Rogers concern for the development of the freedom of the person and her capacity to learn. However, he makes a more detailed analysis of the working of the conscious and of felt guilt than Graham. He distinguishes between the unconscious and the conscious conscience. Each of these has both a positive and negative aspect. The negative unconscious conscience is in fact the superego and would not benefit from confrontation, but the other aspect of the conscience are all able to benefit from caring confrontation (Hoffman 1974).

A crucial element of this confrontation (involving both affirmation or critique) is the establishing of the counsellee's 'right to be', based upon trust - something Hoffman stresses from both Luther and Calvin. Only from that basis can confrontation be effective, both with neurotic guilt and in engaging any moral issue which may emerge. In that light Hoffman is prepared to argue even for confrontation in terms of moral rebuke - should the situation demand.

## Assessing the arguments

Many of the points made in these various critiques and attempts to engage counselling and moral meaning are valuable. However, as a whole they tend to polarise the debate, offering both an inadequate view of counselling and simplistic view of the moral dynamic in the counselling relationship and how this fits into Christian Ethics.

### Therapies

There is no doubt that the medical model of health and healing has its problems. When applied to professional counselling it tends to reinforce the individualist model of care, the exclusion of the community, and the capture of the language and skills of care. Nonetheless, warning of the dangers of professionalisation, and the resulting imbalance of power and possible coercion, is not in itself a critique of counselling.

In addition to this, the critiques of counselling by Graham and Billings are indiscriminate. Firstly, the theoretical differences between different schools are overstated. Orlo Strunk Jr. notes certain features which are present in any healing relationship:

- 'persistent, structured interaction with the therapist;
- the development of trust between client and therapist;

- a desire to change on the part of the client;
- hope that the change will be for the better' (Strunk, 1990).

Secondly, at the heart of this is not so much technique as the therapeutic relationship. Heinz Kohut argues that empathy is the very essence of that relationship, involving a way of knowing and relating. Hence, 'empathy *per se*, the mere presence of empathy, has also a beneficial, in a broad sense, a therapeutic effect - both in the clinical and in the human life in general' (Kohut 1982, 397).

In all this Kohut does not lay claim to empathy as being purely of therapeutic value. He views it as a life skill or quality which may be used in a particular way in therapy. Graham and Billings, in their attempt to guard against the professional captivity of skills and qualities, end up not really valuing these very qualities. I will argue shortly that they are key to the development of spiritual awareness and moral meaning.

Kohut's view also stands out against the idea of scientific technique as the base of therapy. Far from encouraging scientism Kohut focuses on what for him remains something of a mystery, and bases therapy on the quality of the relationship. None of this denies that technique is important. The counselling relationship is one of intentionality - it sets out to help and enable change. Given that, the counsellee can expect a level of competence which enables the skills to be used in an orderly and successful way. This demands that such skills and qualities are effectively reflected on, and developed. There is, moreover, no *a priori* objection to seeing skills and qualities referred to as technique. Any skill or quality has to be embodied and practised, and so requires a way of being realised. The only objection to the idea of technique is where it becomes the major focus and loses the aim of the therapy (Ellul 1965).

Thirdly, whilst the professionalisation of counselling can easily capture what are in effect the life skills of empathy, listening and so on, it is nonetheless also questionable that such skills cannot be learned. All skills and qualities involve some degree of learning, and once acquired need to be developed and maintained.

Fourthly, the idea of the therapeutic model of counselling as being of itself coercive is equally without real substance. It is possible to point to examples of coercion, as it is possible to provide bad examples of any profession. Equally, there is no doubt that the counselling relationship is by definition one of power imbalance. However, the focus of counselling is precisely to provide the environment and resources for the counsellee to effect her own change and healing. Those resources might include frameworks for understanding, such as Transactional Analysis, or possible interpretations. They are, however, precisely tools to be used for the furtherance of the end point of counselling. Even the most neutral form of client centred counselling does have a very clear end in sight, such as development towards the 'fully functioning person' - someone who will takes responsibility for their life, decisions, and response to others. Such a broad end is shared by the majority of counselling approaches. In this light, the critique of Leech holds little water. Rogerian counselling, for instance, is precisely concerned to enable the client *not* to conform, to break away from the oppressive narrative of the family and all that they have internalised from her community.

If counselling and therapy does not encourage conformity it is equally wrong to see it as purely individualistic. The stated principles behind a therapy such as Rational Emotive Behaviour Therapy include acceptance that all humans are fallible and all are equal in humanity (Ellis and Dryden 1999, 204-5). This does not set out an altruistic philosophy but does set the foundation for personal growth which is aware of and responsive to others.

## *Moral Values and Community*

The view that the pastoral counsellor has a clear body of principles in the Christian narrative which are more important than the differences in perspective is questionable.

a. As noted above one approach to this is through middle axioms. The first problem with this is that it is hard to pin down just how substantive such middle axioms might be. R.H. Tawney suggests equality and freedom as middle level principles, William Temple looks to service, social fellowship and freedom (Tawney 1964, Temple 1970). Some writers see the middle axiom as provisional. Others view them as having absolute force (Preston 1983, 148ff.). Secondly, many middle level principles have a variety of meanings. Michael Le Grand, for instance, details the five different meanings of equality in relation to welfare distribution: equality of access, treatment, outcome and so on (Le Grand 1982). Little wonder that the term is used in different ways by different political schools - each trying to 'own' the concept. Thirdly, it is difficult to begin to understand what a middle axiom might mean without some clear indication of how it would be embodied in practice. William Temple advocated the middle axiom approach but increasingly had to set out the policy implications to give substance to the principles (Temple 1976).

Fourthly, liberation theologies have called attention to the agendas underlying the use of principles. The use of principles often depends upon the power context, and principles are often shaped by experience, not least of the oppressed. Attempts to agree upon principles as if they existed in a conceptual vacuum, free from the dynamics of power and underlying affective experience, are simply disingenuous.

b. Graham's rather narrower point about agreement within the church over certain central ideals is equally problematic. Even his view that the church accepts marriage as a life long heterosexual partnership is one which is increasingly questioned. Whilst the ideal of life long commitment remains intact there are questions about the form of the family and about the exclusion of homosexuality. The Church of England's report *Something to Celebrate* rejoices in the diversity of family approaches. The theology of friendship has given new force to the idea of life long homosexual partnerships (Stuart 1995). This leaves a non substantive principle of covenant commitment to the other which might be expressed in several different ways.

Another important example is homosexuality itself. Browning, despite his concern for the freedom of the counsellee sets out a view against homosexuality, partly based on a revised natural law approach and partly on a broad consequentialist approach (Browning 1983, 95 ff.). There are two major problems with this. Firstly, as James Nelson notes, there is a plurality of views within the church, with at least four different commonly held theological views (Nelson 1978). Secondly, there is ambiguity even in main line church documents. The Church of England Bishops' report, *Issues in Human Sexuality*, for instance, holds together several views. On the one hand it affirms life long heterosexual relationships as God's purpose in creation. On the other hand it affirms homosexual relationships which embody a life long covenant - whilst acknowledging that they are not part of God's purpose. It also stands out against practising homosexuals as being allowed to be ordained. None of this is to critique the report. It is to say that the report reflects a very complex situation and tries to hold together several different values which can easily be seen to be contradictory. Part of this is an awareness of the pastoral dimension of the debate and thus a concern not to offend or to fuel fear. More importantly it recognises the complexity of the moral debate, a debate which is changing and developing all the while.

c. This plurality raises major questions about the Christian community and assumptions made about it. Graham and Billings, for instance, assume that the counsellee would come to the pastor /counsellor precisely expecting guidance. The implied conclusion is that they should therefore receive it. However, the fact that the counsellee looks to a pastor for 'guidance' is not in itself a reason for providing it. Paul Avis notes the tendency of the church to build up dependency in its members, and moral guidance can be a part of that (Avis 1989, 77). The danger in that context is of simply paying lip service to the autonomy of the counsellee.

Behind such arguments is the assumption of a model of church as a clearly defined community, and a moral language and discourse well known by all members. However, any Christian community is made up of members and groups from other communities and traditions. As David Fergusson puts it,

'Christians are not and probably never have been hermetically sealed from other traditions. They typically inhabit more communities than the church, and many of the insights and assumptions from other social groupings will inform their Christian practice and witness' (Fergusson 1997, 46).

Secondly, many, perhaps a majority, of church members have not thought through their Christian ethical position. As James Fowler notes, developments in ethical and spiritual thinking often come only as a result of life crisis (Fowler 1996, 71 ff.). Often prior to this, ethical meaning is either accepted uncritically in the different communities to which the person belongs, or is simply not reflected on. Thus when the person comes to the pastor or counsellor she is not being called back to a set of values which have been clearly articulated and which they have previously held. This is far more a matter of learning, about moral meaning and how to take responsibility for that moral meaning in her particular context, and in response to her situation. In this respect the whole process becomes experience led. In the light of this, Meilander's critique of value clarification as part of counselling has much less force. Attempting to clarify values in the context of a particular crisis tends to demonstrate just how inadequate the previous view of values was, and more importantly tends to raise many different, often conflicting values, which have to be understood and addressed. As I note in the following chapters this leads to a process of transformation and discovery which develops moral responsibility, and which cannot be seen as simply returning to well understood moral values.

Such points apply even more to non church members who come to the pastor or pastoral counsellor for help. For them this is by definition a discovery of moral meaning. Conversely, many church members go outside their community for pastoral consultation, precisely because they find it hard to share with the person who they see as a figure of authority and judgement.

## Practice

How the issues of freedom and moral meaning are addressed in practice tends to lead to a stress either on content or process. Graham accepts that ways have to be found of raising value issues which do not abuse the freedom of the counsellee, but he is most concerned about the content which is being communicated. Browning is more concerned for process. He is far more aware of the plurality in and beyond the church and his revised correlational method attempts to enable critical dialogue which can take place in most contexts. However, there are problems with his approach.

Firstly, his approach is too cerebral. He concentrates upon concepts and ideas, without giving weight to the emotional understanding. Hence, there is no effective account taken of the importance of such understanding in development of moral meaning. This also assumes an intellectual capacity which as Pattison notes may not be shared by the average member of the congregation (Pattison 1993, 45). The method is also too complex. If it were pursued with rigor then it would be very time consuming.

Secondly, at the obligational level Browning reveals an uncritical acceptance of the Rawlsian view of equal consideration, seeing this as a useful concept acceptable to all. This is certainly an element within Christian Ethics but is not clear it can be used as the base for agreement amongst all groups. The Christian ethic contains a more extreme notion of responsibility for all and has a very different foundation from the utilitarian approach of Rawls. This will be examined in more detail in the next two chapters.

Thirdly, Elaine Graham argues that the primary language of Browning's approach is that of a 'pre-existent theological ethics', rather than one which is built up in dialogue with and in response to experience. Because of this there is little attention to the power relations within the congregation and to the real concern of the different groups, not least the feminists. The result is that since Browning views values as axiomatic 'he has no mechanism for their contestation or rearticulation' (Graham 1996, 91). As shall be noted in the next chapter, this partly involves Browning not focusing on the spirituality of the counselling process.

When his approach to counselling is viewed in this light we see an uneasy relationship between his *a priori* view of ethics and the process by which he genuinely wants to develop autonomy, with elements of manipulation peering through the critical conversation. Firstly, the pastor is involved in leading the client. Thus he writes in the context of one case discussion, 'pastors are inevitably leading their clients somewhere, even if only by silently drawing certain boundaries and eliminating certain options' (Browning 1983, 96). At another point he refers to covert moral directedness, involved in the way that a pastor can reinforce a particular value. This means positive reinforcement whenever a client expresses a value which the counsellor believes to be right. Not only does this have a degree of manipulation or conditioning, it also is pedagogically suspect, precisely because in such a process there is no critical understanding as to why this might be a good value or why the counsellor is positively supporting it. The counsellor in all this retains the moral high ground with the danger of moving into a moral form of the medical model of health, in which the counsellor 'knows best' and will ultimately guide you into moral health, that is if you listen closely enough to the clues she is giving you. In all this there is danger of losing any sense of mutuality in the counselling process and thus of any genuine sense of critical conversation. In effect this becomes a form of *gradualism*, an approach to moral guidance in pastoral care which simply accepts that the person may not be ready to understand and accept the moral truths, and thus gradually leads her towards them (Gula 1996). It is precisely such a natural law view which is contested.

The focus on empathy and the capacity to both support and confront the counsellee is also a very important attempt to ensure that the moral agenda is part of the whole counselling process and of enabling the freedom of the counsellee to respond to the truth. However, this approach also has difficulties. Once the counsellee is confronted with what is in effect a form of reality testing this does not of itself provide a way into reflection on and development of moral meaning. There is no attempt by Underwood to explore the link between empathy itself and the moral world of the relationship, of counsellee or counsellor. The result is that empathy becomes a pastoral tool, and a part of the process whereby the predetermined content can be eventually communicated. Hence, a division emerges between the initial pastoral 'business', which can establish truth and in Hoffman's terms the 'right to be', and the moral agenda which may be introduced by the counsellor at a later stage. The result is a failure to recognise the moral world of the counsellee as she initially presents it, and the fact that so much of her self view and life view is built around this moral world. As I shall note in more detail in chapter four this inevitably demands a moral dialogue from the word go. Moral meaning is not something to be engaged once the head is cleared. It is actually built into the fabric of relationships, and expressed in tone of voice, body language and so on.

In broader terms this also means that the relationship of self identity to moral meaning, and of the values of pastoral care to Christian Ethics have to be worked through. Pastoral care values and Christian Ethics have to be congruent. On this all sides agree.

## Sin, confession and forgiveness

The criticisms of the person centred approach to counselling centre firmly on the over optimistic view of human nature and the individualism of Rogers. It is important not to state these too crudely not least because Rogers' optimistic view of human nature can be a balance to excessive stress on human sinfulness. In any case Rogers' idea of the failure to be ones authentic self is very close to one understanding of sin, as falling short, or as alienation from the self and others.

Nonetheless, there are major questions of the person centred approach in relation to awareness of sin, confession and forgiveness and the role of the community. Awareness of sin is ultimately a spiritual not simply an ethical matter, about how the person is aware of and relates to herself and others. This includes an awareness of limitations and of the possible ways of responding to those limitations. In fact, neither Rogers nor his critics fully appreciate this dimension. It is precisely awareness at this spiritual level which enables the development of a degree of self acceptance and moves into the possibility of developing quite a different approach to ethical understanding and spirituality, one which is built upon the counselling relationship, but which clearly moves out to affect others. How that occurs has not really been thought through in the debate. The attempt by several writers to differentiate between the false guilt which works against self acceptance and healthy guilt which is possible when the counsellee is able to think rationally and non defensively is important. However, in practice it is not clear what difference this makes. Even healthy guilt is only possible to engage through the positive experience of love and commitment. In theological terms Karl Barth argues that it is precisely the prevenient love of God which not only enables the person to accept the self but also to become aware of that which is sinful in herself (Barth 1956). Prior to that the person spends so much energy on the defence of the self and self justification that they precisely do not see their attitudes or actions as sinful. This would seem to indicate that the accepting environment of the counselling relationship is directly related to the development of moral meaning.

# Conclusions

## Freedoms

This debate demonstrates that the issues of freedom and morality are more complex than has been assumed. All parties tend to emphasise negative freedom - freedom from coercion or manipulation. Indeed all sides seem to accuse each other of abusing negative freedom, be that imposing a moral agenda upon the person or imposing some view of what it is to be healthy. There is no doubt that such freedom is important. There is equally no doubt that such a freedom is not enough. Focusing only on this freedom tends to obscure the need for the equally important freedom to learn. This is stressed by Rogers, but is also something at the heart of any theological anthropology. As Kelly notes, the person is a subject and decision maker but is also constantly emerging, always learning (Kelly 1992). Indeed, the majority of persons in crisis are precisely unable to see themselves or others clearly and thus unable to take rational decisions. The capacity to learn is strongly influenced by a number of factors. Firstly, cultural narratives can often discourage the idea of learning. As John Hull notes, the church itself has a long history of discouraging reflection and learning, based on the belief that to show ignorance is bad (Hull 1991). Secondly, some moral narratives, such as that the primacy of the family can in different ways discourage the practice of publicly engaging difference. Learning precisely involves such engagement and thus some form of disagreement. Without this it would be hard to understand anything new about the self, others, or the social or natural environment. Disagreement, however, can be seen as disobedience or rejection, by nature adversarial - if you disagree with me you do not accept me. From a different angle the need to learn can be seen as weakness or fallibility. If the person has to learn then she must be ignorant, and ignorance is weakness. Such pressures reinforce what might be called a learning shame, associating learning with the feelings of shame.

However, at the heart of any learning is the dynamic of mutual critique. By this I mean mutual testing of the other's view. In learning terms this is non adversarial and aims to simply understand better the narrative of the other. In the context of learning shame such critique is something which itself is perceived as either a threat to the other or to the self. The very value of the self can be put in doubt if a question is raised of behaviour or ideas.

Freedom to learn then is essentially a relational freedom, one which involves seeing the other as both accepting and also as different, as able to disagree and not reject, one which demands acceptance from the other, an experience of accepting community, and thus an acceptance by the person of her own limitations.

The capacity to learn then requires a dynamic which combines both acceptance and critique, of the self and other. Without that lived experience there is little hope of breaking through the kind of oppressive narratives noted above, and beginning to critique them. It is precisely such a relationship which provides what Berlin called *positive freedom*, or enabling freedom (Berlin 1969). This enables the person to disagree, to learn and to respond. By definition this freedom demands a relationship of mutuality in which both parties can test each other in various ways. This relationship will test spiritual and moral meaning affectively as well as cognitively.

Such testing is the basis of genuine dialogue in which the person not only learns about the values and life meaning of the other but also learns about her own moral meaning. As shall be seen in chapter two and three, once the person begins to articulate her own narrative then she becomes aware of untested assumptions, contradictions, and so on. Learning in the context of counselling then also has to be dialogic.

In such a relationship is developed what Michael Novak refers to as moral freedom (Novak 1990). This is essentially the freedom which emerges through the development of the character, and thus, in ethical terms, the virtues. It is precisely the development of the virtues and related skills which enable the person to handle the different moral narratives.

### Morality

The debate on counselling and freedom can easily see freedom as an instrumental value, a value whose task is to enable autonomy. The dynamic of counselling then goes something like, 'Respect the counsellee's autonomy and then we can begin to introduce the ethical agenda'. Such a dynamic stresses only negative freedom and divides this from the very moral agenda we are advocated to engage. However, the dynamic of freedom noted above is central to this very moral meaning, alongside the community which enables it. These are precisely the values which are partially embodied in the counsellor and often in the physical context of the counselling relationship - in tone, in expressed feeling and attitude, in body language, in the books which surround the study, in the ideas which the counsellee tries to work out about the counsellor. As such these values are public, in the sense of being open to more than the self, and part of the counselling relationship. As such they are open to be misinterpreted, not least as authoritarian or judgmental, and to be tested and wrestled with, as much as the narratives which might oppress the counsellee. Such values of course can never be fully embodied and this too may have to be communicated.

'Autonomy' then comes through the relationship and is based in inter-dependence and the acceptance of that. The relationship itself is suffused with moral narratives which are brought to it and tested. Moral meaning emerges from this complex and holistic relationship in a way which is essen-tially creative and transformative, with moral meaning discovered in and through reflection on narrative, practice and relationships. Moral meaning is not brought *to* the relationship by the counsellor, overtly or covertly, but is worked out *in* relationship and does not have to be imposed.

Underlying much of the debate are different views of ethical meaning and how they fit into the development of moral meaning for the person, and in particular the person in counselling. What is emerging from a reflec-tion on this debate is a view that such meaning cannot be communicated in terms of *a priori* concepts, but only discovered through *reflection* on the counsellee's world, not least the crisis of meaning which will be at the cen-tre of that. This can only be achieved in the context of a relationship which both embodies basic human values and enables the counsellee to explore value and meaning in relation to her social and physical environment, and develop a critical capacity which can scrutinise all moral meaning, includ-ing any implicit in the counselling relationship or explicit in the church.

This is a dynamic which points to a morality which might be able to bring together many of the elements so far polarised in the debate, not least inte-gration of: pastoral and ethical dimensions; content and process; affective and cognitive dimensions; the importance of practical context to moral mean-ing; the importance of consistency in meaning and of continual learning and development of meaning.

What enables and informs that dialogue at all its levels is agape. Agape might seem at first the soft option, bringing meaning to everything and solving all problems. In the next two chapters, I will suggest that far from offering easy answers agape faces up to reality and provides a bridge between pastoral care and ethics.

### References
P. Avis, Eros and the Sacred (London: SPCK, 1989).

K. Barth, Church Dogmatics, Vol. IV part 1 (Edinburgh: T and T, Clark, 1956).

I. Berlin, Two Concepts of Liberty, in  A. Quinton (ed.) Political Philosophy (Oxford: Oxford University Press, 1969) 141-153.

A. Billings, Pastors or Counsellors?, Contact 108, 2, 1992, pp. 3-9.

D. Browning, Religious Ethics and Pastoral Care (Philadelphia: Fortress, 1983).

D. Browning, The Moral Context of Pastoral Care (Philadelphia: Westminster, 1976).

W. Brueggemann, Theology of the Old Testament (Minneapolis: Fortress, 1997).

A. Campbell, Moderated Love (London: SPCK, 1984).

H. Clinebell, Basic Types of Pastoral Counseling (Nashville: Abingdon, 1966).

A. Ellis and W. Dryden, The Practice of Rational Emotive Behaviour Therapy (London: Free Association Books, 1999)

J. Ellul, The Technological Society, trans. J. Wilkinson (New York, Vintage Books, 1965)

R. Erikson, Morality and the Practice of Psychotherapy, Pastoral Psychology, Vol. 43, No. 2, 1994.

D. Fergusson, Communitarianism and Liberalism, Studies in Christian Ethics, Vol. 10,1, 1997, 32-48.

J. Fowler, Faithful Change (Nashville: Abingdon, 1996).

P. Gay (ed.), The Enlightenment (New York: Harper and Row,1973).

E. Graham, Transforming Practice: Pastoral Theology in and Age of Uncertainty (London: Mowbray, 1996).

G. Graham, The Idea of Christian Charity (London: Collins, 1990).

R. Gula, Moral Discernment (New York: Paulist Press, 1997).

P. Halmos, The Faith of the Counsellors (London: Constable, 1964).

S. Hiltner, Preface to Pastoral Theology (Nashville: Abingdon, 1958).

J. Hoffman, Ethical Confrontation in Counseling (Chicago: Chicago University Press, 1979).

R. Hogan, Theoretical egocentrism and the problem of compliance, American Psychologist, 30, 1974, 535-540.

J. Hull, What Prevents Christian Adults from Learning? (Philadelphia: Trinity Press, 1991).

K. Kelly, New Directions in Moral Theology (London: Geoffrey Chapman, 1992).

H. Kohut, Introspection, Empathy and the Semi-Circle of Mental Health, International Journal of Psychoanalysis, Vol. 663, 1982, 397.

L. Kohlberg, Essays in Moral Development. Vol. 2 (San Francisco: Harper and Row, 1984).

M. Le Grand, The Strategy of Equality (London: Allen and Unwin, 1982).

K. Leech, The Social God (London: Sheldon, 1981).

J.T. McNeill, A History of the Cure of Souls (New York: Harper and Row, 1977).

W. Meeks, The Origins of Christian Morality (New Haven: Yale University Press, 1993).

G. Meilander, The Theory and Practice of Virtue (Notre Dam; University of Notre Dame Press, 1984).

J. Nelson, Embodiment: An Approach to Sexuality and Christian Theology (London: SPCK, 1978).

M. Novak, Morality Capitalism and Democracy (London: IEA, 1990).

G. Noyce, The Minister as Moral Counselor (Nashville: Abingdon. 1989).

T. Oden, Kerygma and Counselling (Louisville: Westminster, 1966).

S. Pattison, Alive and Kicking (London; SCM, 1989).

S. Pattison, A Critique of Pastoral Care. (London: SCM, 1993)

J. Poling, 'Ethical Reflection and Pastoral Care, Part I', Pastoral Psychology, Vol. 32 (2), Spring, 1984, 106-113.

J. Poling, 'Ethical Reflection and Pastoral Care, Part II', Pastoral Psychology, Vol. 32 (3), Summer 1984, 160-170.

R. H. Preston, Church and Society in the Late Twentieth Century (London: SCM, 1983).

C. Rogers, Freedom to Learn (Columbus: Merrill, 1983).

C. Rogers, Counseling and Psychotherapy (London: Constable, 1942).

W. Schrage, Ethics of the New Testament (Edinburgh: T. and T. Clark, 1988).

P. Selby, Liberating God (London: SPCK, 1983).

E. Stuart, Just Good Friends (London: Mowbray, 1995).

O. Strunk Jr. Psychotherapy, in R. Hunter (ed.) Dictionary of Pastoral Care and Counselling (Nashville: Abingdon, 1990).

R.H. Tawney, Equality (London: Allen and Unwin, 1964).

W. Temple, Christianity and Social Order (London: SPCK, 1976).

R. Underwood, Empathy and Confrontation in Pastoral Care (Philadelphia: Fortress, 1985).

## Reports

Issues in Human Sexuality (London: Church House, 1991).
Something to Celebrate (London: Church House, 1995).

# 2

## The Spirit of Care

*'Feelings alter, fade, return*
*But love stands constant in the will:*
*Its not alone the touching, seeing,*
*It's how to mean the other's being.'* (James McAuley)

*A*gain he said, *'There was once a man who had two sons; and the younger said to his father, "Father give me my share of the property." So he divided his estate between them. A few days later the younger son turned the whole of his share into cash and left home for a distant country, where he squandered it in dissolute living. He had spent it all when a severe famine fell upon that country and he began to be in need. So he went and attached himself to one of the local landowners, who sent him on to his farm to mind his pigs. He would have been glad to fill his belly with the pods that the pigs were eating, but no-one gave him anything. Then he came to his senses: "How many of my of my father's hired servants have more food than they can eat," he said, "and here am I starving to death! I will go at once to my father and say to him 'Father I have sinned against God and against you; I am no longer fit to be called your son; treat me as one of your hired servants." So he set out for his father's house. But whilst he was still a long way off his father saw him, and his heart went out to him; he ran to meet him, flung his arms around him, and kissed him. The son said, "Father I have sinned against God and against you; I am no longer fit to be called your son." But the father said to his servants, "Quick fetch a robe, the best we have, and put it on him; put a ring on his finger and sandals on his feet. Bring the fatted calf and kill it, let us celebrate with a feast. For this son of mine was dead and has come back to life; he was lost and is found." And the festivities began.*

*Now the elder son had been out on the farm; and on his way back, as he approached the house he heard music and dancing. He called one of the servants and asked him what it meant. The servant told him, "Your brother has come home and your father has killed the fatted calf because he has him back safe and sound." But he was angry and refused to go in. His father came out and pleaded with him; but he retorted, "You know how I have slaved for all these years; I never once disobeyed your orders; yet you never gave me so much as a kid to celebrate with my friends. But now that this son of yours turns up, after running through your money with his women, you killed the fatted calf for him."*

*"My boy said the father, you are always with me and everything I have is yours. How could we fail to celebrate this happy day? Your brother here was dead and has come back to life; he was lost and has been found." '*
(St. Luke chap.15, vv. 11-32)

The parable of the prodigal son is entirely unreasonable. It portrays a father who is faithful to his son despite the fact that he squanders his inheritance. This is a father, moreover, who does not attempt to interfere. He gives him the inheritance and leaves it to his son to discover the truth - about his situation and about his relationships. Finally, rather than put the young man in his place and let him know what he has done, and how much he has worried his mother, the father elevates him, calls him to rise from the status of the servant to be his son once more.

Just to make sure we have got the point the father then has a dialogue with his entirely reasonable older son. This son is incensed because there is no fairness in his father's treatment. The reward for irresponsibility and moral laxity is a great feast. The reward for years of labour is nothing. The father does not attempt to justify this view of morality and justice. He simply invites the elder son to join in the celebrations.

The parable tells us something about the nature of agape, God's love for humanity. At one level the father embodies a care which seeks to respond to the need of the son and which, above all, looks to a response which will re-establish and in this case actually deepen their relationship. It is also about moral meaning. The relational morality of the father is contrasted sharply with that of the elder son based upon reasonableness, fairness and the calculation of reward.

This is the love which, I will argue, is the centre of the pastoral counselling relationship, providing both the ground of care and the ground of moral meaning. What enables the two to be held together is the very particular spirituality which agape creates and sustains, making care more than simply technique and moral meaning more than rational reflection on concepts of good, or the application of some a priori conception of the good. Agape in effect spans all of these elements. It is an irreducible moral principle, an attitude, a virtue, indeed the chief virtue, a way of knowing the other, the ground of care for the other. Agape in other words is central to and spans spirituality, pastoral care, and Christian Ethics. Such divisions are in some respects artificial when faced with the phenomenon of agape.

Agape has been the focus of much debate, not least as to whether it has any substantive meaning. It is all too tempting in the light of a post modern society to use the concept as an unfocused catch - all which will somehow enable communication. It will be the task of the next two chapters to put some flesh on the idea of agape and to show how it is uniquely able to build bridges between:

Theory and practice;

Content and process;

Different values.

This chapter will focus on agape and pastoral care, with its underlying spirituality. The next chapter will focus on agape and Christian Ethics.

## *The nature of agape*

As will be seen the meaning of the term agape has at various times been a matter of debate. The term is not simply imported from extra biblical sources where it is a relatively bland meaning of love. In the Septuagint agape translates the Hebrew *aheb*, a love centred on personal physical attraction, but extended on occasions to food or sleep (Gen 29:18, 27:4; Proverbs 20:14). Such a love is characteristically embodied in the love of man and woman which is both physical and long term. In Hebrew there is no attempt to differentiate between erotic love based upon the attraction of the physical and the more cooler and rational love of agape. Hence, even in the Song of Songs agape is used for love. (3: 1-4)

In the Old and New Testaments agape, not least as the love of God, is expressed in a number of vivid pictures, such as a farmer caring for his vineyard, or a shepherd for his sheep (Isa.5: 1-7; John 10: 11-16). It is a love which is even greater than a parent's love. Such a love is essentially practical, embodied, and the extent of it is summed up in John 3 :16, 17,

'God so loved the world that he gave his only Son, that everyone one who has faith in him should not perish but have eternal life. It was not to judge the world that God sent his Son into the world, but that through him the world might be saved.'

This stresses the inclusive aim of God's love and its sacrificial nature. Indeed, the term agape sums up the very nature of God (1 John 4: 8).

The Biblical and subsequent material provides the basis for some key ideas which involve agape as a way of being or relating (Faithfulness); a way of knowing (Truthfulness); a way of empowering. All of these aspects are key to spirituality and to pastoral care.

Further reflections on the idea of agape have inevitably led to major questions about its nature and how it relates to self love, neighbour love and God love. These will be addressed in the next chapter.

## A way of being or relating

Agape is most often characterised by the term unconditional. This is a love which is not based on attraction or achievement or lack of achievement of the other. It is a love of the will, not simply of feeling, and which loves the other simply because they are the other. Some object to the term because it implies that such love will accept the other whatever they have done and thus run the danger of actually reinforcing bad actions or behaviour. This is a non-discriminatory love, a love which does not distinguish between different behaviours. This is to go too far. All it means is a love which does not base itself on the action of the other, a disinterested love which is not based in a partial way on the other.

Such a love is often expressed in the idea of covenant. Based upon examples from the Old Testament, William May argues that this involves several things (May 1987):

Firstly, it is a gift. It is not based upon any contractual terms. It precedes and may well initiate the relationship. In counselling, of course, the immediate relationship is initiated by the counsellee. However, the counsellor and her offer of care is there prior to felt need. Like the medical practitioner, she has a commitment which is part of the total profession's commitment to those in need.

In this respect the commitment is analogous to that of the family. The marriage vows involve unconditional commitment. This is if anything intensified in the experience of families, where children are in need of a care which is there for the child whatever her weakness, difficulty or vulnerability.

Secondly, this disinterested concern for the other is one which is constant.

Agape promises to be there whatever the response from the other. It is not simply that it is there regardless of the rights of the other, it is there whatever the other does. A core meaning here is being there for the other, remaining true to the other. This is seen strongly in Hosea's image of the lover remaining faithful and calling back his lover to the relationship (Hosea 11; 8-9).

Thirdly, the covenant defies precise specification and therefore remains open in terms of possibilities. It also has a growing edge 'which nourishes rather than limits relationships' (May 1987). It is always searching for the good of the other, but is always open to the possibilities of the other.

Fourthly, the covenant is often not about an individual agreement but about one between whole communities, thus raising the possibility of an agreement which can bring many people together into a network of relationships.

May contrasts this with the 'first cousin' of the covenant, the contract. The contract is based upon specific conditions which if broken can lead to the end of the agreement. The contract attempts to sum up obligations in specific terms. This has the effect of seeing the fulfilment of the contract as discharging all responsibility.

The stress in the covenant is upon the underlying relationship, and on being there for the other - any other. This does not mean that the contract approach is wrong or unacceptable. On the contrary, it may be an important way of expressing the underlying attitude of the covenant, indeed of enabling relationships to be established and developed.

Jesus lived out just this faithfulness, not least in the work of the Atonement. As Wesley Carr notes there are many different views of the Atonement (Carr 1989, 7). At one extreme is the idea of Christ's victory, which sees him paying a ransom for the sins of the world. The stress here is on the achievement of Christ and the universal application of his action. At the other extreme is what is seen as the subjectivist approach of the cross as exemplifying God's love. In this theory salvation is located in the relationships with Christ, the recognition of his love and the subsequent response of the believer.

Perhaps the simplest view of the saving work of Christ is to see the cross at one with his life and as part of his covenant faithfulness. He offered his inclusive love and remained faithful - despite humiliation and intense suffering. Even at this point he was able to be concerned for those around him and to forgive those who rejected him. Most of all he remained faithful in and through the ultimate rejection and breaking of the covenant. The resurrection was not so much the conquering of death - after all the

God who creates can also resurrect - but rather the ultimate sign of faithfulness. The sign of faithfulness was beautifully summed up in the figure of the risen Jesus on the shore, not angrily waiting for the very people who had let him down, especially the person who had broken the covenant through denying that he even knew Jesus, but rather waiting to respond to their needs with breakfast (John 21: 8 ff.). Of course the doctrine of the Atonement is one which tries to answer the question as to why God should have done things this way, and such a question has tended to come up with a mechanistic answer about God's power and about the conquest of sin. At the same time it is an answer which conveniently provides a view of suffering. Suffering and sacrifice are instrumental, leading to the greater good of salvation, an argument extended to health. The covenant provides a quite different perspective which stresses not an explanation of suffering but rather the faithful presence of the other in suffering. The experience of that presence is primary, and any meaning emerges from reflection on that experience and that relationship. As such the stress is on holistic awareness of that presence, not simply on the rational explanations of relationships (Campbell 1995).

## A way of knowing

Agape also has an epistemic function. It is the way of revealing the other. This implies that the 'other' is not instantly accessible. Simone Weil, indeed, argues that the other is often invisible, with many factors from prejudice to fear causing this. Hence, she writes, 'If you want to become invisible, there is no surer way than to become poor'. She goes on to say, 'Love sees what is invisible' (quoted in Gaita 2000, xvi). Love goes beyond artificial boundaries to reveal the humanity of the other .

The dynamic of this is expressed in the idea of empathy. Heinz Kohut characterises empathy as follows:

'(1) Empathy, the recognition of the self in the other, is an indispensable tool of observation, without which vast areas of human life …remain unintelligible. (2) Empathy, the expansion of the self to include the other, constitutes a powerful psychological bond …(3) Empathy, the accepting, confirming, and understanding human echo evoked by the self, is a psychological nutriment without which life as we know it could not be sustained' (Kohut 1982, 398).

Max Scheler notes that it is more than fellow feeling, describing it as 'a genuine reaching out and entry into the other person and his individual situation, a true and authentic transcendence of oneself' (Campbell 1984, 77). It is a movement beyond the concerns for the self, including fear and guilt, and with this an expansion or reaching out of the self. This involves not taking the self too seriously, and thus Scheler can write of abandoning 'personal dignity'. This is not a self conscious process but rather one which allows the 'instinctive life to look after itself'. Such a letting go of the self is contrasted with a self conscious concern for the other, where the concern itself begins to dominate and actually get in the way of real openness, and thus of awareness of the other. Scheler bemoans the way in which this natural awareness of the other, including the environment, has been lost not least in a society where instrumentality - where others are used as means rather than ends - dominates.

This movement towards the other does not lose the individuality of the one who cares. Indeed, the movement away from self concern enables distance which allows her to see herself more clearly. It also enhances the value of the other, bring forth the value they possess and enabling them to disclose what is unique about themselves to themselves and to the other. Empathy then is a way of knowing the other and enabling the other to know herself.

Agape lies at the base of empathy. The second part of Kohut's description clearly signals the inclusive acceptance of the other and the psychological bond which this provides. Empathy is very much a working out of, a sign of, agape. Without an assurance of this acceptance it would be difficult for the person to disclose anything of herself. Indeed, without that love, and therefore without any presumed judgement of the other, it would be impossible to see the truth of the other (Barth 1956).

The natural human dynamic is to keep hidden that which is imagined as not acceptable. Hence, there is always a wariness about possible judgement from the other. At the same time if the person enters into the relationship with preconceived judgements she does in effect foreclose the possibilities of actually seeing the other as she is, or of learning about the other.

Alfred Margulies notes four components of empathy:
- *Conceptual empathy*, stressing cognitive understanding of the other;
- *Self experiential empathy*, referring to memories, affects and associations which are stirred in the listener, thus causing her to identify with the experience of the other;

- *Imaginative - imitative empathy*, involving imagining oneself into a model of the other's experience;
- *Resonant empathy*, the experience of affective contagion, where the listener feels the feeling of the other (Margulies 1989, 19).

Empathy involves an interplay of all of these aspects, leading to an openness to the self and others and to the different as aspects of the self, affective, cognitive and somatic. This openness and reaching out to the other means that the empathic engagement does not deal in static truth, looking behind the other to reveal *the* truth. On the contrary, if through reaching out to the other enables her to reveal something of herself then the truth about the other, our awareness of the other, is continuously evolving. Facts and truth are 'a creation of the relationship itself, a continuous coming into being of possibilities requiring further exploration' (Margulies 1989, 12).

In the light of this, empathy is both open to difference and sameness in the other. Openness to difference is characterised by wonder, surprise, curiosity and astonishment, core aspects of spirituality. Jerome Berryman notes that it is precisely in childhood where this sense of surprise and wonder is at its height, not least because young children live at the limit of their experience most of the time (Berryman 1991, 34). The de-centring of the self which Scheler refers to precisely ensures that the listener does not assert her truth on the other but is genuinely surprised by the other.

At the same time the listener comes to know the sameness in the other. As Raymond Gaita is eager to remind us this is not the cognitive recognition of some generalised common humanity, but rather the recognition of what he refers to as the 'preciousness' of the other. This is a recognition that the other is one with you, a brother or sister. The startling thing is that this awareness can only be found in reaching out to the particular, to the unique other. Gaita reminds us that this sense of common bond is not a scientific universality, to do with general truth, or with abstract language, but rather the universality which we recognise in the particular, local, story of the other. Every narrator needs an 'address', needs roots, and we see our common humanity as we experience those roots, and begin to understand the roots of others in their terms and translate that story into our language. Hence,

'In literature, the universality one aspires to is of a kind that is achieved when a story or a poem in a particular natural language, historically rich and dense, shaped by and shaping the life of a people, is translated into other natural languages, historically rich and dense, and shaping the life of different peoples.' (Gaita 2000, xxix)

In this movement empathy involves mutuality, constant revelation of the self and other. The dynamic of this lies at the heart of genuine dialogue, dialogue which can begin to understand the other in their terms, and which can both enable and allow the challenge which comes from difference, and also enjoy the support and acceptance which comes from sameness. Sameness involves not simply being the same as the other, but also the sense of constancy, and therefore a sense of faithfulness. This mutual disclosure is not necessarily symmetrical. On the contrary different relationships will lead to different aspects of each other being revealed. In a caring relationship, for instance, the carer may not reveal intimate details of her life. She will nonetheless reveal, in body language and in words, her attitude and her values, aspects of herself, how she feels about the other. For the person being cared for this becomes a critical narrative that she is reading from the other, as to whether she is accepted or not. For someone who comes to that relationship from a world of conditional value, where life meaning rests on the reactions of others, and where she is used to negative judgements then she is already herself being faced with something new. Indeed, for most people who come from that experience this is so astonishing that it is hard to believe. Hence, part of the mutuality in that relationship begins to emerge through the testing of the carer's narrative.

The mutual discovery of meaning through this process is summed up by Margulies,

'Invariably, in searching for the other in active fashion, we come to our own reflection, the fundamental projective nature of empathy, and the dialectical quality of finding and creating meaning' (Margulies 1989, xii).

## The love of God

Edward Farley suggests a doctrine of God which is based around empathy (Farley 1996). The Incarnation itself is a reaching out to the other which both communicates the particularity of God and at the same time enables the person to open up to her self. Farley contrasts the transcendent otherness of God with this movement of empathy, and thus sees empathy as simply a part of God's being. Paul Fiddes argues, however, that this empathy is central to God's being, expressed in the nature of the Trinity, in with each person has his own purpose and identity, but exists in constant empathy with the others.

Hence, Fiddes sees God's *whole being* as 'empathic without reserve, as a triune event of relational love' (Fiddes 2000, 208).

It may also be said that empathy is precisely not to be simply identified with imminence and contrasted with transcendence. On the contrary empathy enables an awareness and appreciation of both. This brings us to spirituality.

## Empathy and Spirituality

In recent years there has been a tendency to see empathy as a discrete disposition or quality which is very specific to care or counselling, as if it had no relevance to life in general. The dynamic of agape and empathy, however, reveals quite a different picture, that far from being a 'counselling skill' it is a 'life skill', and as such lies at the heart of spirituality and spiritual awareness.

Spirituality, like concepts such as health, can best be viewed as a latent construct, that is 'a complex multidimensional construct underlying a broad array of observable phenomena' (Miller and Thoresen 1999, 4). Viewed as dimension of human experience, and therefore distinct from but related to religion, it may be characterised as:

*Awareness and appreciation of the other;*
*The capacity to respond to the other;*
*The capacity to develop life meaning based upon this awareness and response.*

The 'other' includes the self, the other person, the group or community, the environment, the divine. Awareness of each of these 'others' involves agape holding together in tension what may be termed aporia - things which seem contradictory to hold together and yet are both part of the truth of the other. These include the other:
- as both same and different, one of a group yet unique;
- as both dependant yet free. The other has limitations and yet has the capacity to create;
- as both fully a person (and thus the bearer of human rights) and yet always emerging as a person;
- as both social and individual;
- as both one who can care for me and one who can need me.

It is important then to briefly review each of the 'others' in turn.

## The self

It is reasonable to speak of the self as other. In one sense the self is indeed one amongst others and so is an other to someone else. In another sense it is perfectly possible to speak of transcending the self or framing a distance from the self, enabling dialogue with the self (van der Ven 1998, 108).

The critical awareness of the self involves the most basic, essentially spiritual aporia, the self as both the same and different as others. This may seem to be a perfectly obvious point in conceptual terms. Affectively, however, it is precisely not always easy to be aware of this. The self cannot be understood if it is seen as completely different. Indeed complete difference makes the self a stranger, someone with no point of contact, who cannot be identified with. As shall be seen later a great many people who are suffering see themselves as strangers - people who are unable to be like the others, people who cannot be identified with. It is this difference which often makes them feel ashamed and makes them unable to accept the self. Equally, if the self is simply the same as others then there is  nothing to learn and the danger of a loss of real identity, separateness and any sense of responsibility for the self.

Awareness of the self  leads also to awareness of limitations as well as capacities, of  weaknesses and strengths. This reminds us of the need for agapeic acceptance in any awareness of the self.  Without that acceptance of the self, limitations and needs are often not even perceived.

## Others

As with the self, awareness of others involves recognition of sameness and difference. For the other to be simply different means there is no point of common humanity to relate to. Hence, the person who is seen as purely different is often dehumanised, seen as the stranger or even the enemy.  Equally, to see the other as simply the same can lead to obscuring the particular history of the person, that which makes them unique.

All this means, as noted above, that the agapeic relationship with the other is inevitably dynamic. The sameness in the other provides the basis for initial trust and collaboration, enabling the person to see the other and feel that she belongs. The difference in the other provides the basis for continued disclosure and learning. Empathic awareness of the other also reveals their need and whether they can be a source of  support.

## Communities

Beyond the one to one relationship is corporate spirituality. This group dimension is part of what it means to be human. Hence, as J. Mbiti writes in the context of African spirituality, 'A person cannot detach himself from the religion of his group, for to do so is to be severed from his roots, his foundation, his context of security, his kinship and the entire group of those who make him aware of his own existence' (Mbiti 1990, 2).

This meaning generated through relating to the community is often lost under the stress of western consumerism and individualism. These tend to focus on the contract nature of groups, i.e. groups formed through individual choice, with no historical or moral claim on the person outside that contract. Groups as a result take on a purely instrumental character, simply used by the person for her utility, and thus with not sense of identification with or responsibility for that group.

Increased awareness of the group, however, reveals greater complexity and ambiguity. Every group, for instance has both community elements (ways in which the members relate to and support each other) and institutional elements (ways in which the group manages, orders and maintains itself). The institutional element is often seen as the enemy of the community, with bureaucracy replacing relationships, creating distance, often moral distance, between individuals or sub groups, or defending the group from the outside (Bauman 1989). Nonetheless, the institution is necessary if there is to be the maintenance of the groups and efficient use of limited resources.

Equally the group is important for the development of a sense of belonging and identity, but also may have limitations, indeed might present a threat to autonomy.

## The environment

The term transcendent, being beyond, can be applied to all the 'others' above - moving beyond the self, reaching out to the other or the group. However it is used most often in relation to the environment and the divine.

The environment has a wide definition, from the physical and social environment which we normally inhabit, to that created through art, to wider nature itself. This wider environment is often so vast and 'other' that it seems totally different from the self. A good example is Niagara Falls. As the boat, the Maid of the Mist, approaches the thundering Horseshoe Falls one is simply overcome by the other - sight and sound which are very hard to take in cognitively. As one stands at the base of the Bridal Veil falls, feeling the might of the water on the so called Hurricane Deck, one simply lets go and opens up to the experience of the other. It is impossible not to feel a part of the greater whole, a literally breath taking experience which leads to a momentary loss of the self as separate. However, there have to be boundaries which do separate, not least for safety's sake. Indeed, without such boundary there can be little knowledge of the self over against the other, and thus ultimately no actual awareness of the other.

Moreover, awareness of and the development of meaning about the wider environment as an other presence is not simply about recognising its difference. Emmanuel Lartey, for instance notes the spirituality of the Lakota Indians who perceive their environment in terms of their own social networks of belonging. Hence, a Lakotan can pray for 'all my relatives', including animals, birds, plants, water and rocks (Lartey 1997, 121ff).

Once again authentic awareness of the environment reveals ambiguities and complexities. The environment is both the base of our existence - providing us with sustenance, but also a place of great risk and danger. Whilst we depend upon the environment it also depends upon us - for protection and responsible stewardship. At the heart of this is a sense of interconnectedness which sets up demands upon the human being as person and as society (McFague 1997).

## The divine

The divine is often viewed as radically the other. For some, the very thought of seeing God in human terms is to betray his nature. Hence, we frequently apologise for the inadequacy of our language. This very sense of God as totally the other is one which easily moves into God as a figure to be feared. We cannot be sure of his attitude and actions and this can easily move to attempts to placate or influence him with sacrifices, of whatever form. This leads to a form of religious instrumentality, which sees the religious life as a means to end, not an end in itself. The dynamic then becomes essentially conditional.

In the Christian faith this quite contrary to the dynamic of God. The doctrine of *Imago Dei*, man made in the image of God, clearly sets out the sameness of God (Genesis 1: 27). This sameness is expressed most fully in the Incarnation. God chooses to express himself and embody his attitude in and through humanity. In all this he lets go of power and becomes vulnerable. However, in his embodiment he also becomes intelligible. His love is summed up in his faithfulness and his inclusive care, and in his capacity to identify with his people. He is both different and the same. This partly about God being both divine and human. It is also about God only being known in the particularity of his human narrative. By extension this reinforces the point that love itself must be embodied. If love is not embodied in relationships and action it is not love, but rather the idea of love. As Gaita reminds us, so many Western philosophers have made do simply with love as an idea (Gaita 2000, 276ff).

The embodiment of love in Jesus also highlights the creative tension of that love. He offers the support and acceptance of all others, but at the same time he makes claims upon them, challenges them to respond, and so further reveal themselves. It is a relationship which involves both security and risk.

Loving God then is not simply about the grateful response to God's love for us. It is actually about how we see him, about how we develop empathy for him in and through our dialogue. The very limited but familiar words that we use to try to reach out to him, to do with family for instance, exemplify this empathy, as does the awareness of their limitations.

Empathy then is at the heart of awareness of the 'other', able to hold together the other in all its ambiguities. As C. Schlauch notes this involves three sets of tensions:

### Doubting /Believing

Peter Elbow writes of two basic 'games' which can be played to find the truth. The doubting game 'seeks the truth by seeking error. Doubting an assertion is the best way to find an error in it. To doubt well it helps to make a special effort to extricate yourself form the assertions in question' (quoted in Schlauch 1990, 13). The believing game aims to find 'not errors but truths, and for this it helps to believe ... To do this you must make, not an act of self-extrication, but an act of self insertion, self involvement.'

The doubting game is out to test the edifice of the other's narrative, to see that it really holds together. The believing game enables the person to actually build that story. Hence, Riceour can write of the need for a hermeneutic of suspicion and a hermeneutic of restoration (Riceour 1992).

In all this, doubt is not judgement but is ultimately an honest testing of the integrity of the other's narrative. Together belief and doubt are a powerful force, which give little room to hide or to avoid responsibility for how the other sees the world and how she responds to the other in her life. Nonetheless, they do not direct but give the other the power and responsibility to be aware and to appreciate the other and the self. There is a strong sense of realised eschatology in this tension with judgement actually a function of the relationship enabling the other to see more clearly for herself. As Fiddes notes judgement in this light 'is not an image of exclusion but of healing, brought about through the painful act of admitting what is true about ourselves and others' (Fiddes 2000, 210). The dynamic which Gordon Graham presents is fear of a future judgement demanding present moral confrontation.

### Separated / Connected
Mary Belenky distinguishes two different epistemological orientations. 'Connected knowers' presume a relationship between themselves and the known. 'Separate knowers' stand apart from the other (Belenky 1986, 102).

Agape brings together both these ways of knowing, enabling the lover to see the other as both same and different. With this the person can be both vitally concerned for the other and also be detached. It is precisely this balance which enables the father of the Prodigal Son not to intervene, but rather to give his son the freedom to make his own life, then to wait and finally to genuinely welcome him back.

This sense of distance as well as closeness is essential to continued pastoral care. Without it the person would be swamped by concern for the other. Without it, it would be difficult to care in practice.

### Understanding/ Explanation
Schlauch notes the distinction between understanding the other, which involves identifying with them and their feelings, entering into their affective world, and explaining, which involves looking at dynamics which have caused problems for the other (Schlauch 1990). The one is very much subjective. Explanation claims more objectivity. There is a danger, however, of seeing explanation in terms of the explanatory concepts and theories which are the base of some particular carers - not least psychotherapists. Firstly, such theories have only a hypothetical force and only make sense in relation to the reflection of the person on her situation. Secondly, in the context of care this can give too much power to the therapist to supply the

objective element. As shall be seen any 'objectivity', shared meaning, has to emerge from the developing dialogue.

In all this the dynamic of agape is never 'smooth'. It involves a continued oscillation between the self and other.

## A way of Empowering

The nature of love is to share power and above all not to take away from the other the responsibility for seeing for themselves. Much that is done in the name of love ends up as manipulation. The lover is unable to wait and wants to see the outcome now. Professional carers are very prone to this, not least because professionalism looks for evidence of successful outcome. Such a love might involve doing things for the other and once more the danger of a patronising love which cares for the other *in spite of* her failings (Bauman 1994, 97). This is a love which actually retains the power of conditionality and thus of judgement. It wants to be good to the other but also wants the other to know that they are different.

Agape on the other hand involves a natural openness and is essentially vulnerable, partly because you have to wait and partly because you cannot know the outcome when you share that love. W. H. Vanstone sums this up well:

'The power which love gives to the other is the power to determine the issue of love - its completion or frustration, its triumph or its tragedy. This is the vulnerability of authentic love - that it surrenders to the other power over its own issue, power to determine the triumph or tragedy of love' (Vanstone 1977, 67).

In a real sense any embodiment of love is risky. The father in the prodigal son parable ran the risk of being made to look a fool, or worse still of losing his son. The person who offers care in an a non-formal setting runs the risk of losing her friend or family member. The person who offers care in a more formal setting, as part of a care group, or a professional, runs the risk of 'failing', of seeming to be incompetent. Hence, as Campbell notes, the culture of professional care is often one of carer 'knows best' (Campbell 1984).

As Henri Nouwen reminds us such a culture in turn tends to ignore the vulnerabilities of the healer and their needs and limitations. Their needs have to be addressed by the caring community within which they operate. It would be inappropriate for them to share those in a pastoral care or counselling relationship - other than as an example of how needs can be accepted and met. However, the empathic relationship is one of mutual revelation and the limitations and attitude of the carer can and should be a part of that relationship. The counsellee or client cannot hope to move forward if she does not develop an awareness of the ambiguities of the counsellor - her concern for the other and also the limits of that concern. At one level this is about drawing boundaries which help the person to see her separateness and to see the areas of responsibility. 'This person is concerned for me but she is not going to rescue me, or live my life for me.' At another level it is about enabling the counsellee herself to develop spiritual awareness, to be aware of the other in her ambiguity. At its most basic it is about the counsellee being able to develop faith in and through an other.

This begins to see the dynamic of agape as more than simply one of loving and waiting. The dynamic involves the proactive reaching out with positive concern for the other, enabling response in terms of revelation of the self and testing of the other. It is this dynamic which enables the development of power. Psychotherapist Heinz Kohut sees this clearly when he accepts that empathy itself is the key to therapy (Kohut 1982, 397).

He sees two major aspects in empathy:
- a methodological function. It enables observation and reflection. In this the therapist is not simply giving the person an interpretation but enabling her to make her own.
- As a 'psychological bond' and 'psychological nutriment', the very oxygen of the therapeutic relationship. Empathy in this enables both the acceptance of the self and also the growth of the self. Once again the critical sense of faithfulness and unconditional acceptance is at the core.

As we move more directly from spirituality to pastoral care then agape is very much about giving power to the other to take responsibility for engaging the truth about the self and the other, and power to make appropriate change. It is the same dynamic as spirituality but with a different perspective and intention.

Such empowerment involves the articulation of narrative, reflection on meaning, and the embodiment of response.

### Narration

To begin with agape provides a safe environment within which the person can begin to develop her narrative. Narration is critical to the development of the character, which, as van der Ven notes is refigured 'in the twofold sense of uncovering its concealed dimensions and transforming its experienced dimensions' (van der Ven 1998, 358). Narration is a complex function which brings together all levels of awareness and meaning.

It enables the person to gain distance from the self, and so begin to become aware of experience, the effect of experience on the self, and the meaning and feelings which shape that experience. Mark Freeman refers to this as a stage of *distanciation*, which achieves differentiation, a separation of the self from the self, such that the text of one's experience becomes the object of interpretation (Freeman 1993, 45). In this the self becomes both subject and object leading to the possibility of dialogue *with* the self *about* the self. Articulation of narrative in this sense is not simply a bilateral communication with the other. Yes, it is transmitted to the other, the listener, but it also involves the relationship with the self. The self can hear what is being said and often discovers something new about data, feelings or thoughts, something new about the self and the other. Hence, van der Ven can speak of the development of the dialogic self and of the self as both reader and writer (van der Ven 1998, 358). It is precisely this dynamic which can lead to surprises, and which enables clarification of the person's feelings and values. It is not possible to become aware of that without articulating it. Articulation may occur in different ways, not least through the posture and body language of the person.

## *Reflection*

The more the story is articulated in the presence of another the more it becomes reflective, and the more it focuses on the many different stories within that. As Bahktin notes, these stories are filled with contradictions, creating not simply a universe but a 'pluriverse' or 'heteroverse'. This leads to many different dialogues each with interactions which generate surprise, challenge and possibilities (van der Ven 1998, 359). Such surprise and challenges are the result of contradictions or connections that might be made between the different narratives and often lead to anxiety on the part of the person who is being cared for. Once more the temptation is to reduce that anxiety through reassurance or attempt to resolve the issue for the 'client'. However, as Halmos and Freeman note, it is crucial that the carer firstly enables her to develop the dialogue so that the underlying dissonance can be seen and, secondly, enables her to face and work through the challenges which this faces her with (Halmos 1964; Freeman 1993, 47). Only with the security and support of agape can the person begin to take responsibility for

this process, a process which does four things:
- Clarifies the meaning of the different narratives as they impinge upon her;
- Works out how to deal with the ambiguities and conflicts which emerge. This is something which will involve work on affective as well as cognitive levels;
- Works through to new meaning, based upon a new sense of value, empowered by developing qualities;
- Puts into practice response.

## Clarification

The clarification of meaning involves reflection on the different stories of the relational network, in effect charting the person's spiritual map, seeing how the person's different experiences come together and examining the meaning which is available to the person to guide her through the experiences. This involves reflection on:

1. *Significant others.* These are a critical part of the person's narrative, generating life meaning. The significant other, such as partner or family member may be either a major cause of personal 'dis-ease', pain of shame or a great resource in providing support.

2. *Communities.* Relationship to communities are examined, identifying the core communities and how they give meaning to the life of the person. How far do such communities supply a meaning structure? What roles does the person fulfil in them? The community can be both the source of problems and the basis of survival and security. New Religious Movements, for instance, can typically provide affective security and lack of cognitive reflection (Barker 1992).

3. *The environment.* In one sense the environment might seem to be irrelevant to pastoral care. However, the physical environment can be part of an individual's problem. Experience of the workplace points, for instance, to pathogenic environments, including sick building syndrome, which lead to depression and anxiety.

Equally, awareness of the environment as a supportive resource can be enabled through reflection. A couple, for instance, who had been trying for a child through the IVF programme had suffered a miscarriage. This was a major blow as it appeared this would be their last chance. Once they were told they decided not to have the woman's womb evacuated immediately, but needed rather to 'hold' the fetus for a few more days and then return to the hospital. That evening at the height of their grieving they went to a local moor dominated by imposing and remarkable rock formations. This place was associated by them with a sense of peace and acceptance. Hence, they could speak of going to the place and 'holding' their child whilst the rocks held them. It would be facile to speak of this as a form of pantheism, they were strong Christians. However, they discovered an affective and somatic experience of acceptance in the environment which was for them more powerful than much of the traditional Christian expressions.

4. *The divine.* As R. Gorush and W. Miller *et al.* observe the divine and related religious experience can actually form the basis of problems (Gorush and Miller 1999, 48 ff.). At one level a restrictive religious focus, with a condemning deity can also be an obstacle to treatment. They also note the way in which negative spirituality can reinforce underlying pathology. Such dynamics illustrate well the interconnectedness of the different areas of spirituality with negative attitudes to the self and projections of the person's way of thinking affecting the perception of God.

## Conflicts

Contradictions which emerge between or within such narratives may include those between:

- Ideas, values and feelings;
- Attitude of the person to self and others;
- Different values and beliefs held by the person.
- Different values and belief, and practice;
- The view of the other and 'reality' of the other;
- Attitude and practice in the past and present.

A typical conflict is that between an affective and cognitive narrative. Brian, an elderly Christian went into hospital for a major operation. He prepared himself spiritually for some time before and believed that his faith would hold him up through the experience. He felt nervous before the event, but assumed this would go away once he was in hospital. In fact his anxiety was maintained before the operation and increased afterwards. He found himself experiencing panic attacks and at the same time becoming angry, resentful and ashamed that he should be feeling this. His pastor tried to persuade him to relax, but his presence made Brian feel all the more ashamed. It was one of the nurses who helped him to begin to reflect on the conflict which he was experiencing. At one level his belief system was both conditional and cognitive in nature, along the lines of, 'If you believe in Jesus you will not suffer and all will be well.' This reinforced a narrative learned in the forces and in his family about self reliance and the need to sort out problems swiftly. To leave problems unsolved was a sign of failure. Against this Brian had a strong group of feelings which he had never been allowed to show, including pain and anger at the way in which his family had never given him the affective and somatic support that he craved. It was precisely in this moment of crisis that he felt the need for that kind of support most, the support of 'being held', and no one was there to give to him, hence the increase in anger and anxiety. With the help of the nursing staff Brian was able to articulate these different stories and so to feel firstly that the feelings he began to express were valid. From this he was able to see that the support which his belief system gave him was not what he needed or wanted, and so began to explore a very different view of faith which saw God as neither someone to please nor someone who would fix things but rather someone who was there for him, a faithful presence, in the midst of pain and suffering. He could only begin to understand that because of the example of caring presence from the nurses. In other words, he could only begin to understand this experientially.

The presence of the other then enables the person to examine the different narratives and the tensions between them, to test them, including the reality of any perceptions of the other, and to either affirm meaning or work through to new meaning. Another classic conflict of meaning, which will be explored in the next chapter is that between care for others and care for the self. Often a person will show a strong narrative of concern for others and yet have quite a different narrative with regard to the self, seeing the self as not worthy of care.

### Life Meaning

The development of life meaning is critical to empowerment. It is connected to development of identity and thus the development of the subject. This in turn is connected to questions of self worth and value. This depends upon both a sense of unconditional and conditional worth, a sense of being accepted for the self and also accepted because of the contribution of the self to the community and a recognised purpose. Both of these can be seen as basic human needs, set out by Gershen Kaufman as:

- A close interpersonal relationship which provides an environment of unconditional care. The experience of being nurtured.

- The experience of nurturing. This involves the practice of care for others and the assurance that this a task of value (Kaufman 1980, 65).

Pastoral care which offers agape addresses the need for unconditional acceptance experientially. Because it leads to reflection on the different narratives, it also enables the person to see the unconditional care offered in those relationships, be that offered by the environment or by groups or by God himself. It literally enables the person to develop empathic awareness of these others.

This reflection also begins to address the second need. It looks at the needs and claims of others in the relational network, the way in which they call the person to respond. It tests that calling, and tests out how the person might respond. Testing the calling of the other means a careful reflection on their narrative, what they are demanding and the reason for that demand. This is not an easy process, especially if the demands of the other have formed the basis of the person's identity and life meaning. Hence, it involves working through the narrative at affective and cognitive levels. Brian's view of God's demand, for instance, was one of calling him to perfection, always ready, never depressed. The crisis in his life forced him to reflect upon and test that perception and to realise that it did not make sense. It was having a bad effect on him and at the same time contradicted other views of God and his calling. His response to that call might then have been to leave that relationship with God, or to move into change and discover a new empathic relationship with God which both nurtured him and gave him ways of nurturing others. The nurse enabled him to understand that affective level of knowing God. Once this occurred then he was able to face the pastor and begin to discover ways of contributing to the church life, a reworked contribution and underlying purpose which was seen to be of value and so help him to feel valued. This was a process of negotiation, something which will be examined in detail in chapter six.

A critical part of both response to the narrative of the other and the negotiation of the contribution to community is reflection on and testing of the self and the self narrative. That narrative, of course, is critically connected to the narrative demands of the others in the person's life. However, testing the person's own perception of her life meaning tests this against reality. This in turn enables the person to see the effects of the different narratives upon her, how she relates to them and perhaps most importantly what her limitations might be. Any response to the call of the other demands an awareness of and acceptance of those limitations, something only possible in an environment of agape. This enables the person to re-evaluate life purpose and take responsibility for that purpose.

At the core of this agape is doing far more than simply allowing space for disinterested reflection. It is also far more than simply providing confrontation which tests reality, or reflects back the narrative and its consequences. The full weight of agape's empowering presence is that it is directly calling the other to respond empathically, both by being open to her network of relationships and discovering the meaning, and being open to the self and so responding in a way which affirms unconditional value and the value of the response. The process then is not simply about being open to the other but also about appreciating the other, about accepting, testing and valuing the other. To use Al McFadyen's terms the process is fundamentally about calling the other to personhood (McFadyen 1990). At the centre of this call is the caring relationship itself, where agape offers acceptance and challenge and at the same time invites the other to test its reality, its embodiment.

Such empowerment then is not simply about 'giving power' to the other. It is about both a sharing of power and in some respects a taking of power. The carer recognises the power of the other and enables her to use that power in the process of mutual testing. The context of that is that the caring relationship is already one in which power is imbalanced, in which the person is already in the role of 'failure', 'stranger', 'person in need'. Sharing of power in that context is about breaking down the barriers of those roles, and offering a respect which accepts the other as someone who is equal. In that relationship the person can then begin to take and practice power. For some this will be a difficult and emotive process, involving expressions of anger. Part of the process which enables the person to clarify affective as well as cognitive meaning also enables her to see that taking power need not be adversarial or involve aggression. Taking power in one's life is natural and proper. Part of taking power is the control which comes through self awareness, and through the openness to and testing of the self and others. Taking power is also about developing confidence in and shaping a purpose, one which again is open to testing. Such power sharing then is a process which ultimately looks to embodiment in response to the network of relationships.

This part of the process once more demands the presence of agape not simply to call the other into response but to affirm newly worked through life meaning and to provide ongoing support which enables the person to put her life meaning into practice. This emphasises the need for continued support and for a continued discipline of reflection which enables the person to maintain practice and the testing of practice. As we shall see, this asks great questions of the approach to discipline within the church.

## Qualities

Central to the whole process of empowerment is the development or affirmation of qualities and skills which enable the person to enter into the dialogue described above. I will examine these in more detail in chapter six in considering virtues. At this stage I want to draw attention to one virtue, characterised by R. Solomons as a collection of several, which come together to form a coherent character and identity, integrity (Solomons 1992, 168).

This involves firstly making connections between the different aspects of the self (cognitive, affective and somatic), and the self and practice. This leads to holistic thinking which takes account of how feelings, thoughts and physicality affect each other. As shall be seen in more detail in chapter five this involves learning to think affectively and feel cognitively. In terms of the affective self, Rowan Williams makes the distinction between emotions and feeling. Emotion involves feeling which intrudes and controls the person. Anxiety or shame, for instance, can be felt so intensely that the person responds to them without understanding their genesis or how they are influencing her. Inevitably with such emotion the boundaries of the self are felt as indistinct and insecure. This is contrasted with dispassionate feeling which involves an engagement with feelings that allows an exposure of the self, 'freed from all compulsions to keep itself safe or keep itself under control' (Williams 1989, 11). It involves learning about those feelings and accepting them, hence, as Williams puts it, learning a positive form of detachment, a 'purifying' of thought and feeling.

Somatic awareness is equally important, not least because, as David Ford notes, all action involves communication (Ford 1999). To put another way all action embodies meaning in some way, not least attitude and values. The relatively recent populism of 'body language' came as something of a surprise to the sophisticated cerebral West. In fact somatic awareness is at the base of spirituality in the earliest stages of human development. Daniel Stern notes research on early childhood, including the establishment of shared affect as early as nine months, including an awareness of congruence between the facial expression of another and the baby's own affective state. If the care-taker's face expresses anxiety about a new or dangerous situation the baby will also express this and turn away

64

from the danger. Behind this lies what Stern calls 'affect atunement', a complex, dynamic and ongoing operation which involves the care-taker recognising the affective state of the child and communicating that recognition. It is a communication through tone and body attitude that the care-taker is in resonance, in synchronicity with the experience of the baby (Stern 1985, 129).

Atunement of this kind falls short of full empathy in that it does not involve the mediation of the cognitive processes. Nonetheless, there is the development of a strong awareness through affective and somatic knowledge, communicating meaning. It is precisely this level of communication which is discouraged in different ways as the child develops or which leads to contradictory messages coming from care-takers leading the child to build up a confused and anxious life meaning. Hence, Rogers was precisely right to stress the need for congruence in the attitude of the counsellor. A critical part of the caring process then becomes learning a level of awareness which had been in some way discouraged, and with that learning to trust the embodied other.

Secondly, integrity involves a constancy and consistency between: the self, values and practice; past, present and future; and different relationships, situations and contexts. The response may not be exactly the same in every context but will remain consistent to the identity and purpose of the person. Central to this is the idea of being true to the self and thus faithful to the self.

A third aspect of integrity is honesty. This is partly about an openness to the self and others and partly about remaining focused on the truth of a narrative. Such a truth is, of course, no simple objective truth found apart from the network of relationships. As David Smail notes much of 'truth' about ourselves and others is illusional (Smail 1984). I may see myself as different and strange, unable to cope, and unable to live up to the excellence which is evidenced in others. The other is then seen as well adjusted, content with life and experiencing no stress or dysfunction. This in turn is reinforced by media images, which reinforce standards of adequacy which the person finds it hard to live up to. Hence, for many there is a determination not to disclose the real anxiety and chaos which they experience, even to themselves. As Smail writes, 'most people keep the way they feel about themselves a deep and shameful secret' (Smail 1984, 4). Hence, honesty is very much about how one is able to examine the self and others in a way which both accepts and tests the illusions.

A fourth element in integrity is responsibility. This involves taking responsibility for meaning and purpose. If the person simply accepted the meaning and purpose supplied by the other then there would be no separate identity, and no attempt to relate to the different aspects of experience. Hence an important part of this is the testing and developing of purpose with and in relation to others.

Given the limitations of human beings it is impossible to have complete integrity in any static sense. Hence, integrity is best viewed in terms of a continual learning process, with the person discovering more about the different aspects of the self and others and how these connect. It is not possible to speak of this holism as wholeness. It is possible to speak of the person becoming one with the self and others.

This whole process is one which leads to the development of other key empowering virtues, in particular faith and hope. These, and the dynamic of how they are learned, will be examined more closely in chapter six.

### Embodiment

Finally, agape is embodied in the relationships which the person goes on to form. The meaning which emerges through the empathic relationship can only more fully be understood through embodiment, as we put that meaning into practice, leading to the next cycle of reflection. This embodiment is most of all seen in the development of shalom (peace). Richard Higginson suggests that integrity or wholeness could be an alternative rendering of shalom (Higginson 1996, 58 ff.). Psalm 85 (vv10-13) gives that sense of relationships which are both based in righteousness and which are flourishing, something far more than simply absence of war:

> Love and faithfulness meet together;
> Righteousness and peace kiss each other.
> Faithfulness springs forth from the earth,
> And righteousness looks down from heaven.
> The Lord will indeed give what is good,
> And our land will yield its harvest.
> Righteousness goes before him
> And prepares the way for his steps.

The state of harmony which The Psalmist looks forward to is interestingly between God and his people, between other people, and between the people and the environment. Such embodiment, like integrity, can never be fully achieved. It is constantly being created and aims to include the other as collaborator in the building of such a community.

# Conclusion

In this chapter I have examined agape and how it informs and enables spirituality and pastoral care. Agape provides faithful presence to the other which offers inclusive and unconditional care. It is a way of knowing which involves several different levels of awareness and which develops mutual relationships based upon dialogue. Finally, in pastoral care it empowers, through enabling narrative and through reflective dialogue which calls the person to respond to the needs and demands of the self and others. None of this is the 'easy dialogue' of conversation. Precisely because the person comes to a pastoral relationship in need, and in the majority of cases in the thrall of a conditional view of life meaning and self worth, this dialogue is one which involves mutual testing and challenges as well as acceptance. It is a dialogue which involves learning, about the self and other. If the very process of developing spiritual awareness through empathy leads to surprises then the biggest surprise for most people in need is that of agape being offered to them. It may be said that this is too good to be true, or at least reasonably true. But that truth is precisely what leads to a dialogue and challenges the person to take responsibility for her own thoughts and feelings and for the direction of her life in practice. Hence, the relationship of love thus far outlined is non-directive in essence. It does not tell the other what to do. On the contrary it values the freedom of the other to relate to herself and to others, with a central concern that the person take responsibility for that awareness. The purpose of love is to enable the other to see, and feel and hear for herself, to develop empathic awareness for herself. None of this is to say that love is directionless. On the contrary, the dynamic of agape leads the person ever more towards her humanity, her personhood, calls her to reach out to the different others in her life. It is an essentially creative dynamic, leading to shalom.

In all this agape calls us to appreciate and respond to the other and with others to develop life meaning - meaning which will continue to develop. A critical part of that life meaning is moral meaning, and it is to that, and the way in which moral meaning begins to emerge in response to agape, that we must now turn.

### References

E. Barker, New Religious Movements (London: HMSO, 1992).

K. Barth, Church Dogmatics, Vol. IV part 1 (Edinburgh: T. and T. Clark, 1956).

Z. Bauman, Modernity and the Holocaust (London: Polity, 1989).

Z. Bauman, Postmodern Ethics (Oxford : Blackwells, 1995).

M. Belenky, Womens Ways of Knowing, (New York: Basic Books, 1986).

J. Berryman, Children's spirituality and religious language, British Journal of Religious Education, 7 (3), (Summer, 1985).

A. Campbell, Moderated Love (London ; SPCK, 1984).

A. Campbell, Health as Liberation (Cleveland: Pilgrim Press, 1995).

W. Carr, The Pastor as Theologian ( London: SPCK, 1989).

B.H. Childs, Forgiveness, in R Hunter (ed.) Dictionary of Pastoral Care and Counseling (Nashville; Abingdon, 1990) 438-444.

E. Farley, Divine Empathy (Minneapolis: Fortress, 1996).

D. Ford, Self and Salvation (Cambridge: Cambridge University Press, 1999).

M. Freeman, Rewriting the Self (London: Routledge, 1993).

R. Gaita, A Common Humanity. (Routledge: London, 2000).

R. Gorush and W. Miller, Assessing Spirituality, in W. Miller (ed.) Integrating Spirituality into Treatment (Washington: American Psychological Association, 1999).

P. Halmos, The Faith of the Counsellors (Constable: London, 1964).

R. Higginson, Transforming Leadership (London: SPCK, 1996).

G. Kaufman, Shame: The Power of Caring (Washington: Schenkman, 1980).

H. Kohut, 'Introspection, Empathy and the Semi Circle of Mental Health', International Journal of Psychoanalysis, Vol. 663, 1982.

E. Lartey, In Living Colour (London: Cassell, 1997).

A. McFadyen, The Call to Personhood (Cambridge: Cambridge University Press, 1990).

S. McFague, Super, Natural Christians (London: SCM, 1997).

A. Margulies, The Empathic Imagination (New York: W.W. Norton, 1989).

W. May, Code and Covenant or Philanthropy and Contract? in S. Lammers and A. Verhey (eds.) On Moral Medicine (Grand Rapids: Eerdmans, 1987).

W. Miller and C. Thoresen, Spirituality and Health, in W. Miller (ed.) Integrating Spirituality into Treatment (Washington: American Psychological Association, 1999).

J. Mbiti, African Religions and Philosophy (London : Heinemann, 1990).

H. Nouwen, The Wounded Healer (London : Darton, Longman and Todd, 1994).

P. Riceour, Oneself as Another (Chicago: University of Chicago Press, 1992).

S. Rudman, Concepts of the Christian Person and Christian Ethics (Cambridge University Press: Cambridge, 1997).

C. Schlauch, 'Empathy as the Essence of Pastoral Psychotherapy', in The Journal of Pastoral Care, Spring 1990, Vol.XLIV, No. 1, 3-17.

D. Smail, Illusion and Reality: The Meaning of Anxiety (London: J.M. Dent, 1984).

R. Solomons, Ethics and Excellence (Oxford: Oxford University Press, 1992).

D. Stern, The Interpersonal World of the Infant (New York: Basic Books, 1985).

W.H. Vanstone, Loves Endeavour, Loves Expense (London: Darton, Longman and Todd, 1977).

J. van der Ven, Formation of the Moral Self (Grand Rapids: Eerdmans, 1998).

R. Williams, Christianity and the Ideal of Detachment (Oxford : Clinical Theology Association, 1989).

# 3

## Agape and Moral Meaning

*When the Pharisees heard that [Jesus] had silenced the Sadducees they came together. And one of them, a lawyer, asked him a question to test him. "Teacher, which is the greatest commandment in the law?" And he said to him, "You shall love the Lord your God with all your heart, and with all your soul, and with all your mind. This is the greatest and first commandment. And the second is like it, You shall love your neighbour as yourself. On these commandments hang all the law and the prophets" (Matt. 22: 34-40).*

*'The moral self is always haunted by the suspicion that it is not moral enough' (Zygmunt Bauman).*

*'You may not be able to complete the work but that does not mean you are not required to start it' (Emil Fackenham).*

It is one thing to see agape as providing a foundation of spirituality and even providing the basis for pastoral care, with its concern for equal care embodied in practice. It is quite another thing to see agape as the basis for a coherent Christian ethic. Stanley Hauerwas, for instance, argues that 'the ethics of love is often but a cover for what is fundamentally an assertion of ethical relativism' (Hauerwas 1981, 124). The meaning of agape has itself become debased in popular discourse, leading, it is argued, to the reduction of the meaning of love simply to inclusiveness, abandoning the idea of sacrifice, discipline, repentance and transformation. Hauerwas concludes;

'The ethic of the gospel is not a love ethic, but it is an ethic of adherence to this man [Jesus] as he has bound our destiny to his, as he makes the story of our life his story. As an ethic of love the ethic of the Gospels would be

69

at our disposal, since we would fill in the context of love by our wishes.' (Hauerwas 1981, 115) Such an ethic, argues Hauerwas, can only be summed up in the narrative of the cross.

Richard Hays develops this argument by suggesting that love cannot be used as a focal image for New Testament Ethics precisely because it is not an image, but rather the interpretation of an image, the *cross* (Hays 1996, 202). According to Hays the cross is one of three central images which act as focus for the New Testament ethic, the others being community and new creation. What the New Testament means by love is exactly embodied in the cross. Hence as St John writes, 'We know love by this that he lay down his life for us - and we ought to lay down our lives for one another'(1 John 4:10, 11). Apart from this message of the cross then the term love has no meaning.

Hays further suggests that love cannot be used as an image to bring together New Testament ethics because four major witnesses - Mark, Acts, Hebrews and Revelation - resist the attempt to use love to synthesise their moral vision.

Such arguments alert us to the need to take great care with any ethic of love. However, they do not provide grounds for dismissal of such an ethic. Firstly, Hauerwas simply assumes that there is no practical content to agape. From this he proposes that we can fill in the moral meaning in whatever way we want. This is an argument very similar to Graham's concern about opening the door to liberal ethics, and it depends upon using simply one view of love. Not only is this arbitrary, but it also ignores any attempt at discovering the substantive moral content of agape. Secondly, Hauerwas' concern with discipline infers that agape itself cannot challenge or be the basis of discipline. Once again this doesn't begin to explore either the idea or means of discipline. As shall be seen in chapter seven, it is possible to view agape as the basis of a much more effective and profound view of discipline, based ultimately on process and community. It is precisely such a dynamic of love which leads to reconciliation, forgiveness and transformation - of both the person and the community. In short Hauerwas does not begin to analyse the content of agape or how it relates even to the virtues which are the base of his ethical view.

Hays' points are equally problematic. The cross is certainly an embodiment of God's love, but then so is the saving act of Jesus in the resurrection, to say nothing of the presence of God's kingdom embodied in the miracles and reflected on in the parables. His concentration on the theology of the

Atonement leads him to ignore the theology of the Trinity with its emphasis upon a present love of mutuality. In this light Hays' suggestion that there are three major images in the New Testament on which to rest an ethic, the cross, community and the new creation is simply arbitrary.

Secondly, Hays confuses two things. He speaks of the concept of love as embodied in the cross and yet also of love as an interpretation of the cross. In the first of these love precedes, or at the very least is part of, the embodiment. Love may then be discovered in and through reflection on that action. This is quite a different logic from reflection on the image of the cross and using love as an interpretation of the crucifixion. The first approach sees love as an attitude which is experienced in practice. The second sees love as simply an interpretative concept. As an attitude it is hard to see how this could be one amongst many others in the New Testament. In any case as we shall see, the very nature of agape is not of the same logical order as concepts such as creation or sacrifice. Agape in fact provides a hermeneutical basis from which such concepts can be examined and tested.

Thirdly, the view that agape cannot be used as a basis for New Testament ethics simply because four writers do not use it to synthesize their ethic is to ignore the importance it plays in other writings, both explicit and implicit. At the very least agape has a strong part to play in the view of any Christian Ethic, as both Outka and Schrage note (Outka 1972; Schrage 1988, 68-107).

Building on this brief review of Hauerwas and Hays, I will argue in this chapter that:
- agape is the irreducible ground of Christian Ethics, a moral attitude which precedes rational reflection;
- agape provides an ethic of relationality and care;
- this does not preclude the need for ethical principles, but these do not form the basis of Christian Ethics. We rather see a dynamic relationship between the agape and the principles, enabling mutual critique. At the base of this agape has a substantive moral content which informs principles and holds together further ethical aporia.
- agapeic ethics is essentially social and not individual, demanding that responsibility be taken and shared.
- agape involves an ethic of response and transformation, at the heart of which are ethical aporia.

# The ground of ethics

## Relationality

Agape as an ethical concept grows out of its spirituality and thus is primarily an ethics of relationality, summed up in the double commandment above. It is about how I relate to my God, my neighbour and myself. Placed in the form of a command it clearly precedes any use of rules in ethics, and Linda Woodhead contrasts this with the view of morality which is concerned 'with the regulation of the competing claims of individuals rather than with the establishment of loving personal relationships' (Woodhead 1992, 60). The first of these is achieved by 'a formal hierarchy of moral laws or rights.' The laws apply to all people and rights are possessed by all. Underlying this view is a concern for justice and fairness, and an attempt to apply ethics in a discernibly consistent, and even objective way. However, as Simone Weil notes, any rights have to be founded themselves on some sense of prior obligation, and this is an obligation to the other which must be based upon need (See Woodhead 1992, 63). Hence, agape always precedes ethics. The ethical impulse, the impulse to see the other as valuable, as humanity, precedes any attempt to calculate ends. Zygmunt Bauman even suggests that the moral impulse, to see the other as humanity, precedes thought and that being moral precedes any idea or appreciation of society (Bauman 1993, 58). The critical underlying point is that agape moves the person away from the role of spectator, or as Bauman suggests tourist, to direct relationship, direct awareness of the other as brother or sister, and therefore to a sense of responsibility which precedes any reflection on the particular moral response. In the terms of philosophers such as Wittgenstein or Winch, this is the 'primitive reaction' which is the condition of being aware of others as beings with states of consciousness like ourselves (Gaita 2000, 266).

Daryl Koehn sees this as an ethic of care, based upon what she terms broad empathy, such as was outlined in the last chapter. She stresses that this is not distant appreciation of the other but a concern for them which seeks to know them and to enable their good, a concern which presumes and sets up a mutuality in the relationship (Koehn 1998, 57 ff.).

## Beyond rationality

Secondly, the agapeic ethic always exceeds a justice or rights morality. As Helen Oppenheimer writes:

'Christianity is not "fair"...Christ's demands exceed legality and ask more of us than can "reasonably" be expected...The teaching of Christ is that a man does not insist even on his own rights, that he loves his enemies, that he turns the other cheek' (Woodhead 1992, 64).

In one sense this is a love which is beyond possibility, though as Oppenheimer notes it can be embodied to some degree in human practice, not least in the example of parenting (Oppenheimer 1983). This is the classic example of nonconditional love, and of attention which goes beyond simple fairness. Importantly, this means that the ethical attitude is not rational or simply calculative. Indeed, Bauman sees the starting point of morality as 'endemically and irremediably *non rational*' (Bauman 1993, 60). Here the meaning of rationality is about survival and the capacity to calculate one's interest, something essentially defensive. Dihl goes further in arguing that the law of love is unnatural (see Schrage 1988, 77). It is far more natural to defend one's own interest.

## *The challenge of inclusivity*

Such love is impossibly demanding. It is a love which is unconditional and thus sets up an inclusivity. L. Schotroff reminds us that this is partly an attitude of inclusivity but that it must lead to a concrete social event, something summed up in the command to go beyond love of neighbour to love of enemy:

'The Christian is challenged to include the persecutor in his own community...The command to love the enemy is an appeal to take up a missionary attitude towards one's persecutors...Even the enemies of the community are to be given a place in its common life and in the kingly rule of God' (Schotroff 1978, 23).

This is not a fairy tale world in which the enemy suddenly becomes one of us. It may be that the enemy remains the enemy, we nonetheless have to love her. This sets up an attitude of responsibility for the other in every situation.

Alongside this, however, is the problem that agape cannot be precise in ethical guidance. Indeed, Bauman suggests that there is an inescapable aporia in any attempt to decide what is the right course - an ambiguity which admits of no easy solution. The responsibility to do something about this, to respond, nonetheless remains with the individual. Bauman contrasts the precise order or rule with the ethical demand, which is 'abominably vague, confused and confusing, indeed barely audible. It forces the moral self to be her own interpreter, and as with all other interpreters - remains for ever unsure about the correctness of the interpretation. However radical the interpretation, one can never be fully convinced that it matched the radicality of the demand' (Bauman 1997, 8). This may be seen as the core aporia of agape, that it demands responsibility for the other and therefore some response, but at the same time we can never know if that response is absolutely right.

Faced by this demand Bauman suggests that there are two dangers. Firstly, demand can be defused by narrowing its focus. Hence, as Schrage notes the Hebrew command to love the neighbour (Leviticus 19.18) was originally inclusive but over time was narrowed down to Israelites or full proselytes (Schrage 1988, 73). Hence the Samaritan in the parable was the least likely to be seen as neighbour (Luke 10: 30-37). Bauman reminds us that the key dynamic of the Holocaust was to see the Jews and others as outside the moral claims of humanity (Bauman 1993, see also Gaita 2000).

Secondly, a code of ethics can be developed. The more detailed the code, with application in many different contexts, the less the person has to take responsibility for the moral response. Indeed, the ethical rule becomes the basis of responsibility. Hence, when things go wrong there is always the plea that one was simply following the rules. This dynamic is sharply challenged in the New Testament stress on love. The command to love exactly has no limits, and 'love does not reach a boundary beyond which nothing is required' (Schrage 1988, 74). This is exactly the logic behind Jesus' stress on ethical attitudes in the Sermon on the Mount. The exhortation to forgive the other seventy times seven precisely expresses a constant attitude of forgiveness, contrasted with the 'rule' of forgiving seven times, after which the person no longer needs to take moral responsibility (Matt. 18: 21-22).

## Particularity

In one sense, the moral claim of the other is based upon the sameness of the other, recognition and acceptance of the common humanity. Hence, Kierkegaard can write of the 'common mark' illuminated by 'the light of the eternal' (Kierkegaard 1946, 73). However. agape also looks to the value of the particular. Hence, R. H. Tawney was able to see equality in the light not of equal treatment for everyone but rather different treatment dependant upon the need of the other (Tawney 1964). However, as Oppenheimer notes such a love which responds to the particular is not simply about responding to need. It is also an appreciative love, i.e., one which is aware of and appreciates the other.

'It is a kind of love which looks at what people see in themselves, that positively elicits their own special character and then is glad of it: a love that creates enjoyment and enjoys creation' (Oppenheimer 1982, 120).

This involves the empathic relationship noted in the last chapter which enables the disclosure of the other. The particularity of the other is very much about the difference of the other, and this difference is the basis of a continual learning about the other. It is precisely in and through this disclosure that the real good of the other is learned. Moreover, that good is something which always is being revealed, it is not predetermined. Hence, even the value of beneficence is radically affected by agape. Concern for the good of other can only be realised through this process of constant revelation (Koehn 1998, 57).

In this light Oppenheimer is concerned to see love of the other as responsive and not simply given or endowed through the grace of the lover. The dynamic of bestowing value on the other assumes that they have no value in themselves, leading precisely to the kind of patronising love noted in the last chapter. This leads to an instrumental form of agapism which simply seeks to treat every one in the same way.

## Self love

The stress on particularity and the revelation of this through love inevitably leads to a view of agape as involving mutuality. A major strand in Christian thought is suspicious of the idea of self and the idea that there can be any mutuality in the love of God for man and man for God. Anders Nygren focused this on the discussion of agape and eros. Eros, he argued, was the opposite of agape, and was defined as a 'natural self love, which extends its scope to embrace also benefactors of the self' (Nygren 1932, 97). Such self love is the root cause of sin, searching for reward and finding value in the attractiveness of the other. Hence, Nygren categorically states,

'Christianity does not recognise self-love as a legitimate form of love. Christian love moves in two directions, towards God and towards its neighbour; and in self love finds its chief adversary which must be fought and conquered' (Nygren 1932, 217).

In contrast agape is a disinterested love which is exemplified in God's love for sinners. This is not motivated by any desire for personal gain, and is not based upon the attractive qualities of the other. Nor is such love based upon the need of the lover. In the first place God has no need and in the second there is little in sinful humanity which could attract God. Agape then is a love which enables the unlovable to be valued. Such love is fundamentally about self sacrifice, 'a love that gives itself away, that sacrifices itself even to the uttermost' (Nygren 1932, 118). It is a theocentric love which comes to the sinner and is then shared with others. Such love is rooted in the sacrifice of Christ himself, 'the self giving majesty' of his love (Nygren 1932, 741). Hence the Atonement is stressed in Nygren's view of love.

A similar stress is found in Reinhold Niebuhr and Gene Outka. For Niebuhr only selfless love can overcome the excessive concern for the self. Such love is characterised by a refusal to use power on one's own behalf. Hence it must remain 'history's impossible possibility' relevant to personal life not politics (Niebuhr 1943, 76).

Outka also sees agape as other regard. However, he does distinguish between other regard and self sacrifice. It is possible to love the other and feel a due sense of reward and happiness. Hence, other regard and self interest are not incompatible (Outka, 1972).

The resulting polarisation of other love and self love which such views encourage can be very problematic:

a. Concentration on the Atonement and the unlovableness of the human being risks not recognising the goodness in God's creation. Oppenheimer suggests that there is no need to bestow value but rather seek it out. The distinction should be drawn between the appreciation of the material/physical which involves awareness of the whole other, and focus which is purely on the material as a means to gratification. Paul Avis argues that such an appreciation of the material world is experienced by God, a proper response to creation as it is - 'and God saw that it was good' (Genesis 1:21). The consequences of not finding such an eros in God are serious, with human beings having 'no source, analogy or hope of redemption in God. It means that our erotic nature in itself alienates us from God' (Avis 1989). Hence, the disastrous dualism between the spiritual and material is perpetuated.

Avis further reinforces a positive view of eros by reminding us that Nygren's interpretation of the Platonic and neo-Platonic view of love, something important to the definition of eros, was flawed. Plato's view of eros is creative and overflowing, concerned not just to give but to receive. Plotinus also sees eros as the creative act, writing of its unitive role in the 'ultimate union of soul with the One' (Avis 1989, 132). When this positive view of love is applied to a relationship with God, it is found in both the energy which drives the person towards God and in the experience of the presence of God. The first of these involves transcendence of the self, not unlike the empathy described by Scheler. The second focuses on the religious experience - the sense of ecstasy at being at one with the Other (Avis 1989, 129).

b. The idea of 'one way' love flies in the face of the expressed dynamic of God's love. As Oppenheimer notes we love God because he loves us. God loves us and desires a response, hence the making of covenant and the building up of trust. The very dynamic of empathy assumes mutuality not least because just as empathy enables the other to disclose herself, at the same time it involves a disclosure of the one who offers empathy. This may not be a symmetrical mutuality, but certainly leads to mutual disclosure and mutual trust. Oppenheimer refers to this as the give and take which is part of loving relationships and which is exemplified in the Trinity and the mutual caring of each person (Oppenheimer 1983, 114). God, as Fiddes puts it, is receptive, seeking and delighting in our response (Fiddes 2000, 213). There has always been difficulty in this idea for some in that it implies a need on God's part. However, as Vincent Brummer notes, if we can find a part for 'need love' in healthy relationships there is no ground for seeing such need as unacceptable or bad, and no reason why we should not find an analogy in God (Brummer 1993).

c. Nygren ignores the mutuality of the two great commandments. The second commandment has the implication of equality. The neighbour is to be loved as the self. Scharge suggests that this should be seen as in place of the self (Schrage 1988, 79). However, there is no evidence to suggest that this should be the interpretation. More impressive is the argument that underlying agape as an inclusive ethic is an equality of regard which demands that the self is not excluded from this love. As noted in the last chapter, there is a real sense in which we can see the self as an other. To exclude the self from the love of the self would, therefore, be both inequitable and also a form of moral pride, with the self as being very different from others and not needing the concern, support and nurture of others. As Oppenheimer puts it,
'If any creature is to be loved and cherished, then sooner or later we ourselves are likewise to be loved and cherished...To shut our eyes to this for ever would be inverted pride or faithlessness rather than Christian humility' (Oppenheimer 1983, 103).

d.  It is precisely such considerations which lead Paul Tillich to look for a balanced view of love, which can take in all the forms of love and see them as one. He points to four forms - epithymia (desire), eros (the search for value), philia (friendship) and agape (the depth of love). Each of these forms requires the others to maintain a balance. Agape has a special relationship with the others, ensuring that they do not become distorted. Eros without agape, for instance, could tend towards the idolatry of the other (Tillich 1963, 89).

However, whilst Tillich looks to one love with these discernibly different aspects in balance, there is still more than a hint of the hierarchy of loves - with agape at the top and eros at the bottom. Woodhead argues that the subtext of such hierarchies is again negative about the material world, and in particular to sexuality. Hence, many feminists would want to invert such hierarchies, placing embodied love as the highest form and seeing the disinterested love referred to as agape as relegated to a sub Christian level (Woodhead 1992).

Such debates, however, can easily polarise and not take full account of the breadth of spirituality. As noted in the last chapter, love is not possible without embodiment, involving awareness of ideas, affects and the material. Agape itself gives equal weight to all the elements of disinterestedness and closeness, difference and sameness and so on. In this light, it is perfectly possible to speak of a love which both desires the other for their uniqueness and also loves them without condition. Eberhard Jungel can thus write of agape as 'a power which integrates eros' (Jungel 1983, 320).

At the heart of this is a key battle, frequently fought between the feminists and others. This is between the view that value is bestowed upon the other, and value is recognised in the other. The Nygren argument can do little else but see value as bestowed, given his view of sin. The feminist view counters this but in its attempt to get away from the patronising view of the person does not always strike the right balance. Once again, the balance is found in the dynamic of agape. The unconditionality of agape presumes value and does indeed bestow value upon the other. The other, even the enemy is given the value of the neighbour. However, such valuation does not in any sense mean that the other has not intrinsic value. On the contrary, such value is confirmed in the agapeic relationship, as agape and empathy enable the disclosure of the other and the self, the development of the self and the embodiment of the other's value in the development of relationships. Hence, the recognition of the value of the other only really occurs within the dynamic relationship which enables the revelation of the other. All of this process of valuation occurs in embodied fashion, i.e. in a way which clearly is relevant to the particular life of the self and other.

e. The characterisation of love as simply other oriented also tends to stress the sacrificial elements of love, the love which will inevitably involve suffering. Feminists note the way in which such a view can easily lead to oppression. The woman is given the role of carer. Caring is seen as sacrificial. The ethical framework of this imposes guilt on the woman who tries breaks out of such sacrifice and looks to fulfilment.

It is hard to not see some connection between suffering, sacrifice and agape. The very unlimited and inclusive nature of the concern inevitably means that there will be suffering in trying to achieve that. The dynamic of empathy itself is sacrificial, reaching out beyond the self and beyond the concerns of the self. However, too great a stress on suffering and sacrifice comes from assuming an individualist mode of operation, and with that an inability to accept limitation. Agape is more than the working through of individual responsibility. By definition, the community is also responsible for the other. Hence, mutuality extends responsibility. This recognition also enables the person to begin to explore interdependency and, as we shall see, acts as the basis for negotiation of responsibility. This sense of mutual responsibility is at the heart of the two great commandments and also of the Trinity itself. Jesus demands that we love God, the neighbour, and the self. The term neighbour is perhaps the most complex of the three. It could involve simply an other, or a group or even the environment. All of these neighbours are interconnected. Reasonably then the responsibility for them should be shared, as exemplified by the Trinity. As Douglas Meeks notes, the persons of the Trinity are responsible together for each other and for creation and salvation. At the same time each has his own particular task in that work (Meeks 1989). The ultimate conclusion of its ethic of mutuality is that agape is in essence social, embodied in community.

In that context, the aporia which van der Ven points to, between self-love and other-love, love for significant others and for the marginalised, and love for those in short term or long term relations, are far from problematic. On the contrary, they are the very stuff of a creative ethic which in van der Ven's words, refuses 'to be caught in the pitfalls of cultural and religious conventionalism on the one hand or principled fanaticism and rigid idealism on the other' (van der Ven 1998, 378).

It is precisely the holding in tension of these various aporia which compels an ethical response which, as we shall see is both transformative and shalomic. However, before examining this response it is necessary to see how the content of agape relates to this dynamic.

## Agape and moral content

As noted above, there are commentators who would argue that agape does not have substantive meaning. Some would say that this means that use of the word leads to filling in the meaning with whatever we want. Others argue that meaning is found not in agape but in the development of middle axioms, such as equality.

### Substantive meaning

Agape does, in fact, have substantive meaning which can be expressed in general principles. The stress on inclusivity which sees the other as part of common humanity leads to the principles of *community* or *fellowship* - something which fits in to the basic human need of belonging. Concern for particularity of the other leads to the principle of *freedom* and diversity. The concern for inclusivity naturally leads to the principle of *equality of respect*. Arising from these are a number of other principles such as participation and mutual responsibility.

These principles are not of themselves axiomatic in the sense of commonly accepted. The term equality, for instance, has at least 100 logically distinct meanings (Rae 1981). Hence, there is no simple meaning which all might agree upon. More importantly each of these general principles is informed by agape, and by each other. Community is not about the solidarity of a community over against others and the rest of the world but rather about an inclusiveness which opens communities to others, and which is thus outward looking and also self critical. The idea of freedom is not simply negative freedom (freedom from oppression or constraint) or positive freedom (freedom which enables), but involves freedom to learn, to develop, to take responsibility for the self and for the other.

The concept of equality is not simply about equal outcomes or equal regard. Despite Outka's attempt to see this as the same as agape, equal regard is too bland, too much inclined to fairness. Equality is concerned about diversity of treatment rather than equal outcomes - real meeting of the particular needs of each (R.H Tawney 1964).

In all this it is important to note that agape holds together all these principles, almost as a community of principles. The principles then enable a constant dialogue, questioning and clarifying each other. Such principles remain constant, applying in all situations, but never absolute in the sense of being applied *to* all situations. They enable a consistency of moral meaning but at the same time can only fully discover moral meaning in the situation, through reflection on practice (van der Ven 1996, 260). The history of ideas is peppered with writers who would argue for the supremacy of one of these above the others. Agape requires that *all* are taken into account as part of ethical decision making.

In the light of this, it becomes clear that agape relates directly to any moral rules. The moral content of agape provides the criteria to judge the understanding and use of any principle. The moral principle 'honour your parents' is a good example. The idea of honouring parents does not mean accepting all things which are said by the parent or obeying them in all things. The meaning itself is tested in relation to the basic content of agape. Hence, honouring involves an acceptance of the parents freedom, respect for their point of view, the capacity to challenge, respect for their place in the family, and also concern for the development of mutuality. In practice this leads to a response to parents which will involve empathic listening, dialogue and mutual challenge which establishes purpose, and which recognises and enables the contribution of the parents and children. This set of criteria, far from eroding moral rules and principles, actually strengthens them.

## Moral meaning and self worth

There is a direct relationship between self worth and moral meaning. In the last chapter, we noted the way in which the discovery of reality was related to the sense of self worth. There are those whose sense of self worth tends to focus on the groups or persons who they perceive as setting the conditions of worth, who will give them value once the conditions have been fulfilled. This discourages an empathic attitude towards the other, and thus any attempt at finding out about the other outside the significant group. Concern is precisely for approval from the other rather than knowing the other.

This in turn leads to the dangers of stereotyping others and polarising values. This can lead to use of ethics in terms of the defence of the self or group, exemplified by the use of ethical rules by the doctors of the Law in the gospels. Ethical rules then become used to exclude and control.

However, self worth which is based purely on unconditionality, which does not challenge the person to respond, and in particular to contribute to community, thus confirming worth in action, can easily move into non-reflective self-esteem. As Richard Erikson notes, the global goal of enhancing self esteem 'on the assumption that happiness, success and responsible behaviour will automatically follow' leads to a confused ethic which does not begin to engage with the challenges and demands of the relational network (Erikson 1987, 163).

A conditional view of self worth, then, tends to express itself in conditional ethics, stressing concern for self reliance, adherence to rules and so on. A purely unconditional view ignores the ethical narrative of tradition and focuses on the self. A balanced view of self worth leads to dialogue with the different narratives which make up the person's life.

Hence, a critical first stage in the development of any ethical thinking has to be to work at the sense of worth, aiming for the balance outlined in the last chapter. This signals also that it is not possible to work through any ethical decision making without reference to the affective understanding of those involved, without some awareness of the affective agenda which might be controlling the use of ethical principles.

Given that rules can be used to oppress the other, then it is important to continually test the use of moral principles. Even the finest of principles can be misused. Faithfulness in marriage, for instance, can be used to support oppression and abuse. Part of this is perhaps to do with patriarchal oppression. Part of it also involves the build up of an alternative reality based upon conditional worth which does not see the abuse. A similar dynamic occurs in certain cults, where the conditional belief system is attached to self worth. The concern to please the leader becomes paramount. This in turn makes it difficult to see abusive, controlling behaviour (Barker 1992, chap. 2).

Enabling a response to such situations cannot be seen simply in terms of seeking justice, or even raising the consciousness of the person. At the core there is the need to work through the question of self worth, how this is connected to relationships, and its connection to moral meaning. This in turn will enable the person to work through to a different moral identity and so to begin to develop empathy, and thus an awareness of the truth, and the connected values of agape. From this, the previous value system can be critiqued and justice can be developed. This will be examined more closely in chapter seven.

### Agape and the virtues

Just as agape provides criteria to test any moral principle and its use, it also provides criteria for judging virtues. Virtues of themselves are neutral - qualities which are there to develop skills and to fulfil a purpose or function. Ultimately, their ethical status depends upon the nature of the end(s) they serve. Agape provides ends which ensure that virtues do not serve simply a conditional end.

Agape is, of course, itself a virtue, one which provides the irreducible moral attitude and quality. As such it acts as the foundation of all other virtues, informing the meaning of faith, hope, wisdom, and so on.

Agape then provides the base of a morality which is based in relationality, grounded in empathic awareness of the other and the self. It brings to together affective, cognitive and somatic knowledge in reflection on and critique of moral narratives, of the self and of the other. It informs the meaning of ethical principles, providing clear broad criteria for the critique of moral narratives. Its meaning can only fully be explored in practice. At the same time such practice can never fully express the nature of agape. The embodiment of agape is always insufficient. Nonetheless, the community can point beyond itself to that agape.

Inevitably then, agape can only be realised in and through the process of commitment to relationship and dialogue, leading in turn to a transformative ethic.

## Dialogue and transformation

### Case

*A Christian Student group executive (Christian Action, CA) called an emergency meeting of its honorary advisors - from local churches and Chaplaincy. The president explained that the president of another student Christian group (Gospel Outreach, GO) had been suspended by the Student Union because it was alleged that he had been aggressively homophobic in the Union building. He had been preaching from the Bible and had harangued homosexual members of the Student Union executive, calling upon them to repent. The Student Union were thinking of expelling the whole society.*

*The president introduced the issue saying that it was quite clear what the Bible had to say about homosexuality and we could not ignore that. Moreover, if CA did not support the suspended student and his society, this would send the message that the society did not support the gospel, and that they were happy with an ethic of confusing liberalism. CA should also stand up for a broader principle, the right of students to share Biblical truth in the Union building. The Union had at one point actually banned the public use of the Bible there. In short, for the president this was both a matter of gospel truth, and of justice and rights. CA must stand up for these even if that meant them also being banned from the Union. Sacrifice here was the price to pay for staying loyal to the gospel. This view was supported by two of the executive and by one of the honorary advisors, who was concerned not to water down the Pauline view of homosexuality.*

*The first objection to this came from the communication secretary who was concerned what message this would send to the rest of the campus:*

*'We have worked for years to be accepted on the campus as real human beings who are not trying to Bible bash. If we go down this line we will appear censorious, lose all our credibility and not be able to seriously work with our one-to-one outreach.' Recently the group had made a conscious move away from major mission to outreach which depended upon building up friendships.*

*Another member of the executive who was also on the Union executive objected to the idea that the suggested sacrifice was gospel based. For her the Union had a point. The gospel was not about shouting and harassing another student, whoever they were. We may want to question homosexuality but nowhere does the gospel say that we should condemn homosexuals. 'Aren't we supposed to love them?' This brought to the surface a discussion about rights and justice and the importance of being open to what secular views of ethics had to say. One member (who later 'came out' as a homosexual) argued that Christian should not be afraid to take on board such views, and developed the view that the Bible did not actually condemn homosexuality, not least because none of the references to it understood it as a sexual orientation per se.*

*The internal secretary tried to earth the discussion by reminding the group that this issue was liable to divide the 300 members of the society. They had worked for the whole year to keep the group together, despite many problems, and had managed to do that on a ticket of evangelism and outreach. If they failed to hold on to that now they would ruin all their work.*

*The discussion ranged far and wide for several hours, not least because a decision was required for a Student Union emergency meeting the next day, with an increasing appreciation of both the emotional and rational content of the arguments. The final conclusion involved the following:*

*- The executive were to challenge GO about the way in which they communicated*

*the gospel. This was not to be a public condemnation but rather to invite the group to reflect on the gospel ethic, how this sat with an aggressive presentation, and how it related to the Union ethical stance on rights.*

*- The executive, along with churches and the chaplaincy, were to set up a series of public reflections on the issue of homosexuality. This would involve representatives from the Christian Gay and Lesbian groups, and evangelical leaders with very different views. This in itself would enable the membership to be aware of the complexity of the issue.*

*- The executive was to challenge the policy of the Union to ban use of the Bible from public spaces in the Union building. At the same time they affirmed the importance of Union discipline and the basic rights which it sought to uphold*

These actions had several consequences. Firstly, they transformed the dialogue and openness of the CA. There was an increasing awareness of the need to accept limitations and accept the help of other groups. Secondly, they developed increasingly secure alliances and work with other groups. Thirdly, this led to increased respect on campus amongst secular groups. Fourthly, members of the executive became increasingly aware of the need to move beyond their group, leading to three of them successfully standing for the Student Union executive. Fifthly, the group became more confident in how to approach ethical issues. Thoughtful reflection, the avoidance of knee jerk reactions and an awareness of the ambiguities in the situation had not led to a breakdown of moral meaning in the group. It had led to greater assurance in 'prophetic action'. Overall the response had led to significant changes in the CA itself, how they related to others and to significant changes in the other groups.

### Virtue Ethics

It would be very tempting to view this case in terms of the virtue ethics of Stanley Hauwerwas. Indeed, several of the people involved did want to see it in that way, not least because Hauerwas argues that the Ethics of the Christian Community is very distinctive and should have very different things to say from the secular value systems.

Hauerwas argues that Christian Ethics is not about foundation principles 'but rather about how the self must be transformed to see the world truthfully'. For Christians this perception 'develops through schooling in a narrative which teaches us how to use the language of sin not only about ourselves but about others' (Hauerwas 1984, 33). The narrative is the essential way of developing any ethic, and this narrative is focused and embodied in the Christian community. A great deal of Hauerwas' concern focuses upon the development of the self, and the Christian taking responsibility for the ethic, with the personal narrative reacting in some way to the community narrative and building up the virtues which are enshrined in those narratives. Attempts to somehow place the Christian ethic into the public forum, and thus enquire how Christian principles might be applied to that context, are always doomed to failure, not least because they 'fail to recognise that all accounts of the moral life are narrative dependent' (Hauerwas 1984, 61). In order to understand the Christian ethic we have to enter the community and relate to the narrative and so become a part of the community. The Christian ethic then does not have universal application, except through revelation.

This parallels the concerns of an agapeic ethic with reflection on the self and the others and an openness to the truth. Equally it involves a concern for process as much as content. The Christian Ethic provides both the motivation for the good and also the content of the good.

However, there are several problems with Hauerwas' virtue ethics, and these are highlighted in the case of Christian Action. Firstly, Hauerwas fails to understand the complexity of community and narrative. Despite the fact that the CA group had a strong evangelical identity, it was neither simple nor single focused.

a. In the same meeting there were many different ethical perspectives, reflecting several different perspectives on homosexuality and the Bible, including acceptance, qualified acceptance, non-punitive rejection. The group also represented the different narratives which Brueggemann points to in the Old Testament theology - prophecy, wisdom, law, worship community and so on (Brueggemann 1997).

b. The group was not a single homogeneous body. On the contrary, there were many different groups represented within it, including: a representative of the national CA organisation; several different local church leaders of very different ecclesiologies; the Chaplaincy; a member of the academic staff; a member of the Student Union executive. Hence, far from there being a clear church community seen as something quite distinct from the narratives in secular society, the meeting shared the diversity of the academic community, with members who were a part of several other different communities, bringing with them fragments of their different community narrative.

c. There were very different personal narratives. Some of these were connected to the group's narratives and a role or function within the group. The president, for instance, was concerned about the danger of splitting the society, or losing its mission oriented identity. Part of this involved fear of his own failure. Other members brought with them sexuality narratives which were still being worked through.

Alongside such personal narratives, there were very different views about the responsibility of members of the group and of the student society itself. The president, for instance, saw the CA as in some way being responsible for the fate of GO.

In short there was no single narrative upon which the group might reflect, and members of the group brought many different personal and community narratives to the dialogue. Indeed, the group, like any church group, was a microcosm of post modern life (Fergusson 1997). Hauerwas, perceives the church community as clearly delineated over against the world outside. The truth is more likely that whilst it does have boundaries, that these boundaries are negotiated and that the community is both different and the same as the wider community.

Secondly, Hauerwas does not begin to work through what the place of dialogue is in this diversity. For instance, he infers that the personal narrative is taken up into the community narrative, but does not explain how this process works, and importantly, therefore, does not offer an understanding of personal autonomy in the light of the community narrative. Indeed, he takes no account of the importance of the personal narrative testing and critiquing the gospel narrative as set in the community.

Thirdly, the danger of an ethic which is simply wedded to a community narrative is that it is not open to the challenge or critique of external narratives.

This challenge of diversity occurs on three levels:
- testing the values which are held by the community. This is a cognitive exercise which clarifies the meaning of values and principles;
- testing the embodiment of those values. This reflects back the practice and how that seems to fit with stated values;
- testing the ground and use of values. This raises questions about the affective and cognitive ground of values, helping to identify any underlying agenda such as personal need or power struggles which might dominate ethical thinking.

Openness to the critique emerging from dialogue with external narratives reminds the church that its embodiment of the gospel ethic is and always has been flawed. Once the limitations of any embodiment are accepted, then the need for a dialogue with the different narratives outside the church becomes apparent. Such external narratives provide the real test of the congruence of any church community, how far its embodiment is at least reflecting something of the underlying covenant ethic. Such dialogue itself enables the witness of the church to be better articulated and understood, not least at the level of confirming aspects of community life such as faithfulness.

Fourthly, Hauerwas' understanding of narrative is too restricted. As van der Ven notes, narrative is more than reciting or hearing a story (van der Ven 1998, 385). The articulation of narrative involves reflection and learning. The subject is both writer and reader, speaker and listener, and thus discovers new aspects of her own life meaning and practice in and through the articulation of the narrative, and learns to evaluate and critique her own narrative. What is true of the individual and of the dialogues within the community, is also true of the relationship of the community to the outside world. The church needs to engage in dialogue to discover how its narrative in the fullest sense is being embodied.

Fifthly, Hauerwas' stress on the distinctiveness of the Christian community and its narrative makes it difficult for the church to genuinely collaborate with other groups. This is tied to a flawed spirituality which cannot see the sameness as well as difference between different communities. This is a basic aporia which Hauerwas' approach to ethics does not grasp, and leads to a lack of moral confidence - involving a constant need to assert difference. In contrast, the ethical reflection of the CA group led to clear acknowledgement of the sameness and difference between their ethical narrative and those of the Student Union and the GO. Precisely because of this acknowledgement, they were able to affirm the value of the other narratives, to challenge other narratives and to offer clear way of collaborating with those narratives. At no point did they lose their identity. On the contrary, their identity was clearly articulated in and through dialogue.

Hauerwas' focus on the importance of the particular community always runs the danger of making ethics inherently relativist, always dependant upon the particular community.

Finally, Hauerwas does not give enough emphasis to a critical point of narrative, that it be relevant dialogue. A great deal of writing about dialogic or community ethics focuses on the exchange of ideas and world views per se. If, however, as agapeic ethics suggests, the ethical meaning is only worked through in relation to practice, then the dialogue itself has to be based in reflection on practical issues which are of concern, make a difference. It is precisely the area of shared concern which enables the development of a broader shared narrative, a narrative which builds up shared responsibility.

## Dialogue

The idea of shared narrative and dialogue brings us to the attempts of J. Habermas and S. Benhabib. These are important because they work on the possibility of dialogue enabling a common ground for ethics. In the case of Habermas, he looks to the development of conditions that will enable clear communication of values. He sees these values and the associated realm of symbolic discourse as forming the 'life world'. This life world has been obscured by the instrumental reason which is driven by monitarisation and power, precisely not by discourse and consensus. He looks therefore to procedures which will enable just such discourse and the development of shared - inter subjective - ethical meaning, meaning which can include a meta-critical ranking of norms. In order to reach such an end, Habermas proposes a procedural view of morality which does not presuppose any ethical judgement. Indeed, he distinguishes between *ethics* - rules or principles which emerge from local communities - and morality which is more about the process of discovering moral meaning beyond the local expression of rules.

The process of morality involves three important conditions:
- Mutual recognition by all participants of each other as rational, autonomous subjects. The claims of the participants should be acknowledged when supported by valid arguments.
- All should be able to participate equally in the discussion. Hence there must be no social or political constraints to this.
- All 'ethical norms' should be open to challenge, and rational disputation.

In effect discourse ethics forms the basis of a contract ethic, i.e. agreement on ethical meaning which has been arrived at through dialogue (Habermas 1992).

Habermas' vision is very attractive and is an important step forward in trying to balance an ethic which is both universal and particular. However, in the end it looks to the development of an ideal speech situation which has little empirical evidence to support it. In this respect Habermas parallels the 'original position' of Rawl's view of justice. Such ideal situations simply do not exist, and any dialogue, even within the church, takes place in the context of constraints - involving imbalance of power, inequalities, lack of freedom, lack of respect. Just as important as such external constraints are the psychological constraints which may prevent individuals from being open to the other in dialogue.

Benhabib takes such points into account and attempts to develop the Habermas approach (Benhabib 1992). She notes that though the process may begin to generate moral understanding, it actually depends upon some shared moral assumptions. In other words, there have to be basic conditions for the conversation to begin, not least the underlying need for universal moral respect for all conversation partners and egalitarian reciprocity. This in turn demands the development of communication skills, and in effect, empathy, to enable the conversion to develop (Benhabib, 52).

However, even Benhabib does not go far enough. Underlying such a determinedly rational view has to be the covenant stance of agape. Firstly, discourse demands a pre-rational commitment to the other, which minimally commits the person to conversation and provides the basis of initial trust. Without this initial stance of openness to the other, further development of trust becomes difficult. Secondly, it points to a relational ethic which is as much about the development of mutual trust and personal development as it is about the clarifying of ethical meaning. A discourse ethic then becomes itself transformative, enabling a learning process in which the personal, structural, and cultural constraints to conversation are actually worked at in and through the conversation. The conversation then becomes the focus of growth, not something which is enabled after growth, or once the people are ready to converse. Hence, discourse enables all levels of moral meaning to be addressed. The discourse itself is an embodiment of agape, testing and engaging both at affective and cognitive levels.

Thirdly, agape also informs the ethical meaning which develops in that discourse, making explicit what Benhabib refers to as simply underlying moral assumptions. Such 'underlying' moral meaning, is not simply instrumental - enabling discourse to occur - it is in fact the basis for shared understanding of moral meaning. That moral meaning may be articulated in different ways, through attitude, body language, and the very communication skills which Benhabib advocates. Explicit moral meaning can then be developed in and through reflection on the relationship. Again, this is not a matter of establishing trust and then being able to hold a discourse and develop moral meaning. The development of moral meaning occurs in and through the discourse and the relational demonstration of the meaning of agape - so that the participants feel they have the *freedom* to develop their narrative, and feel a sense of belonging to a wider *community*. This actually demonstrates the basic principles of freedom and community.

Fourthly, in particular, this moral meaning provides the criteria for the conversation. If we unpack the criteria set out by Habermas they lead to values such as those articulated by Benhabib, e.g. equal respect. The concept of agape provides the following:

- Freedom. Autonomy is respected, and enabled with the sharing of power ;
- Participation. Involvement in the process. Here is no simple democratisation, but rather the taking of responsibility, the ownership of ideas and openness to others. Without this, the ethical response does not come to life. Hence, in terms of community growth Jean Vanier can speak of each person being responsible for the whole community (Vanier 1979, 157ff.).
- Openness to challenge and change. This is a learning process of ethics, involving the development of transparency at all levels. The importance of transparency is that it forces al participants to think about their views, and reinforces the question of responsibility.
- The capacity to live with the difficulties and ambiguities, to handle the different aporias. This is critical to any discourse ethics. There will never be any precise agreement on principles in their conceptual or abstract form, and in reflecting on practice, there will always be aporia.

Finally, agape takes dialogue beyond the idea of consensus or simple pragmatic solutions, into mutual learning, collaboration around practice, and creativity which enables the different groups to see the resource of each other and utilise them for the creative end. Hence the shalom, which was seen to be a part of the pastoral process, is also the end of the ethical reflection. Feminists such as Koehn come to similar conclusions in noting that dialogic ethics focus on the essential relatedness of all human beings, and that dialogic ethics evolves naturally from an ethic of care (Koehn 1998, 147ff.).

All this can now be illustrated with a return to the case of the CA. Firstly, the group, as it worked through the problem before it, was profoundly aware of its limitations and of the need to be open to all the members. This, covenant stance was signalled from the word go through prayer and through an explicit commitment to all the stakeholders and to an honest working through of all the issues. This is not to say that immediate and profound trust is required or was felt from the word go. There certainly had to be sufficient trust at least for the narrative to be started, for each member to feel secure enough to articulate their narrative as fully as they could.

Secondly, the narratives were articulated, often in a fragmentary way in relation to the 'problem'. This led to a long analysis of the underlying issues and values involved in the different narratives of all the stakeholders.

In this several things occurred:

- Values were clarified and tested. This included values and attitudes displayed about each other and other stakeholders. The homosexual members consistently tested the view of the majority that they could possibly both hate the sin of homosexuality but love the 'sinner'. As the meeting progressed so the idea of loving the 'sinner' became less and less used, replaced by 'accepting the other'. The difference was critical in the development of trust. The phrase 'loving the sinner' may be well meant but actually bespoke a condescending dynamic such as that which Bauman objected to. The impulse of agape as we have seen is one of openness and mutuality, and not of a residual judgement. Even this clarification, which enabled those who held a view antihomosexual practice to review why they held it, had a relational element to it. The gay members could see the limitations and difficulties faced by the CA members and the advisors, and could begin to develop trust of the other despite ambiguities. Indeed, acceptance involved living with uncertainties and ambiguities.

- Further discussion articulated key values held by different groups and how these related to the situation. It did not take long, for example, for the group to see that both GO and the Student Union were the same as and different from the CA. The initial attempt to polarise the GO and CA against the SU did not work. The SU had a concern for all societies including the CA. They also stood out on values which the committee recognised as valid, even if not directly gospel inspired - freedom of speech, defence of minorities etc. GO shared many concerns for the gospel. However, their way of addressing the other, in this case the homosexual, was as an enemy. The CA executive accepted that this was not congruent with the ethic of agape. This also led the group to accept that there were many different views about homosexuality, even based on the Bible, and within the 'evangelical wing' of the churches.

- The sameness and difference of the two groups and their values enabled the CA executive to begin to empathise with both groups, and to challenge them. They could understand core shared values and were able to reflect back to the two groups the incongruity and lack of integrity in their positions. At the same time both groups were able to test the values of the CA executive. The concern to communicate the gospel was imperative and was part of the aims of the organisation. However, this had to remain congruent with basic values of equal respect and freedom. Because the executive listened to the other values it was able also to learn more about the other groups, understand their problems and so challenge them, not from an adversarial or judgmental position but from one of acceptance.

- The questions of responsibility were then pursued. This was particularly important in the light of the concern of the president and vice president to take responsibility for the actions of GO. The implication was that because they were of the evangelical wing and therefore 'one of us' the CA should stand by them, in effect take some responsibility for them. However, it was clear on reflection that GO had overstepped the mark and that it was their responsibility to sort that out. If they could not convince the SU executive of their good intent then it was probably better that they were not part of the Student's Union. In looking at the various factors then the CA aimed to ensure that responsibility for dealing with this was properly shared.

- In the light of all this the outworking of this problem led the CA to remain faithful to all the other 'stakeholders' but also to reflect the incongruities of their responses back to them and challenge them to take responsibility for this. In the case of the SU this meant endorsing its values and aims and challenging them in the light of values such as free speech should they want to ban the Bible from the SU building. In the case of the GO this involved reflection on the incongruity of a love which can be expressed acrimoniously. In both cases, agape was the basis for a moral critique.
  The effect, however, went beyond the simple problem to transformation of individuals and relationships. On the individual level two members of the CA felt called to stand for the SU executive, having seen the importance of this group. Two other members took the first

steps in coming to terms with their sexuality and how this related to their faith.

The SU executive committee developed a broader awareness of religious rights and needs. Prior to this they had tended to stress religious rights in a combative way, championing world faiths over against what they saw as an imperialist Christian faith.

This extended to the whole issue of homosexuality and the church and led the committee to put in place further reflections that would enable the CA as a whole to move away from a judgmental attitude into further dialogue. The knock-on effect of this was a number of 'talk-ins' and events which involved many local churches, which moved the whole debate beyond sterile stereotypes.

Critically this meant that the whole process was at all levels transformative. This was not a fairy tale ending with all parties singing from the same moral hymn book. The subsequent dialogues revealed many differences and conflicts. This approach had rather set up on-going relationships which embodied integrity and shalom, and thus allowed those differences to be held together, enabled by continued faithfulness and challenge.

### Transformative ethic

Agape is the basis for an ethic which is in essence transformative. It is not based on principles which are applied to a situation or standards which have to be lived up to. It is based upon a relationship of agape which enables the transformation of data, values and principles, responsibility, practice:

- The data of any narrative is not surface material to be read off. It demands empathic, holistic understanding of the social and physical environment. The gathering of this data is a function of dialogue and thus by definition is a social, collaborative activity which enables the continual discovery of the other and the self. This has important implications for prophetic activity as we shall see more closely in chapter eight.
- Agape itself informs core principles and attitudes which form the basis of moral meaning. Dialogue tests their embodiment, how they are used in practice. This involves clarification of the meaning of those principles but also the experience of the attitudes in practice, the faithfulness of the other and so on. Moreover, learning about the values of the other is a further stage in empathic awareness of the other. All of this involves mutual learning and the transformation of previous

views, especially where the previous views involve conditional ethic of some kind.

- Reflection on responsibility and how the person begins to respond to the call of the other also leads to transformation. At one level this is inevitable, given the changes which occur in life, leading to crises of responsibility, such as suddenly becoming responsible for dependant parents. The transformation of agape is, however, more fundamental in that it looks to a transformation in perceived responsibility, moving to mutual responsibility and accepting limitations and interdependency.
- Finally, practice and relationship are transformed. The spirit of collaboration emerges, with relationships which aim to enable co-creation. The inclusive nature of this reaches out to affect those beyond any group, so that the care of the empathic ethic does not stop at the group boundary.

All of this points to an ethic which not only holds together various aporia, but actually embodies aporia (see Bauman 1993). An ethic which is inclusive, applies to all, and yet can only be communicated and realised in particular relationships or community. It is an ethic which informs both content and process. It is also an ethic which is constant and depends upon faithfulness but which is always transforming and being realised. This is why it is not entirely true to view the agapeic ethic as provisional. It is precisely both provisional *and* constant. An ethic which values the person for who they are but also impels them to develop and grow. An ethic which takes seriously responsibility for the individual but also looks to mutual responsibility. An ethic which has clear content but which cannot be fully understood without embodiment and in particular without the experience of the ethic in relationship. An ethic which has to be embodied to make real sense at this affective level and yet can never be fully realised.

It is an ethic which values principles and aims to strengthen and sustain them but which can never be summed up in terms of principles *per se*. They are simply another limited embodiment of the ethic. It is an ethic which by definition is non-directive. This means that by definition, it seeks to enhance and nurture the freedom and responsibility of the person. Hence, the dynamic is not to tell the other what to do. At the same time, it is profoundly directional in that the response which it seeks is to do with the growth and development of the human person, and the dynamic of being human.

This is an ethic which always involves something more. It never allows the person to be satisfied with the response that is made. The logic of any response is that it is an embodiment of the person and no embodiment can fully realise agape. At the same time, it is an ethic which seeks to confirm the value of the person and thus enable her to live with the limitations of the self and especially the limitations of the moral response. This demands constant reflection in a supportive community, to ensure that the ethical response neither overwhelms the person, nor becomes sterile. In all this, the pastoral and ethical become one.

### Agape and forgiveness

At the core of this transformative ethic is forgiveness. Forgiveness is not about forgetting. Agape focuses on truthfulness as well as faithfulness, including the truth of the past. Forgiveness also does not begin with judgement. That is rather a contractual approach which assumes that the person can only re-enter the relationship if she seeks forgiveness. This is ultimately a conditional ethic, which is precisely of the kind that the Prodigal Son's brother espoused. That begins from difference, stressing the injury done to the other and the contrast with the other who is not guilty.

However, as B.H. Childs argues, forgiveness starts from the position of sameness. It involves

'...a realisation that we are more *like* those who have offended us than we are *different* from them. Forgiveness from this perspective is a realisation of this fact rather than an act of condescension by a righteous person towards a sinful one' (Childs 1990, 438).

Forgiveness in this ethic is precisely what sets to one side all shame, all that divides the person from the other, and all that stops the person living as a unique other. As Stanley Rudman notes, forgiveness cannot make wrong actions right, or ignore the past and its consequences,

'What it can do is to snap certain links in the connecting chain of evil and make a new start possible. Forgiveness restores a person to fellowship with others, and, in the case of the Christian faith this is understood in the context of God's family' (Rudman 1997, 282).

In all this, forgiveness becomes identified with the dynamic of empathy. Hence, Fiddes can write,

'However untidy it appears, we find that the initiating act of identification and empathy with a wrongdoer *is* forgiveness' (Fiddes 2000, 217).

Whatever follows, in terms of moral meaning, justice and so on, follows in the light of this. This is untidy. There are no formulae or rules which can short cut the need to reach out to the other, and in the light of narrative reflection, to face the past, respond to present need and create the future. Justice is worked through in the light of this relationship, and as shall be seen in chapter six and eight can take many forms. What is clear is that the demand for truth, and for right relationships as well as faithfulness means that justice cannot be avoided. The tension of faithfulness and truthfulness is the aporia at the centre of this and demands that justice is worked out in the transformative ethics of shalom.

### Ethics and Pluralism

The view of ethics outlined above sees pluralism as an essential part of moral dialogue. At one level, this is a matter of pragmatism. Bauman in his reflection on the Holocaust, notes that 'pluralism is the best preventative medicine against morally normal people engaging in morally abnormal actions' (Bauman 1989, 165). Ethical pluralism in effect ensures that all beliefs are challenged.

At another level, the creative dialogue of pluralism is enabled by agape, which says at its core that it is possible to think differently and be accepted, and that despite different views, it is possible to work together for good.

# The Love of God

The concern for an ethic of care which precedes moral reflection is not uniquely Christian. It has been reasserted in recent decades because of the rise of the liberation theologies and philosophies, and especially feminism, where the concern for care is primary. Perhaps even more important in the rise of such an ethic has been the experience of the Holocaust. This has posed most intensely the question about what happens when we do not begin with the assumption of humanity in the other, when we do not begin with the view that the other is neighbour, when we do not begin with the assumption that we have responsibility for the other. The answer is that unless we consciously begin our ethic from that attitude, then we run the danger of first ignoring and then denying the humanity of the other. The step from denial of humanity to destruction of humanity is short. Bauman and Gaita amongst many others remind us that what happened in the Holocaust is extreme but not rare.

What difference does God make to such a perspective? The Christian narrative takes more seriously than any other not simply the need for a pre-rational ethic, an attitude of care and concern which precedes any moral rules. It takes most seriously the need for the other, the one who embodies such an attitude, and thus who initiates the care. Such care does not make sense simply as an idea. It only begins to make sense in the experience of an agapeic relationship, in the practice of response, and in the meaning which emerges from that. It is an ethic then which is built upon spirituality. This involves the development of an empathic awareness of God, as one who is faithful, truthful and free, something only possible in the light of a love experienced, a love which enables us to articulate our narrative and to reflect, on ourselves our social and physical environment and our God, a love which accepts us and challenges us. This is a love which speaks to us at all levels, cognitive, affective, somatic and social and so enables us to develop empathy for ourselves and challenges ourselves. The freedom to be aware of the different narrative at all these levels and to critique them is only possible in the light of agapeic community.

Loving God then becomes a central part of the Christian ethical dynamic. It is not simply a matter of grateful response. It is a matter of coming to know him, not as a distant deity, but as one who is beyond our awareness and at the same time as one who loves us. This means a relationship in which we are always testing out what that love means in every new situation. With each situation the nature of that love is tested, often sorely, and our understanding of it grows as our empathy develops. Like all relationships this demands disciplined practice, not least in worship. Effective worship will then not be simply a thankful response but an experience which enables empathy, and thus enables the holding of all the related aporia, and a response based on that. As Fiddes reminds us this relationship is summed up in the very being of God as Trinity. Loving God is about participating in that community, coming to know and live its real nature (Fiddes 2000).

We must now see how this ethic might apply to pastoral counselling.

### References

P. Avis, Eros and the Sacred ( London: SPCK, 1989).
E. Barker, New Religious Movements (London: HMSO, 1992).
Z. Bauman, Postmodern Ethics (Oxford: Blackwell, 1993).
Z. Bauman, Modernity and the Holocaust (London: Polity Press, 1989).
S. Benhabib, Situating the Self (London: Polity Press, 1992).
V. Brummer, The Model of Love (Cambridge: Cambridge University Press, 1993).
R. Erikson, 'The Psychology of Self-Esteem: Promise or Peril?' Pastoral Psychology, Vol. 35 (3), Spring 1987, 163-171.

D. Fergusson, 'Communitarianism and Liberalism', Studies in Christian Ethics, Vol. 10, 1, 1997, 32-48.

P. Fiddes, Participating in God (London: Darton, Longman and Todd, 2000).

J. Fletcher, Situation Ethics (Philadelphia: Westminster, 1966).

R. Gaita, A Common Humanity (London: Routledge, 2000).

J. Habermas, Moral Consciousness and Communicative Action (London: Polity Press, 1992).

S. Hauerwas, The Peaceable Kingdom (London: SCM, 1984).

S. Hauerwas, Vision and Virtue (Notre Dame: University of Notre Dame Press, 1981).

Richard Hays, The Moral Vision of the New Testament (Edinburgh: T and T Clark, 1996 ).

E. Jungel, God as the Mystery of the World, trans. D. Guder (Edinburgh, T and T Clark 1983)

G. Kaufman, Shame: The Power of Caring (Washington: Schenkman, 1980).

S. Kierkegaard, Works of Love (Princeton: Princeton University Press, 1946).

D. Koehn, Rethinking Feminist Ethics (London: Routledge, 1998).

D. Meeks, God the Economist: the doctrine of God and the political economy (Minneapolis: Fortress, 1989)

R. Niebuhr, The Nature and Destiny of Man Vol. II (New York: Charles Scribners Sons, 1943).

A. Nygren, Agape and Eros (Philadelphia: Westminster Press, 1932).

H. Oppenheimer, The Hope of Happiness (London; SCM, 1983).

G. Outka. Agape An Ethical Analysis (New Haven: Yale University Press, 1972 ).

D. Rae, Equalities (Cambridge Mass.: Harvard University Press, 1981).

S. Rudman, Concepts of Person and Christian Ethics (Cambridge: Cambridge University Press, 1997).

W. Scharge, The Ethics of the New Testament (Edinburgh: T. and T. Clark, 1988).

L. Schotroff, Non-violence and the Love of ones Enemies, in R.H. Fuller (ed.) Essays on the Love Commandment (Minneapolis: Fortress,1978) 9-39.

R. H. Tawney, Equality (London: Allen and Unwin, 1964).

P. Tillich, Morality and Beyond (New York : Harper and Row, 1963).

J. van der Ven, Formation of the Moral Self (Grand Rapids: Eerdmans, 1998).

J. Vanier, Community and Growth (London; Darton, Longman and Todd, 1979).

L. Woodhead, Feminism and Christian Ethics, in L.K. Daly (ed.) Womens Voices: essays in contemporary feminist theology (London: Marshall Pickering, 1992).

# 4

## The Moral World of the Counsellee

*'Love sees what is invisible' ( Simone Weil).*

In turning now to the counselling relationship, I will suggest something of the moral dialogue at its centre. I argue that this is not something which emerges late in the relationship but is there from the beginning. First, it leads to the articulation of moral narrative, with the counsellee able to look at her moral world, and the truth of events in the past and present. In a second stage the values underlying the narrative are clarified. I argue in chapter five that this is a complex dialogue with affective as well as cognitive elements, involving a learning process. A third stage, in chapter six, looks at the moral and spiritual change which occurs in the counselling process. This involves a conscious change in terms of faith and hope and the grounds for these virtues, showing clearly that addressing morality in the pastoral situation demands attention to the whole belief system, what the counsellee puts her faith in. This determines any moral response and enables the person to begin to take responsibility for her ethical meaning.

## Case

*Anna came to the pastoral counsellor in a neighbouring church because her marriage was collapsing and she did not know where to turn. She was distressed and preoccupied, unable to sit still, taking deep breaths and sighing and frequently apologising for being there.*

*The counsellor encouraged her to talk about how she was feeling and she began to speak about her marriage. Married to John for three years, their relationship gave the public impression of a stable and loving relationship.*

*'Its a sham though. Any stability is down to me. I sort out all the money and all*

*the plans. All he does is spend hours preparing for work ( teaching RE at secondary school) and spending money on the credit card. It isn't fair. He says he will change, take responsibility but never does. I can't take any more. If I don't leave now I can't see the point of going on.'*

*She suspected that her husband was being unfaithful, and spoke as if she could trust no one. Each part of the faltering story was accompanied by an apology - 'I know this sounds awful,' 'You must think I am terrible to even think this sort of thing'. She hinted also that there was much more that she could talk about, but couldn't. 'I know what I really want and need but I can't say it. I shouldn't really be here - I'm wasting your time.'*

*As Anna left the first meeting she agreed to come back despite a sense of failure at having to come to a pastoral counsellor. Her body language showed that she was more than simply feeling failure. Her neck and face were flushed, and despite a little more evidence of control there was a haunted look in her eyes.*

*Anna was late for her second session and was once more uncomfortable and unsure of herself. At points she was also defensive, interpreting comments of the counsellor as implicit judgements about her. At this point the counsellor began to suggest some form of contract which could establish aims and practice of their work together. Anna was unsure to begin with but agreed to a short term contract. She was very keen to 'get things sorted - see an end to all this.'*

*Soon after this she moved into her fears and concerns about work. She was P.A. to an administrator in the a large health service organisation, and prided herself at sorting out problems. She 'looked after' her boss, making sure that he was not under pressure. Now things were changing, with greater pressures and stress with the result that her boss was finding it less easy to cope. The knock-on effect for Anna was that she was less able to solve problems for him, and less able to cope with the volume of work she received and the pressure and negative attitude which she saw as coming from the MD. She felt as if under siege and spent a long time at work including weekends. She also felt exhausted. 'It is so unfair that I should end up doing every-thing'. She described how she was increasingly losing her temper with her colleagues. As she left the meeting she informed the counsellor that she had agreed a trial sepa-ration from her husband.*

*Anna's next session revealed a further side to her in church life. She was Parochial Church Council secretary, and used to enjoy solving problems for the min-ister. Now the weekend work was pushing out the possibility of church attendance, and she felt that she was getting nothing out of the services she did get to. In fact, the services more often made her feel angry and resentful. 'I stand there and sing cho-ruses and thank God when I know I am miserable. I look at the others and see their smiling faces and I start to hate them.'*

*She admitted, reluctantly, that she felt like suicide. She had recurring images of smashing her wrist through glass.*

*The only time that she found peace was when she took her dog for a walk. This was to do with her dog, who she loved, and the countryside where they walked - part of a local national park. 'Sometimes' she said, 'I just want let go of everything - I don't want to go back to the world'.*

*The short term contract came up for review and developed into a long term therapeutic relationship, where it gradually became clear that at the base of Anna's despair was childhood which had involved emotional and sexual abuse from more than one person.*

The first stage of the pastoral counselling relationship is often thought of in terms of a 'value free zone'. This is the time when trust is established and pastoral issues focused on. Gershen Kaufman argues that this is the time for building the interpersonal bridge (Kaufman 1980; Pattison 1989, chap 3). The ethical agenda can be established later, the argument goes. For now it is safer not to raise issues of morality.

Such a view runs the risk of seeing the 'ethical agenda' as just that, issues and dilemmas that can be examined and discussed. Moreover, these issues are to be brought into the relationship as if they are something quite distinct from the caring relationship. For the counsellor who worked with Anna this could easily have involved focusing on the issue of marriage and the danger of a break up.

However, Anna's experience reveals that the counsellee already inhabits a distinctive moral universe. This is something which, far from being absent or hidden, she is at pains to assert. Such a universe involves how she perceives the others in her life, what she sees as the core values, how she sees possibilities and what ground she has for hope. All of this, and the relationships she has with others, give her a sense of moral identity. For her, such a moral identity is well established but also already being disturbed by the emotional pain she is experiencing and, above all, her sense of worthlessness. Her spiritual and moral identity, then, is something she feels compelled to hang on to but is already proving inadequate when faced by the demands of life. The question of marital breakdown then far from being an 'ethical issue' which has to be raised at some point is a life crisis, amongst others, which is testing Anna's spiritual and moral identity, indeed her moral and spiritual universe. The discomfort which she displays even in the first sessions suggests strongly that her spiritual and moral view of life is not sufficient to sustain her.

From the word go then, the counsellee has an agenda suffused in moral meaning, communicated through body language, as much as through ideas or feelings expressed. The counsellor does not have to introduce an ethical agenda but rather has to respond to the difficult, often confused, moral world of the counsellee.

The important first stage is to enable the counsellee to articulate this moral world, and for the counsellor to begin to engage it. Though the language is of enabling, with power imbalance which is implicit in that, the relationship actually develops the character of a dialogue, one which does not attempt to assume what the moral meaning might be, and takes totally seriously what the counsellee presents. The counsellor's task is to help the counsellee 'make sense' of this moral world, and take responsibility for it.

In this chapter I will also note that moral meaning itself has a direct effect on the way in which the person perceives the truth - about others, the self and the past, present and future. Attention to that truth is a critical part of the developing counselling relationship, and of any development in ethical meaning, not least because of Joseph Fletcher's beloved 'situation'. In his situation ethics Fletcher rightly argued that great attention should be paid to the situation surrounding any moral problem (Fletcher 1966). Without a clear understanding of such data, the moral decision making cannot be effective. The difficulty with this view is that it sees the situation as something which can be 'read off', which is accessible. In fact the 'situation' is made up of many different relationships each of which involves personal perspectives. These perspectives, all of which involve explicit or implicit moral views, themselves affect any understanding of the situation and often lead either to an obscuring of the reality of the situation, or to hasty judgements. To discover the truth about the situation involves reflection which takes time to test those perspectives, and enable them to be worked through.

The explorations of the moral world of the counsellee and of the truth of the situation come together in the articulation of her narrative. The presence of agape provides the secure environment within which the counsellee can begin this articulation. However, this is not a simple process, and as shall be seen, the establishing of that trust in itself involves careful work with moral meaning, and moral dialogue.

It may be said that the experience of Anna is extreme. However, as James Fowler notes, few lives are not built to some degree around moral values which are held in place by some form of shame (Fowler 1996, chap. 6).

## Moral Narrative

From the word go, Anna was revealing in different ways a faltering moral narrative. As noted above, the key point of narrative is that articulation enables the person to disclose something about herself, not simply to the other but also to herself. At the base of this is the presence of the other, signalling the faithfulness of agape. However, the first part of the articulation of narrative is quite a studied piece of 'disclosure'. As Gordon Lynch and David Willows note,

'When we tell stories we usually make judgements about what would represent interesting or appropriate content for those stories given the particular audience that we are telling them to. The way in which we tell stories about ourselves is typically shaped by our desire to appear to our audience to be if not morally commendable, then at least not morally blameworthy' (Lynch and Willows 1998, 17).

Viv Burr's social constructionist view confirms this, viewing people,

'as located within a local moral order within which they have to negotiate a viable position for the themselves. The functions which their constructed accounts serve for them are primarily those of offering explanations and excuses, making justifications, apportioning blame and making accusations. People are actors in a moral universe concerned with negotiating for themselves a credible (and creditable) moral position' (Burr 1995, 120).

Anna begins then by disclosing what she thinks is reasonable to hear. She wants the counsellor to hear a view of her which is acceptable and good. For her this meant firstly assuring the counsellor that though she was in pain she was 'really alright'. This said two things: that she was self sufficient and could solve this problem and that the counsellor did not need to feel pity. In one sense this was actually the beginning of a narrative designed not reveal the truth about herself. Of course, the pain which she tentatively referred to was true, but this was to be pain that could be dealt with. Hence, the first part of this 'disclosure' is to assure the counsellor that she need not worry. The message which she presented was 'I am really a very self-reliant person - I am not strange or different, and I am here to get this sorted out'. She was trying to justify herself morally and also to reassure herself that the counsellor would accept her. As such there was an implicit assumption that the counsellor would only accept her if she demonstrated that she was capable and not in need. At one level there was an assumption that the counsellor inhabited the same moral world. However, precisely because narrative articulation was new to her she worked hard at ensuring that the counsellor was drawn into her moral world.

Part of this pre-narrative dialogue was in trying to establish a clear way through the counselling process. Anna was consistently concerned about when this would finish and how she would know that she was 'better'. In effect she was trying to draw the counsellor into the medical model of 'talk therapy' which sets out a clear method for dealing with a problem and looks to a cure. The cure for her was to be relieved of the emotional pain. Three things were going on for Anna in this. Firstly, she was anxious about facing up to and working through the immense pain she was experiencing. Secondly, there was a contrary hope, which she later pinpointed, that she might be able to get rid of the pain without having to 'face it' and work through it. Thirdly, she was also signalling that she did not want to become dependant on someone else. The longer any therapeutic relationship goes on for the more she felt there would be a chance of this. These concerns came across as a suspicion and a testing of the counsellor. Would she be able to achieve this 'cure' for her? How far could she rely on her? From the beginning there was a clear assertion about a moral world which was based on self reliance, and attempts to find a way that would give her back this independence, but also an underlying question about how far she could trust the counsellor. She signalled ambivalence on this. On the one hand, she did not want to trust her as an other human being, but rather as a therapeutic practitioner, someone who would sort things out for her. She wanted the counsellor to reassure her that this would happen. On the other hand, she had been through other therapeutic relationships and had seen these 'fail to deliver the goods'. She had a sense that maybe a different kind of relationship was important. Indeed, this was why she came to a pastoral counsellor, and not another psychologist. The counsellor had to ensure that she was not drawn into the role of expert who could solve all things, and at the same time help Anna to explore what it meant to trust another.

The testing continued in this early phase with Anna showing more strong ambivalence. She wanted to know more about how the counsellor could help her. At the same time she devalued the work of pastoral counselling and therapy as a whole, asserting that there was really no hope for her. This showed itself in suspicion about the words of the counsellor. At one point, for instance, the counsellor said that she would be happy to arrange an initial series of six counselling sessions and then review the situation. Anna wanted to know what this implied. Did it mean that everything would be sorted in six sessions, or did it mean that the counsellor was only going to give six sessions and would not stay with her? Any ambiguous phrase was tested to see whether it contained a judgement about her or about the process.

The task of the counsellor, then, was not to be drawn into this moral world and reinforce it but to enable the counsellee to articulate it more fully and begin to examine it. However, the whole point of Anna's initial moral narrative was to ensure that she would be seen as acceptable. Hence, a lack of overt reinforcement for that narrative was something which Anna found hard to handle. For her it was hard to trust someone who had a different view of values from her. Not to share her values was seen as a sign of disapproval, indeed a questioning of her worth.

It was important for the counsellor to establish and maintain a sense of acceptance, sameness, which also reflected difference such that Anna would not see failure to support her moral world as rejection. This dynamic already involves a dialogue, in which moral meaning is tested and explored. The faithfulness of the counsellor, communicated through body language and tone of voice, especially in reaction to the developing narrative, not only enables the narrative articulation but also sets up the possibility of dialogue between the perspectives of conditionality and unconditionality. Hence, agape is not simply a condition of narrative articulation. It is also an intimate part of the dialogue which enables that narrative to develop. Critical to this is mutual testing. Anna's view of moral meaning continually tested the acceptance of the counsellor and the counsellor's faithfulness continually tested the Anna's moral view. It is important to note the continual surprise that can be experienced by the counsellee in facing a moral world which is so starkly different from hers. For Anna there was the hope that someone might be there 'for her' but she found it a surprise that the counsellor could actually not be part of her moral view. Indeed, such was the surprise that it took her a long time to actually believe it. Looking back at the first weeks of counselling she said, 'I found it all unreal. I was desperate for acceptance but could not believe that you accepted me. It was nice to feel accepted but I kept thinking that there must be some other reason for that - it was your job, you pitied me, and so on...'

## Moral meaning and care contract

Establishing a therapeutic contract enables the beginnings of a shared moral meaning to emerge, one based around the counselling relationship. Such a contract is spoken rather than written, and negotiating it enables ethical reflection and the testing out of that meaning. Most importantly, once an initial contract has been arrived at this provides the bench mark for future ethical reflection, which in turn may lead to a revision and development of the contract and its moral meaning. By the end of the second session, in response to Anna's testing, they had agreed a broad contract which involved the following:

- A short term contract of six sessions. The progress would be reviewed in the sixth session with option for renewing the contract, including making it a long term one. This stressed the freedom of the counsellee, she would be in control. It also stressed the limitations of the counselling process. The relationship might not work for her and she could move out of it if she felt that this was not working or she could not work with the counsellor.
- The counsellor would be available to Anna for one hour confidential sessions. Both would abide by the times agreed, and be punctual. The counsellor would be non-judgmental and open to any challenges from the counsellee about their relationship and its meaning. There would be mutual respect for feelings and ideas.
- The aim of the whole process is not to effect a sudden and magical change but rather to enable the counsellee to work through her own change at her own pace

This summed up elements of agape: nonconditional care/community (with limitations of delivery), concern for the autonomy of the other, equality and mutuality - the counsellee could raise objections to the counsellor about where the relationship was going at any point. The clarification of boundaries also helped to focus on attainable objectives and as such gave a framework which could empower the counsellee.

Though this was accepted as a starting point, the counsellee was still clearly wary of three things: the genuineness of the counsellors care; the openness of the process, she was still left with uncertainty as to how the process could end; and the responsibility which the process placed upon her.

The initial contract then begins to embody agape, providing an explicit framework for the relationship. However, it cannot be fully understood without further reflection and mutual testing as the relationship continues. Is it really safe to challenge? How do I know the counsellor really does accept me? Is it really safe to say what I feel? Sometimes this leads to the extension and development of a contract.

### Developing the contract

The most pressing thing on Anna's mind in the first sessions was a strong sense of a felt need and the question as to whether she could share it, and how the counsellor would react to something which went against Anna's own sense of what was ethically acceptable. Typically, at the end of the session, as she was about to leave, she would make remarks such as, 'I know what I really need and it is so simple'. She eventually articulated this as an overwhelming need to be hugged and held. As she said this she avoided eye contact and mumbled an excuse about this being childish and in any case she knew it was not possible. For Anna this reflected and raised massive ambivalence.

Raising the idea of the physical touch was both a strong yearning, but also an area of danger. The sexual abuse she had experienced in childhood, not at this point revealed to the counsellor, had emerged from what she had thought initially was non-erotic touch. Equally, emotional abuse, received from another important figure, was such that physicality and touch were devalued.

Revealing need for dependency, moreover, went against the basic moral position and identity which she had been trying to get across to the counsellor. Alongside this was a fear of disapproval from the counsellor and the possibility of moral judgement. This was a very delicate time, not least because the counsellor needed to affirm this as an acceptable need - but also begin to work through how this need might be met.

The need to affirm the need as one which was morally acceptable was clear from how she presented the need. 'Here I am' she said, 'a married woman of thirty five and I am talking about wanting a hug to someone who is virtually a stranger. Now that is weird. You must think me so strange.' Anna felt herself to be quite different from others and, therefore, a target for disapproval. As she shared those words she did not look up, as if waiting for a blow. When she raised her head in response to the counsellor's comments she scanned her face for any signs of judgement. The counsellor did not disapprove and encouraged her to articulate this felt need more, and talk about what it meant for her. She began to articulate the need in terms of security, safety, 'wiping away tears'. Even this was tested further, though, with Anna characterising it as a childish need. 'It's fine for children to get hugged and have their pain kissed better, but I am past that now. I cannot catch up on that now'.

Again the counsellor did not confirm her assertion and invited her to talk about what the feeling meant to her now, and also about the sense of loss which seemed to be at the back of it. The more she talked about this with no sign of disapproval from the counsellor, the more she became practised in articulating need and thus aware that this might be something that adults are allowed to feel. As she gained a certain level of confidence in expressing this she then asked the counsellor if she might at some point in the sessions hold her.

This was a very tentative request with a fear that it might embarrass the counsellor or put her into difficult position - raising all the questions about professional probity, and the question of touch in the caring situation. For Anna there was the additional factor that she had been in one professional medical relationship which had gone wrong, again something which would become apparent later.

Margaret Lyall provides an important reflection on the use of touch in therapy . She notes the key professional ethics questions involving the safety of the client and the competence and limits of the counsellor. The issues here are very much attached to the question of power, and the danger of professional abuse (Lyall 1997, 22 ff.). At the same time Lyall explores the importance of non-erotic touch. In effect, touch can be an embodiment of the agapeic concern. It locks, in a unique way, into the presence of the other reassuring the counsellee of the faithfulness of the other, reinforcing somatic awareness of the other. Lyall notes a strong body of empirical evidence which shows the positive effect of touch in human development (Lyall 1997, 11 ff.).

All this provided then an opportunity for a reflection on the contract. Anna and the counsellor were able to talk about why touch was important to her, what it meant to her. In allowing that to be articulated she was also beginning to see that the felt need was not strange - nor the intensity of that need.  This was beginning to move into a spiritual awareness of one aspect of the self as same and different. It would inevitably move on to the expression of the feeling of fear which lay behind the intensity of that need.  As she talked through the need Anna very carefully differentiated the touch she hoped for from erotic touch, and accepted that she had no right to ask for such a response, but that it might perhaps be negotiated.

The counsellor then moved to talking through her position. She was concerned about safety of her self and Anna. She was concerned about her own limitations. She also encouraged Anna to look at alternatives to human touch:

- providing a big comfortable sofa which might 'enfold' her.

- Having an object which Anna could hug such as a big cushion or even a teddy. Lyall notes from her own experience as a hospital patient the importance of touching an object which, in her case a teddy, could sum up the significant faith relationships in ones life, and thus act as reminder of her 'spirit', her sense of self (Lyall 1997, 4 ff.). For Anna there were few such relationships which to reflect on.

Hence, they began to negotiate ways in which touch might be arranged.

Lyall notes five areas in which touch may appropriate:
- As a social ritual, e.g. on entering or leaving a room. Here touch is stylised, through a shaking of hands or a hug of greeting.
- At the moment of crisis. This may involve grief or trauma, where the counsellee needs to be 'grounded' and assured of the presence of an other.
- To focus the counsellee's attention if not able to concentrate. This literally involves a brief moment of contact to bring her back to the present.
- To emphasise a verbal statement. If the counsellor is reassuring the counsellee that she is present for her then the touch reinforces this message.
- To 'unblock a client'. As Lyall notes, it was Freud who discovered in his early days the importance of skin to skin contact in releasing repressed material (Lyall 1997, 28ff).

For Anna two areas of touch were eventually negotiated:
- She greeted the counsellor with a hug at the beginning and end of each session. This was a ritual, almost public act. It was a physical reaffirmation of her self, something very important when in the first sessions she was very nervous before each meeting, and often left the meeting with unanswered questions and anxieties in her own mind. Above all, that was the direct message of faithfulness.
- Touch was to be initiated by Anna when she felt that she needed reassurance, especially when recalling painful parts of her narrative. The counsellor agreed not to move forward towards her, and to ensure that her personal space was respected.
The working through of this contract of touch is simply one example of how a contract might be extended. The question of touch is not one that is being advocated *per se*. As J. Older notes, this may involve less

than 10% of therapy time (Older 1982). It also involves a clear experiential factor of power sharing and freedom, and above all of sanctioning of acceptable feelings and seeking their fulfilment.

All of this provides a way in which the agape offered by the counsellor can be felt at affective and somatic levels. It is important that the cognitive level be included, reflection on the meaning of the hug, not least because this is part of the experience in which the counsellee is beginning to find new meaning, in and through the relationship. The formal nature of the contract might seem to go against what in essence is a spontaneous show of care, to hug someone. However, the careful negotiation of touch was essential. Firstly, Anna needed to learn how to communicate the need for touch and how to accept it. She had literally been starved of this as a child, and this meant that she had to practice. It became real for her the more she focused on her narrative and the associated pain. Secondly, it was important in establishing boundaries. She was able to see that in physical contact she need not lose control or be overcome by the other, and that physical contact which had been thought through as part of the relationship could establish boundaries. Thirdly, a great deal of her moral world had been built up through her interpretation of the body language of significant others - her mother's sigh or silence, her father's dark glances, all of which reinforced her conditional and secretive moral world. It was precisely the same body language of rejection or abuse, which she was searching for and more than half expecting from her counsellor. Hence, it was critical for her to test and make explicit the connection between the attitude of the counsellor and the body language and response. Through this she was beginning to make connections between somatic awareness of the self and other, awareness of the affect and attitude of the other and the meaning of these. All of these were central to the challenging of her moral world. Together they began to add up to an *experience* of agape, a connection of moral meaning to relationship. The contract was the first step in enabling Anna to learn to receive that love.

The contract then provides the basis for reflecting on the relationships and the problems that may arise and above all provides the basis for the equalising of power. It also provides the basis for the spiritual discernment of ambiguity both in the self and in the counsellor as other. At one level this helps the counsellee to see that nonconditional care can be offered, but that the counsellor has limitations of time and energy. At another level it demonstrates that agape does not preclude testing. On the contrary, the contract and its extension involved continual mutual testing. The counsellee tested the counsellor's narrative of agape. At the same time, the counsellor tested the counsellee's narrative and its meaning, enabling a dialogue around different moral perspectives. At some points there was an agreement about negotiated moral meaning, which gave the basic criteria for assessing the relationship. The meaning, however, was not static and continued to be tested throughout the relationship. There is often the assumption on the part of the counsellee that the kindness of the other should not be tested. This would be to doubt the counsellor, who is, after all trying to help. This, however, is all part of the conditional moral world which aims above all to please or at least not to offend.

The very idea of dialogue, of course, was for Anna risky. It meant that the meaning which she had held together, and that through very hard times, was now threatened. Counselling makes meaning, and the search for meaning, public, in the sense that it sets up a conversation beyond the self which in turns leads to a dialogue with the self and a critical examination of values. For Anna this was the very opposite of the dynamic of her moral world. Her world was secretive and defensive. Her identity was about maintaining values, both to keep her sanity and to protect her from the rest of the world. Addressing those values in and through the counselling relationship would not simply imply rejection but also reinforce the major horrors at the heart of her self.

At one level, she was experiencing the desolation of knowing that her parents were not there for her, leading to the belief that she was unlovable. Only two things held her together faced by that ultimate lack of meaning and value. Firstly, there was the belief that her parents might yet love her. Hence, she went back to her mother time after time to try to establish a relationship, and so bring to life a fairy-tale ending. This was of course something her mother was not capable of. Secondly, she looked for worth that was conditional, value that could be quantified. This was central to her sense of self worth. Hence, to question that sense of worth and that perception of the truth would threaten her entire self. The only thing that could enable her to work through that fear and maintain course for change was love embodied in the counsellor. 'Unconditional positive regard' is a distant cousin of agape, and is too anodyne by half. The very phrase smacks of politeness, albeit a form of genuine concern. Agape is about a faithfulness and loyalty which allows itself to be tested in very intense ways and which will still be there whether the counsellee reveals despair, or aggression. Despair was something Anna did not want to reveal to herself or the counsellor. After all, the conditional moral agenda was about pleasing people, including the counsellor. She wanted her to feel happy that she had 'got better'. The counsellor had to show her that she did not want to be pleased but rather to develop a mutual relationship in agape.

Far from being marginal then her moral world was at the core of her life and her sense of conditionality clearly gave her the basis for her moral principles. Moral value and truth about who she was were all tied up together. Her moral narrative had to be expressed and faced.

### The moral narrative

Once the contract was initially established the counsellor encouraged Anna to continue with her narrative. In one sense Anna was happy to do this, 'I know I have to talk this through'. However, she still wanted to present an acceptable moral world to the counsellor. This was a world she had to look at directly and was characterised by moral individualism, moral heroism, and moral perfectionism.

### Moral individualism

Anna was concerned, as we saw, with the values of self sufficiency, tough mindedness and independence. The great vice was dependency and the admission of this. To seek help from another is seen as not simply moral failure, but to question her very identity. By extension Anna at first appeared to deny that she had needs. This was not so much a form of moral hubris as the belief that any needs should not be expressed and should be put out to one side. She had here a clear sense of justice as desert. People had to live with the consequences of their actions. 'I know it sounds tough, but if they have been stupid then they have to live with it. We get what we deserve.'

This often led her to judge others quite harshly. They should be sorting out their own problems, especially if they were autonomous adults. Conversely, life for her was often unjust or unfair. She could deal with all of the problems set before her if only she were not borne down by the others. At other points, the fairness took on a wider view - life itself is not fair - it does not give space to her, allow her to catch up or to be.

Part of Anna's task was to draw the counsellor in to this characterisation of justice and begin to accept this view of fairness at the centre of her moral world.

Once more the counsellor had to be careful not to collude in the presented moral world and thus the final view of unfairness but, at the same time, demonstrate she is there with non-judgmental love for the counsellee. This affirmed her worth and allowed a relationship in which she could have the luxury of talking about herself and her fears.

Presented by the direct question, 'Do you think this is fair?' the counsellor could have gone several ways. She avoided being drawn in and spoke to the underlying pain, 'I am hearing that you feel very hurt about this'. This was then explored at an affective level - not just feeling hurt but feeling rejected, not appreciated - 'no one asks me how I am'. Once again the counsellor was not drawn into this world but rather encouraged Anna to return to the narrative and talk about the events and to reflect more clearly on the relationship which are seen to be unfair. The counsellor encouraged her to be specific, to work through just what was said, how she reacted. As we shall see in the next chapter this approach is not simply trying to establish truth but also is in effect reflection on moral meaning with an invitation to consider the basis of it.

## Moral heroism

Moral heroism involves a sacrificial altruism, especially for those who are vulnerable. At one level this involved non-maleficence, a concern to defend the other from oppression, this ranged from 'innocent adults' to children to animals. At another level Anna explicitly held the value of beneficence, an active seeking of the good of the other. The concern for the good of the vulnerable was such that it overrode the good of others including Anna herself. 'I am not important' she said. 'What is important is that the people who need help get it'. This led Anna to care for a local elderly woman whose family did not visit her, a number of children at church, children of a close friend and certain colleagues at work.

## Moral perfectionism

Along with the heroism and individualism was a perfectionism which demanded that she maintain the highest of standards and that she does that for all the people who she cared for. There was no question of mutuality in her moral world. All the moral demands which she was faced by she had to take responsibility for immediately. This meant that there were no boundaries to her care, often caring for people who were part of other care groups, such as the elderly mother of the vicar. Indeed, at points, she chose to exclude other possible carers, or to make up for their deficiencies in caring especially for children. This in turn meant that she could never really make such care 'public', and that she in turn was not recognised for it. Her pain in this was clear to see, but she had a moral injunction against 'boasting'. When the counsellor commented on how tiring this taking of responsibility must be Anna's initial response was to see this as an affirmation. Exhaustion was at least a sign that she had done all that could be done, even if that was not enough. Hence, the affirmation was tinged with regret.

At the same time this almost idealised view of rescue and caring for the powerless was one which precluded any anger. Anger for Anna was by definition wrong. It was wrong because it hurt others, another example of nonmaleficence. The idea that she might actually express anger was anathema. Anna and the counsellor spent more time on identifying and owning anger, differentiating it from aggression and violence (see chapter five for a more detailed examination of anger and moral reflection).

### Shame

At the heart of Anna's moral world were two narratives, one of survival and one of shame. Anna had survived despite the pain and she had survived with what she defined as integrity, which meant being 'honest' with people. She could not stand the dissembling of people and told them so.

Like many survivors of childhood abuse, Anna had developed a strong sense of moral identity, summed up in the role of the care-taker. Even at the beginning of the narrative there were problems appearing with this identity, but Anna was not going to let go of this identity at all easily. The clear moral values and concerns were part of her coping mechanisms. They had given her a sense of worth. It had to be worth her while letting go of that identity and the spiritual and moral meaning which was at the base of it. There had to be some alternative that she could believe in. Hence it was important for her to continue testing that the other was there for her.

In chapter seven the different types of shame will be examined more closely. Here it is sufficient to distinguish between healthy shame and toxic shame. Healthy shame is at the base of learning, enabling the person to acknowledge to herself and others things which are wrong and to seeking forgiveness for the things which ought to be addressed.

Toxic shame is rather centred upon the person herself, involving an acute sense of exposure of personal deficiencies, and a powerlessness to deal with them, often accompanied by self loathing or contempt. It is not simply that the person feels shame but that she believes her very self to be shameful and unworthy. Any amount of assurance or ritual will not allow her to feel or accept forgiveness, any more than she can forgive others. She can only deal with what she perceives as moral failure by repeatedly trying to get the tasks she faces right. This means continuously trying to make up for her shame.

Two critical dynamics lead to the development of this shame, both experienced by Anna. The first is the dynamic of conditionality. Gershen Kaufman notes this as the failure to establish the inter-personal bridge, resulting in the failure to develop mutuality in key relationships (Kaufman 1980, 106). At the heart of this is the experience of a personal environment built upon unfulfilled conditionality. The parent treats the child as a means to an end, setting up the expectation for the child that if that end is achieved she will be fully accepted, only for the child to be humiliated when she cannot meet the often impossible task.

In terms of moral development this in effect led to Anna being blocked at the early part of what Kohlberg sees as the conventional stage (Kohlberg 1984). In this moral decisions are based on a desire to conform to the expectations of significant communities. Hence, doing good becomes a matter of pleasing other people. For Anna, however, the pleasing of others was ultimately not about school or work norms but about the conditional norms of her parents. Because the emotional abuse in childhood leads to this desire to please, the person never moves on to a more mature ethic or to the usual development phases, not least the ones associated with adolescence and the move away from the parent - something associated with the awareness of the limitations of the parent and the clear expression of anger and frustration.

A second dynamic was that of secrecy, leading to a double bind situation. For Anna the abuse that she suffered could not be shared, not even within the family. For some children, such as in the families of alcoholics, the emotional abuse is clear but cannot be shared outside the family. Hence, the child has to build up a defensive wall. As Al McFadyen notes, the pressure to keep up such secrecy prevents the child from actually processing the data of what she experienced (McFadyen 1996, 94ff.). It is therefore interpreted in terms of the moral framework of the child at the time. This involves both the belief that the parent is good and the belief that goodness involves pleasing the parent. In the light of that, the experience of abuse must either be not real, and many abuse survivors do doubt the veracity of the flash back experiences, or seen as something which was not the parent's fault but hers. The survivor then takes on the responsibility for the abuse.

All of this results in the sustaining of a 'false self' which denies to the world or the rest of the family any problems. At the same time the pain and ambivalence towards her parents is suppressed, requiring considerable psychic energy. Alice Miller sums up much of this with reference to anger and parental care in general:

'The greatest cruelty that can be inflicted on children is to refuse to allow them to express their anger and suffering except at the risk of losing their parents' love and affection. The anger stemming from early childhood is stored up in the unconscious, and since it represents a healthy, vital source of energy, an equal amount of energy must be expended to repress it' (quoted in Fowler 1996, 126).

This leads to a shame about the self which pushes down the elements of the victim's experience which are unbearable. In turn this leads to the development of shame binds, shame associated with particular aspects of the self. For Anna this involved *affect shame*, *drive shame*, and *need shame*.

Affect shame associates emotions such as fear with shame. Even the feeling of fear and pain associated with the original abuse is itself infected with shame. It cannot be expressed, and thus to a great extent cannot even be recognised. Hence, as we shall see in the next chapter, feelings tend to be hard to understand.

Drive shame is associated within any of the pleasure drives, most obviously sex. The very drive to please the self can become shameworthy. Hence, Anna cannot begin to put herself first. The idea of self nurture is itself shameful.

Need shame refers to basic human needs. Gershen Kaufman notes the six basic human needs, each of which Anna felt shame about in various ways:
- the need for close interpersonal relationships;
- the need for touching and holding, the ground for security and trust;
- the need to identify with others, to feel some sense of belonging;
- the need for differentiation, to experience the self as a separate being capable of mastering major tasks of personal development;
- the need to nurture, involving the practice of care for others, and an assurance that this is of intrinsic worth;
- the need for unconditional affirmation, being valued for ones uniqueness (Kaufman 1980, 65).

## The Narrative of truth

The continued articulation of the narrative enabled Anna to see more clearly her moral world for what it was. This process is taken further through reflection on the narrative which clarifies the values, something to be examined more closely in the next chapter. However, the articulation of the narrative also begins to enable a narrative of truth, allowing the truth of the past and the present to emerge from behind the counsellee's moral world. In effect, this involves the development of empathic reflection, upon the self and others.

### The self

For Anna, there was no sense of distinctive self. In one sense her self was simply an extension of her parents. Her desire still to please them meant that she had no identity apart from them. As Fowler notes, this leads to difficulty in developing a clear sense of 'boundaries for the self' (Fowler 1996, 123). In any case Anna was reluctant to look back and see herself, precisely because she was so ashamed of herself and fearful. It is the fear which kept asserting itself through flash backs to the time of the abuse which she began to experience in the early morning.

As the narrative is encouraged so the counsellee begins to establish a distance, and is able to see the self. She could only begin to articulate that narrative in the light of a very secure presence of the counsellor. This led to a further development of the contract of touch which had the counsellor sitting back to back with her and holding her hand. This was first to avoid the eye contact of the counsellor. Any eye contact made her feel her shame more strongly. Secondly, holding the hand of the counsellor was a strong indication of her presence and a reassurance that whatever was said would not make her turn away, thus enabling Anna herself not to turn away, but to keep looking at herself.

Several other techniques can help the counsellee to gain distance from the self, such as fantasy journey or memory retrieval exercises (Parks 1994, 176ff.). These enable the counsellee to distance herself from her situation but 'return' to the place where the abuse occurred. For Anna this was a very powerful approach. From the clear position of adult she could see her self as the 'other', and begin to feel for herself.

Two important factors emerged from this reflective work: a greater awareness of the truth of the situation and the beginnings of an alternative moral meaning. For Anna her moral view was actually getting in the way of the truth about the past. As noted, the experience of child abuse survivors is often that they begin to doubt the reality of what happened, despite the increasing experience of flash backs. These were half remembered parts of the experience which came vividly back to her mind at moments of relaxation, such as early morning before rising.

She also believed that she wanted to harm herself, based on the recurring image of her putting her fist through glass. The more she moved back into her story the more it became apparent that this images was not in fact a desire for suicide or self harm but rather an image from her memory. When she was suffering the actions of abuse this was often in a room where there was a window, close by the bed which reflected light from the street. She was not able to articulate any sound to struggle against the abuse. All she could do was look to the light of the window, a window she could not quite reach, and wish that she could smash it to stop the abuser.

In effect, Anna's moral view with its great stress on guilt and on the feeling that she might have been responsible for the action, had entirely altered the perception of the past experience. Her moral world-view had reinterpreted the data which the brain was giving it, leading her to assume that this recurring image must be a desire for self harm.

This was a critical break-through and one which began to radically affect the moral view of Anna. In exploring this view of the past and the pain which was associated with it she began to move into a different view of the self. At the very least this was an ambiguous view. She felt that she was partly responsible for what happened because the first time had involved her being dressed attractively, and spending time alone with the abuser. She felt that she had 'allowed herself' to get into a position where things might go wrong. Now, alongside that picture of the person who was responsible and ashamed, was the view of the victim, a vulnerable child.

The narrative had enabled a distance from which Anna could begin to view herself. This did not lead immediately to empathy for her self. However, from the beginning there was clearly affect atunement. She spoke of resonating with the feelings of the child, but not really knowing what it meant. Empathy began to develop fully as Anna brought more cognitive reflection to the affective and somatic work, and she began to want to know more about herself and her past.

As the different moral picture emerged so Anna began to be aware of the different feelings which had been kept down for so long. As we shall see in the next chapter, this introduces the next part of the moral work. At this stage, however, the important dynamic of the relationship was to keep bringing the counsellee back to the reality of what did happen, with agape enabling her to become more open to the past. The more that she was able to articulate the past in whatever form, the more she was able to become not simply the teller of the story but also the hearer. This process enables the person to take responsibility for the remembering.

## The Other

For Anna, others were in general not to be trusted. She sympathised with those who were victims, though this never became genuine empathy. She tended to project her own experience on to them and not be aware of any ambiguities in their behaviour. At the same time she could not begin to sympathise with herself, as one who was responsible. Hence, though she was able to relate to these perceived victims, there was no mutuality involved. With the reflection upon the significant others in her life she noted a few who she felt she could rely upon, but these never stayed for long in her life, and none of them realised what a bad time she had at home. With most others she was unable to develop any trust. She saw them as either oppressors of the vulnerable or as people who were simply unaware of others. With several relationships, including her husband, this tended to be reinforced. Hence, there were no people who Anna could actually put her faith in. For her, others were a source of either approval or disapproval. Hence, her view of the other was to watch simply for the possible dangers, and attempt to avoid them. She could not begin to let go of her self concern and so see herself over against others. With this she could not begin to know or understand them, still less see them as both source of faith and risk, the ambiguous other.

As the narrative continued so Anna focused more on her parents and wider family. Anna had constructed split images of both parents. Her father had been seen as a saviour, someone who would take her away from her mother. She could not cast him in the role of the abuser. At the same time, her mother was someone who she continued to hope would accept her. The more that she continued with the narrative the more these views were challenged. Alongside the 'saviour' was a weak man who was concerned to please but also had no sense of responsibility. Alongside the hope of her mother's change was a sense of her unremitting dislike of her daughter. At this stage the important point was that the narrative began to reveal complexities and ambiguities which had to be worked through. The picture of black or white others was changing. As shall be seen in the next chapters this paves the way for seeing others as they are and where appropriate for beginning to let go and grieve for others or the images of others which have been central to the counsellee.

## Environment

For Anna the physical environment was very important, and yet it was undervalued and underused. This side of spirituality can be very important in providing the ground for trust, enabling the person in need to lock into an identity which might not be possible to articulate in conceptual terms.

Bass and Davis describe the importance of such spirituality in healing:

'A healing spirituality is...a passion for life, a feeling of connection, of being a part of the life around you. Many people experience this in nature, watching the ocean roll in, looking over the vast prairie, walking in the desert. When you are truly intimate with an other...when you are in touch with something bigger than yourself' (Bass and Davis 1998, p.156).

Hilary Cashman also quotes one abuse survivor for whom an awareness of her physical environment, a farm she would sometimes go away to, was critical to her healing:

'When I was little I would lie on the ground and cuddle into the earth and listen to the trees. I got my mothering from the landscape then, and I do now, and that's where I feel closest to God. There I have no doubt about my faith. I feel held, but not healed. Something is holding onto me while I am going through the pain, but it doesn't lessen or shorten it' (Cashman 1993,86).

The environment was a very important part of Anna's spirituality. She frequently took walks in the nearby moors, and had recently begun to explore snorkelling on holiday. When she reflected on both of these areas she spoke of a sense of peace.

Anna, however, had not begun to realise the truth of these experiences for her. They were in a part of her life which seemed not to have relevance to others. Increasingly, through the articulation of her narrative, she became aware of how important these relationships were to her. With that she began to nurture them. This would become very important as change occurred so that she could begin to make connections with the other parts of life.

### God

God for Anna was not so much a help as part of the problem. Her Christian faith was a bleak one. God was seen as severe, without any sense of concern for her. Her moral world dictated that she had to please him. Hence, she could find no sense of relief in him. Above all, there was no sense of faith in a divine other. Indeed, she had no sense of a divine other. God was found in church buildings and in the moral injunctions of the church. This led to a strong sense of the fearfulness of God.

She still harboured hopes of the Christian faith taking her through this crisis. But this was about being a good Christian and earning the pleasure of the church and God. The truth about God would emerge as she learned more about the unconditional acceptance at the heart of the counselling relationship and began to reflect on the nature of God.

Narrative began to open up the past, revealing the truth. As the truth emerged so the old moral world which held in place the distortions of the past began to be challenged. The agapeic support of the counsellor provided the condition for perceiving that truth. Prior to this she had a very fixed view of her relational network one which could be viewed in terms of sin.

## Sin

It may seem problematic to introduce the idea of sin at this point. However, it is shame experienced by the counsellee which binds her into a world of sin. It is precisely the sins of her parents which were visited upon her. Sin in this involves:
- a fragmented world in which the person is alienated from her herself, others and God;
- a distortion of reality;
- a denial or distortion of moral responsibility;
- a denial of hope, with no ground of faith in the other.

Anna was in the ultimate double bind. She really only had her self as the ground of hope. Value depended upon her pleasing the other, something she could never achieve. Hence, she was in an unforgiving cycle. Forgiveness was not actually possible for her. The admission that she had got something wrong would simply confirm her lack of worth. Equally she could not then begin to forgive others, not least because there was no recognition of sameness.

None of this is to condemn the counsellee. Far from it. It is to recognise the reality of her moral world and the consequences that this reality has for her life meaning and relationships (Cavanagh 1992). None of this is to deny the sins of others and often of groups which have caused her to see the world in this way and generate such moral meaning. Nonetheless, this cannot obscure the sense in which Anna was responsible for the continuation of this sin, that she chose to cling to the conditional view of the world and that she chose to continue to view others in a distorted way.

The agapeic support of the counsellor began to help her to see a different picture behind this wall of sin. The next step was to see what this meant and to take responsibility for it, and for change.

# Conclusion

In this first part of the counselling process agape enables what has been invisible to be seen - the past, the self and others. It does more, in that through enabling the articulation of narrative it begins to develop meta-cognition. The counsellee is not just looking at her world, her story, she begins to look at how she sees her world, and think about how she thinks about her world. This enables her to re-examine her world and her experience of it and so to begin to see that this depends upon her sense of value, of her self and others. Reality is a social construct and a value construct.

This places the counsellee in essentially a social situation where ideas and feelings which were unformed or felt in secret have to be given the form of publicly accessible language. As such they are made available for testing and questioning. The same is true of powerful socially constructed symbols which might be part of any narrative. Even as the narration is created and the response to the narration is tested, so the counsellee and counsellor begin to develop rules of dialogue and the development of meaning. These may be summed up in the contract, or may simply arise along the way. During counselling Anna showed concern, for instance, about the response of the counsellor. She worried about judgement of her but also about the fact that the counsellor did not always reflect back what she, Anna, was feeling. She and the counsellor agreed that if either was unsure about what the other meant they should challenge her to clarify. They thus agreed that the meaning of any ideas should be checked and agreed upon by both parties. Such a rule was important for Anna to feel safe, and established speedily the possibility of critique. At the same time it established that the development of meaning was collaborative and that if either person did not fully hear what the other was getting at this did not matter. More important was the mutual commitment to working through meaning. This would take some time to practice, not least the experience of disclosing the self.

Agape in all this was not simply the *condition* of perceiving truth, rather was it the very way of seeing it. In and through that relationship, with both its distance and publicness, and closeness and safety, Anna began to look at meaning and experience new ways of seeing her story. In and through the relationship she struggled with meaning and identity. As Habermas notes " 'Who' I am is tied up with that narrative meaning which lies within my actions and binds them together into a single meaningful plot or personal story" (Habermas1972, 214).

Because of this the dialogue which emerges is neither easy nor civilised.

The dialogue itself involves a learning process - learning how to articulate, test and look at the different affective as well as cognitive factors which affect it. The necessary trust and related skills of dialogue which Benhabib noted were important are developed in and through that dialogue, and are dependant upon developing a relationship with the other.

With the dialogue begun the question now arises as to what moral meaning emerges in the relationship, and how far this is directly informed by agape.

### References
E. Bass and L. Davis, The Courage to Heal (New York: Harper and Row, 1988).

V. Burr, An Introduction to Social Constructionism (London: Routledge, 1995).

H. Cashman, Christianity and Child Sexual Abuse (London: SPCK, 1993).

M. Cavanagh, 'The Concept of Sin in Pastoral Counseling', Pastoral Psychology, Vol 41, No.2, 1992, 81-87.

J. Fletcher, Situation Ethics (Philadelphia: Westminster, 1966).

J. Fowler, Faithful Change (Nashville: Abingdon, 1996)

J. Habermas, Knowledge and Human Interests (London: Heinemann, 1972).

G. Kaufman, Shame: The Power of Caring (Washington: Schenkman, 1980).

L. Kohlberg, Essays on Moral Development, Vol. 2 (San Francisco: Harper Row, 1984).

M. Lyall, The Pastoral Counselling Relationship: A touching place? (Edinburgh: Contact Pastoral Trust, 1997).

G. Lynch and D. Willows, Telling Tales: The narrative dimension of pastoral care and counselling (Edinburgh: Contact Pastoral Trust, 1998).

A. McFadyen, Healing the Damaged in D. Ford and D. Stamps (eds.) Essentials of Christian Community (Edinburgh: T and T Clark, 1996).

J. Older, Touching is Healing (London: Stein and Day, 1982).

P. Parks, Parks Inner Child Therapy (London: Souvenir, 1994).

S. Pattison, A Critique of Pastoral Care (London: SCM, 1988).

# 5

## Say What You Mean or Mean What You Say

" 'Then you should say what you mean' the March Hare went on.
'I do' Alice hastily replied; 'at least - at least I mean what I say - that's the same thing you know'
'Not the same thing a bit!' said the Hatter. 'Why you might as well say that "I see what I eat is the same thing as I eat what I see" ' "
(Lewis Carroll, Alice in Wonderland, chapter seven)

### Case

Laura was a single mature university student who came to a parish priest, who was a pastoral counsellor, with problems related to her academic work and church life. Her academic work was adequate but she was constantly missing deadlines, leading to a cycle of anxiety. She said that she felt unable to get her ideas on to paper because she felt she could never get them right. She was fearful of failing to meet the standards she felt were necessary. Her church life was 'interesting' and 'important' but never really seemed to satisfy her, leaving her lonely and depressed.

Subsequent counselling sessions revealed that Laura's view of life was very much conditioned by her response to her mother. Her mother had been very demanding, something frequently expressed through psychological and physical illness. Laura's role had become the care-taker, attempting to supply all her needs. This often involved staying off school to be with her. Rarely if ever was her mother satisfied with her attempts, often leading to aggressive and dramatic put-downs. On one occasion her mother was taken to hospital whilst Laura had been staying over night with a friend. On hearing this next day Laura went to the hospital, to be met by a hostile mother who slapped her in full view of the ward and said that she was no daughter of hers.

Only later did Laura realise that her mother was in hospital as the result of a suicide attempt, something which further reinforced her sense of guilt and the shame at *not being able to satisfy her mother. The cycle of guilt and shame continued throughout Laura's school days resulting in failure at school. After several years employment she discovered real academic aptitude, and began to do night classes with a view to late entrance into Higher Education. She worked hard at this, gaining the reputation at work of an 'intellectual'. Church had always been in the background, through school and the town where she grew up, and now she began to go more to Sunday worship.*

*Meantime, she continued to work hard to support her mother, with little support from anywhere else. Her father was a passive man who withdrew from family life. Her younger brothers did well in Higher Education and moved quickly out. One got a good job in industry, and the other two married early but found it hard to stay in employment. Hence, Laura was more and more isolated in her care.*

*Avenues then began to open up for moving out of the family. She did A levels in her late twenties, and found a boy friend. There was friction between the boyfriend and mother, but the relationship was sustained. Then Laura's mother suddenly died. She and Laura had a violent argument and under the influence of alcohol her mother had fallen down the stairs in front of her. Laura had to organise the ambulance, her father unable to take responsibility. She stayed with her mother for her final day in hospital, and had to deal with all the hospital care and the funeral. All this further reinforced her sense of responsibility for her mother's death.*

*Soon after, her boyfriend left and Laura felt this as a second bereavement. All her attention was now focused on academia and the church. She worked long hours in different part-time jobs to get the money to go to university.*

*She saw success in academia as the only way to achieve independence and break away from her family. At the same time, she did not feel 'entitled' to success. In later counselling sessions she returned more and more to the sight of her mother dying before her eyes and her responsibility for her death.*

*After several weeks of counselling Laura came to a session very upset. The previous day she had been at the Mothering Sunday church service.*

*'I feel so angry. The preacher kept banging on about the family, how important it was - how it was a school for morals and all that. Mothers in particular were ever so important. We have to cherish them and make a fuss of them. It didn't take long for him to get round to honouring parents. What the hell does he know about living in a family. Not everybody has a family with a sweet mummy. But I felt so bad as well. It was as if he was pointing to me and saying you have failed to honour your mother, and there is no way back. By the time we got to the next hymn, going on about the joys of the family I felt I could not breath, I had to get out of the church.*

*I can still feel it. It is as if I am caught in a vice, with the church telling me what a whore I am and my mother still there, with that accusing look. I have no breath left to fight.'*

By this time Laura had begun to articulate her narrative and it was becoming clear how complex it was. The next stage was to begin to clarify the values and to begin to see how they related, especially where there were conflicts. In this chapter I will briefly examine the idea and practice of value clarification and then how this began to take shape for Laura. Finally, I will examine in more detail two major approaches to value clarification, the affective and cognitive, both of which are common in counselling. What is less common is to draw out the moral dimensions of these approaches and show how moral meaning is developed through them.

## Value Clarification

With the articulation of narrative and the emergence of the counsellee's moral world the values which are important to her can now be clarified.

Raths, Harmin and Simon, in the broader context of moral education, see the term value clarification as consisting of three processes and seven elements (Raths *et al* 1978). The three processes are choosing, prizing and acting. Choosing involves three elements: (a) freedom in the choice of value; (b) choosing from amongst alternative values; (c) consideration of the consequences of holding such a value. Prizing involves: (a) cherishing the choice and being happy with it; (b) being able to articulate this choice and affirm it in public. Acting involves (a) putting the choice into practice and (b) doing this repeatedly.

Several problems emerge from this initial approach. Firstly, it is not clear what counts as a value. Put another way anything can count as a value provided that the person cherishes it and has arrived at it in an orderly and rational way. This returns us to the view of personal values being private and non challengeable. Secondly, at the base of this approach there is the assumption that the person is already a rational individual and, given the right conditions, will make a reasonable choice. Hence, Rogers sees articulation leading to value clarification and from there to self actualisation. Discovering the values of the self is both a liberation from values which have been imposed and a discovery of the autonomous self.

'There is an organismic base for an organised valuing process within the human individual ...This valuing process in the human being is effective in achieving self enhancement to the degree that the individual is open to the experiencing which is going on within himself' (Rogers 1983, 251).

This view must not be dismissed lightly, not least because of his stress on freedom. Nonetheless, it raises the question as to what is going on within the person. Simply to open oneself to one's inner experience runs the danger of arriving at moral and spiritual meaning which is not tested (Mielander 1984,78). Moreover, as already noted, the person who comes for pastoral care is not simply a 'rational agent'. In initial stages she will at least be confused about meaning. Behind this may be a much more profound confusion involving:

a. a series of very different moral narratives or fragments of narratives which she is involved in. There is no simple moral position for her to clarify .
b. moral narratives which drive her at an affective and somatic level as well as cognitive, the power of which she may not be conscious of.
c. inability to distinguish the way in which her affective, cognitive and somatic life affect the different narratives and thus to establish any criteria for deciding between the different narratives.

The person then may need to learn several things:
- how to articulate moral meaning, both feelings and thoughts;
- how to take responsibility for moral ideas;
- how to distinguish between and judge different values, and the allied moral ideas.

Clarification demands the development of these skills and involves not so much settling for any values that the person happens to hold, but rather learning how to be responsible for values tested in community, and in relation to the demands of her network of relationships.

Such clarification is essentially dialogic. In counselling the central dialogue is between the counsellor and counsellee, and this begins, as we shall see, to exemplify supportive, open and challenging dialogue, enabling communication and hermeneutic. The very process of counselling, as we noted in the last chapter, is one which is social, opening up language which is publicly accessible and thus open to discussion and the discovery of meaning. However, the language opens up not simply one narrative but a whole collection of 'oral texts' developed through family, school, work and so on, and so to a whole series of dialogues. These texts are embodied in the life of the person through habits, behaviour patterns, rules, rituals, explicit values and principles, and explicit qualities and virtues. The different texts might relate in a variety of ways:

- mutual reinforcement of the whole of one text from another;
- partial reinforcement of one text for another or part of an other;
- conflict between the meanings of each text;
- the holding of several very different texts which are not congruent. In this case the question is raised as to how such different views can be held. Typically at this stage the counsellee will be 'discovering' texts she never realised she had or did not realise were so important. Laura, for instance, spoke of being surprised by the intensity of feeling underlying one text to do with her brothers. She had not realised how important it was until it began to engage in dialogue with other texts.

Van der Ven notes that through narrative articulation and dialogue, 'all kinds of connections are made between these oral texts as well as between oral and written texts' (van der Ven 1998, 259 ff.). This 'intertextuality' is developed as part of any reflective process and through this something of the person's own identity begins to emerge.

Three levels of clarification then begin to operate, not in any order:
- clarifying the different texts in the persons life;
- clarifying the meaning of each text;
- clarifying how these texts relate to each other. Note here that any text may be ambiguous and that this needs to be worked through. It is often ambiguity or conflict which is the starting point for clarification. For Anna this had brought the moral narrative which viewed her as responsible for the abuse sharply up against the narrative of herself as the victim, one who needs both care and justice. For Laura, as we shall see, there were several conflicts.

The educationalist Van der Plas suggests that clarification as a process of communication has to go through four phases:
- explicit formulation of the value and feelings.
- explicit formulation of the value and feelings of others.
- relating of ones own values and feelings to those of others.
- validating values and feelings (see van der Ven 1998, 266).

In this process several things are going on:
- the clarification of how values relate to feelings - examining congruence;

- development of empathy with the other, which may mean the need for testing perceptions about others, and how far they project the persons own world view on to the other;
- the comparison of the different views, enabling testing, clarification and development of both.

It is important to note that the affective dimension remains throughout this and that just as the validation of values depends upon working through feelings, so the validation of feelings involves working through values. Counselling literature has tended to stress simply the affective side. Yet, as we shall see in the reflection on Laura's anger, validation of a feeling inevitably involves validation of an ethical perspective, and this inevitably involves moral challenge and hopefully moral learning.

Van der Ven suggests four criteria for the learning process of moral education in general, each of which apply to the moral dimension of dialogue in the counselling situation:

- the 'reader' of the different texts must try to bracket her own prejudice. This requires an awareness of the affective dimension of values held, but also reasons for holding values. This can only be seen in *actu*, through the example of the counsellor or the example of someone who the counsellee is reflecting about. The clearest example of this in practice is the response of the counsellor to the confrontation of the counsellee. For instance, when the counsellee has gained some confidence she can begin to confront the counsellor on responses of the counsellor which cause her discomfort or pain. A response of the counsellor which demonstrates that she has heard the pain, that the challenge of the counsellee will not cause her to return anger, and that she did not intend to make a judgmental comment, will embody the possibility of not responding from her own prejudices or becoming locked into a dynamic of blame and counter blame. Agape remains at the heart of this dynamic, enabling a dialogue which establishes the possibility of seeing relationships differently.
- The text should be seen not from the person's perspective but from that of the text and the text community. This is critically the perspective of empathy, trying to see what the different texts are actually getting at and how they express something of the nature of the other. Requiring a leap of imagination, the development of this empathy is an important learning point. It enables a better appreciation of the moral situation and the different people involved. It also enables a

genuine dialogue to be set up between the different values, testing the person's own and the reasons she has for holding them. The person can also begin to see how she is the same as others - in terms of both challenges faced and values held.

- The truth of any value can only be discovered and understood in relation to the situation. The value is only learned in a situation where it is embodied. Hence as Gademar notes 'truth and application correlate with each other' (Gademar 1960, 290-323), and 'there is no understanding without application' (Riceour 1973). Once again this is critically so with the counselling situation. The reflection on value has to emerge from the narrative and the underlying experience.

- van der Ven's fourth criterion is to do with what he terms the 'hermeneutics of the good'. This involves a dialectical process between the free individual and whatever authority she recognises in moral terms. This demands that the person be free to critique and 'wrestle with' that authority. Fleischacker notes here two aspects of a process which involve transcendence. At one level, this involves moving beyond the 'father figure' or group who embodies the moral authority. This is a liberation from the constraining elements of that relationship, and a discovery of ones own moral meaning. At another level, this wrestling is about accepting the limitation of the other and finding the good which transcends them, which cannot be fully embodied by them. As Fleischacker puts it,

'You need to go beyond your biological, literary and ethical fathers not just because they are psychological hindrances to your development but because their function is to teach you a truth which goes beyond anything they can embody' (Fleischacker 1994, 108). How that truth is discovered will vary with each relationship. What is critical is the wrestling with the authority, something that will inevitably highlight the limitations of any embodiment of moral meaning, be that in the family or the institution such as the church. The very awareness of such limitations leads to the development of moral meaning and taking responsibility for such meaning. It may mean a total breaking away from the 'fathers' or an acceptance of ambiguity, accepting some values and not others in such organisations. This wrestling is also a life long process. In counselling terms this means that the aim of moral reflection should not be 'sort out' moral meaning completely but rather to enable the person to have the tools to continue this hermeneutical process.

Clarification then emerges then not through simplistic reflection but through dialogue with the different texts, with all the conflict and tension that this involves. There is no need to clarify and work hard at clarifying if there is no tension or complexity. Once more, this is a clarification which involves the person taking responsibility for the process (Halmos 1964).

There are major parallels in this clarification with Jurgen Haberemas and his conditions for Discourse Ethics, not least the freedom to challenge tradition norms and open up moral meaning to rational discourse (see Reader, 1997, 104). Such rational discourse, however, does not emerge from rational reflection *per se*. It needs an environment of trust and love to enable learning. This is even more important in counselling where the kind of challenge and openness which Habermas points to are often associated by the counsellee with rejection and shame. The possibility of critique which began to emerge as the narrative was articulated is now something experienced directly, as the very way in which the counsellee sees her self and others, and related values, is the focus of dialogue which handles difference and conflict, sameness and security.

For the counsellee this process of clarification leads to the development of moral identity which does not simply discard the values of the different narratives but both challenges them and takes them seriously as narratives which may contribute towards the values she can commit herself to. We can begin to see some of these issues in Laura's narrative and the different texts or fragments of texts which they reveal.

## Laura's Narrative

Laura had little capacity to engage with the self. Her moral identity was really a whole series of values and needs which were driving her on, and she could not begin to see herself apart from those values. Hence, she had no way of actually examining those values 'objectively'. The important thing then was to enable her to look at the self which she had created in response to her spiritual and social environment and thus begin to see if she could discover a self that she could own and like.

In a real sense then she could not begin to look at herself until she had looked at her self as someone interacting with others and with a set of moral ideas that gave those interactions meaning.

## 1. Family

The core narrative which gave meaning to Laura's life were that of her family. At the centre of the family her mother aimed to keep control of Laura. From the earliest age Laura remembered that her mother communicated through put-downs. 'I was to blame for all her ills. She kept reminding me that if I hadn't been born she could have made a life for herself, even gone to university'. Three major moral injunctions came from this relationship: the importance of service, caring for her mother, and not thinking of herself; an injunction against expressing feelings (leading to affect shame); an injunction against any expression of sexuality (thus developing need shame). She would often place Laura into a double bind both referring to her as 'a whore' when she was going out with her boyfriend but also criticising her dowdy appearance.

Laura's father was the centre of a moral vacuum. He did not so much collude with his wife as opt out of all responsibility for her behaviour. He cared for his daughter but was not able to express this, thus reinforcing any affect shame. He also let go of any general responsibility for the family as a whole. As a result that responsibility was taken on by Laura. On the frequent occasion when her mother was ill she took over house work and cooking and even finance matters. Gradually, this led her to take over such functions all the time. Her brothers grew to depend on her.

From this experience a view of care developed which had a passive sense of peace at the centre. Her brothers would quite often quarrel openly with her mother, leading to a conflict of two moral imperatives, of pleasing her mother, and of caring for her brothers, both of whom she was responsible for. From this emerged the crucial moral imperative to seek peace at all costs, with an intense fear of expressed anger. The conflicts were never actually faced or resolved and she was often seen as the one in the middle and blamed by both sides. The blame was acceptable providing the conflict stopped. As we shall see this was part of the moral perspective which affected her view of anger. It also radically affected her view of fairness and justice.

Laura still prided herself on this whole area of caring, and even at the time of counselling, felt responsible for her brothers. At the same time she felt that they were unaware and that the two who had children, and their wives, were bad parents. In turn, she felt that she was responsible for their children, identifying them as victims, and had to protect them in some way.

## 2. Boyfriend

Laura's boy friend, Alan, was like an oasis in her life. The relationship with him was one in which he made her feel special. He showed her something of unconditional care, doing things for her without expecting return. At first she found this relationship very difficult, and would not react to his attentions. She was surprised by his persistence and looked forward to their times together. She did her best to insulate those relationships from her mother. Nonetheless, her mother saw her boyfriend as competing with her for attention and made Laura feel ashamed of her sexual needs and identity, setting up a conflict between a narrative of attraction and pleasure and one of shame. When she was with him she had tried to work on her behaviour and appearance, including extensive work on neglected teeth. This level of conflict often made her feel angry, an anger she could not begin to express.

*3. Education*

The moral text of Laura's school and subsequent education had several sub texts:

- Nurture. A teacher accepted her and tried to nurture her, for the first two years in secondary school. She communicated a sense of worth, but this positive narrative was isolated from the rest of Laura's world. It was never seen as 'really counting'. She consistently was unable to connect any positive aspects with the rest of her life.
- Learning shame. This was a radical fear of making a fool of the self in class, reinforced by teachers who shamed her. Still strong in Laura's mind, and again a real surprise to her, was the shame of one occasion when a teacher who she respected asked the class what they thought of the book they were reading. Laura raised her hand, and said that she found it hard to read and that she did not like the heroine. The teacher's sharp response was that if that was what she thought she could stand outside the class room for the rest of the lesson.
- Alongside this, she was brought up in a city with a strong university tradition, with students dominating the inner city. After school she began to see the academic life as a way of getting out of her family life and of achieving acceptance. At least this had a quantifiable end which could display her value, and she wanted to be in the same world as the students. Eventually, this led to university. This put up a view of conditional acceptance she thought was worth aspiring to. However, because it was essentially negative, aiming for worth through avoiding the shame of ignorance, it led to a moral view of others which judged and condemned those who failed or did not try. Because it was conditional it led to a view of others which was conditional. All this led to

great difficulty with the university course. The learning shame conflicted directly with the instrumental use of academia and led her to find it very hard to get things out on time. This led to a great gap between her hope and the reality of poor marks because of her lateness. Fear of failure led her to believe that she could not achieve. Hence, when a tutor congratulated her on one essay which got 2:1 marks, even after penalties for lateness, her immediate thought was that he had been reading the wrong essay. Here then were several moral texts in conflict - pride in achievement, injunction against taking pride, injunction against revealing ignorance. All this led to her to go for difficult subjects to read, to prove her worth, and to freeze at moments before assessment and for fear of rejection.

## 4. Work

For Laura work narrative was difficult. She could always get jobs in offices as clerk, but this was associated with shame, as not achieving. Work, therefore, led her to look hard at vocation. Academia could provide some way out but it could not go on for ever. Real problems with finding jobs subsequently emerged. She aimed too high, to get out of her previous life, but became involved in intense competition and did not succeed.

## 5. The Church

The church was a profoundly important place for Laura:
- It was a place where she could be anonymous. Sitting at the back of a service she did not have to be challenged. At times she felt like a child, being held by the church. She could belong but did not feel she had to contribute.
- It was a place where the narrative of the academia was continued. By definition it had to be intellectually proper. Free thinking in this context was acceptable not least because it was actively encouraged. It brought acceptance, and made her feel superior to non-intellectual church groups.
- The church was a place of escape, from conflict to peace, from working class to middle class and so on. The result of this, and the strong emphasis on intellectual theology, was a second-hand faith, one which did not involve reflection on self or needs, and which did not engage her affective life.
- There were also conflicting sub texts within the church. Many of the sermons she heard reinforced her shame about family life, and about

sexuality, thus fuelling anger. This made her increasingly uncomfortable with the church and forced her to examine the ambiguity of a community which she felt was 'good' for her and moral authority which made her increasingly feel worse, between a narrative of acceptance at the somatic and affective level and a narrative of judgement at the cognitive level, which reinforced her feelings of shame.

### 6. The environment

Laura had little awareness of the physicality of the 'other'. The physical was a threat to her. Hence, at different times she would cut herself off from her environment, avoided eating, distance herself from her boy friend. She associated physical awareness and enjoyment with self gratification, something which should be avoided. Along with this was a very poor body image.

She had two points where she began to feel some spiritual effect of the environment. Firstly, Alan would take her out on his bike, an experience which was fun and made her open up to her environment. Secondly, the simple physicality of the church building made her feel secure and cared for. It felt good to hear the choir and smell the incense and see the stain glass. It could not be called ecstatic experience but it did feel good to be a part of this physical experience.

### 7. God

It was hard to say that Laura viewed God at all. At one level he was an object of conversation who was part of the strong intellectual environment which she wanted to be a part of. At another level there was no actual connection between her view of God and the environment in which she was. He certainly was not in her work place. He was not even consciously in the aesthetic church experience.

If she felt him anywhere it was in the church's reinforcement of the moral injunctions. She saw him as judge and someone who she had to please. But he was hard to please. She referred to him at one point as the God of the perfect ones, who did not forgive.

Laura had to begin to wrestle with several 'fathers' in these narratives and did not want to be simply shorn of the moral meaning which came from any of them. Sometimes, this meant her building bridges between the different relational narratives to see where similar values were held. This making of connections was critical. As the sessions developed she began to make connections between the acceptance she received from church services and God;

between Alan's concern for her and God's concern; between the narrative of her nurturing teacher and her academic work, and so on. The positive aspects of these 'texts' along with the environment of the counselling sessions began to show her the possibility of her value.

More often the texts gave rise to a number of conflicting dialogues and the counsellor invited Laura to focus on the areas which were important to her. Two major kinds of dialogue began to emerge, which would themselves enable Laura to see connections between different areas in her life:

    a. Dialogue of affect. Laura had the emotions of shame and anger in equal intensity, expressed in dialogue within the family and between her, the family and the church.

    b. Dialogue of cognition. This examined the ideas held in different narratives and began to see what held them and what might be put in their place.

These two will now be examined, looking at how they can be creatively handled as part of the development of moral meaning and identity.


## Letting off Steam?

A popular view of the emotions in pastoral care is that they should be 'ventilated'. By letting off steam this does one good, releasing the tension and so leading to a return to normal. Doubtless for those who find it difficult to express feelings ventilation will be important for such a reason. However, there is the danger of seeing this as a mechanistic activity which will somehow effect cure of itself. It has something of the medical model of health about it, and as such can lead to counsellors actively seeking to make the counsellee ventilate feelings 'for her own good'.

Equally, this approach tends to be value neutral. It does not see feelings in the context of moral meaning, or see the possibility that working with feelings might begin to explore moral meaning. In fact, the dialogue with feelings is critical to reflection on moral meaning and the development of moral dialogue in pastoral counselling.

With Laura one of the most important emotions to appear was anger. It was often beneath the surface of the counselling relationship, expressed in sarcasm and attempts to put down the counsellor, thinly veiled in humour. She reported increasing annoyance with her brothers and with co-workers, snapping at them if they had not got things right, but did not recognise this as anger. Perhaps most often she reported anger focused upon herself, usually for not achieving what she hoped for. Most of the time it would remain firmly under control. Attempts to address this anger were difficult for several reasons:

1. Laura did not want to be seen as angry. The thought made her feel ashamed, unacceptable. Above all, she did not want a priest to see what she felt was her bad nature.

2. Secondly, she had built up a strong moral carapace based on the argument that anger was by definition wrong. It always led to conflict and conflict was by definition bad. This meant, of course, that for the most part Laura tried to avoid conflict or to directly initiate it, never to attempt to creatively engage it. A great deal of this came from her childhood experience of conflict between her mother and brothers, noted above. This was elevated into moral injunction with the belief that anger is always wrong, causing others pain, therefore it must always be avoided in herself and others. Behind this was strong affect shame.

3. The repression of feelings meant that Laura simply did not know how to express them. She did not have any practice at saying what she felt and thus in a real sense did not actually know what she felt.

4. Feelings in any case do not appear as discrete entities which can easily be identified. As C. Tavris writes,
'our emotions are not especially distinctive. They tend to come in bunches like grapes, and it is very rare to find a single emotion causing trouble on its own' (Tavris 1982, 96).

In the light of all this it is hardly surprising that in the early stages of the counselling relationship Laura would resist attempts to focus on her feelings. This would most often take the form of trying to bring the dialogue round to some aspect of the church and attempt to draw the priest into this, including some intellectual problem of theology, an overdue assignment, or some aspect of church activities. The counsellor had to check out this and ensure that he was not being drawn away to the 'false security' of the church conversation.

The process of clarification for Laura was broadly the same as the one outlined by Alastair Campbell in dealing with anger (Campbell 1986, 68 ff.). As this is worked through the moral dynamic begins to emerge. The process involves:

- Acknowledgement.
- Ventilation.
- Identification.

- Understanding.
- Validation - part of the dialogue with self and others.
- Communication - moral dialogue with the others.
- Action.

This does not involve the slavish following of stages. Many of these factors may occur together and even after actions the person may return to other parts of the process. As noted in chapter two the dynamic of dialogue is such that the person is always looking at the other and then back at the self and so on, and may move backwards and forwards between these different parts of the process. Through this the moral perspective of the counsellee begins to emerge, and moral stance worked through.

## Acknowledgement

The issue of feelings was explicitly and most successfully raised when Laura came to a counselling session showing barely suppressed anger. She had been to church on the anniversary of her break up with her boyfriend. The priest had been preaching about the importance of loving the enemy and the problem with anger. 'Who was your enemy?' he had said. The feelings she experienced were so powerful that she left early and was physically sick.

The counsellor asked her what she had been feeling. She was able to report the physical and emotional effects but could not begin to say what the feelings actually were. As she reported this she was smiling. She looked pale and drawn and her foot kept tapping on the floor. The counsellor reflected back what he saw, not least her body language, and the contrast with her speech.

At first, Laura was unaware of this incongruence. As she began to reflect on it she said, 'Yes you're right. It feels so unreal. I actually feel as if I am seething under here, but at the same time I feel I have to smile for you'.

Here was a crucial acknowledgement that she had feelings and that these were intense, even though she could not even describe them. She could also acknowledge her own ambivalence, and the underlying conflict between the feelings and the moral imperative not to show these feelings, indeed to reveal opposite feelings.

## Ventilation

The counsellor invited her to return to the moment when she had felt the intense feelings and simply to talk about what was going on in her head at the time and explain the images or the 'voices' she could hear.

Three pictures emerged each with their own text or text fragment, each of which had a strand of moral meaning attached to them:

a. On the anniversary of their split she pictured Alan. This memory alone made her feel sadness and loss, but also anger - something she had not previously acknowledged about her boyfriend. He had deserted her just at the moment she thought she might have begun to get things together. She had never really acknowledged this anger about him.

b. She also had the picture of the church before her, no longer as a place where she could feel secure but rather as somewhere which reinforced her sense of guilt. She felt angry, betrayed, ashamed. She also felt powerless, unable to actually respond to the priest and tell him how she felt. The shame was paralysing her.

c. Behind these images was the image of her mother, insisting that she was no good, making her feel ashamed of all her efforts.

As she focused on the relationships so she began to let go and broke down sobbing and thumping the cushion in the chair next to her. At one level this allowed her to release the pressure which was causing real stress.

## Identification

At another level, she could now begin to identify the feelings, a cluster involving: pain; anger at several people, church, boyfriend mother; shame at feeling and expressing feelings she should not share; anger at the counsellor for 'making her' share these feelings; despair and hopelessness at seeing no way out of her hell - one way lies experience of pain, the other the pain of intense shame; regret at not taking opportunities. She oscillated at this point between great intensity of feelings and a feeling of exhaustion. In these moments she felt beaten down and there was no point in getting angry. It would not change anything. The counsellor stayed with her through these feelings enabling her to focus more on the context of the feelings.

## Understanding

The various feelings could only begin to be identified and understood in context, in the light of the relationships which gave rise to them. This involved revisiting those experiences. Through telling the story of those relationships so she began to form a distance and to analyse the dynamic which gave rise to them. Taking the 'texts' side by side, she was also able to compare the demands of the different people, and with this begin to examine the different moral worlds which generated them. The shame was very much generated by her mother and held in place by the church at one level. Over against this was the anger which directly fed into the pain and the sense of loss. Her loss of Alan was intense and she blamed herself for this. It was as if the final attempt to face up to her mother had failed, was doomed to fail. The more she worked through these relationships the more she saw herself as a victim rather then a failure, beginning to question why her mother treated her in this way. The more affective distance she gained from which to view that relationship the more she began to form empathy for her mother. This did not mean that she felt love for her, but rather that she began to see her as an other, an ordinary human being with problems which led her to treat her daughter in this way.

All this enabled her to see more clearly the basis of her moral meaning, where the moral injunctions she held onto were coming from.

## Validation

Validation is not a simple or discrete stage but rather has two levels to it. By letting go and allowing the counsellor to see her in 'a state' Laura made the first step in acknowledging that it was acceptable to show feelings. The sharing of feelings and the anger which was at the heart of it was validated affectively. It is precisely such validation which enabled her to begin to distinguish between competing feelings. When she reflected later on her progress she marked out the moment as being when she first experienced the juxtaposition of anger and love. It was not sufficient to understand the idea of unconditional love, she had to experience the faithfulness of the counsellor at the very point when she revealed to herself and the other the anger which she had kept secret for so long. This was not a one off event, after which all would be well. She had to get used to being treated in this way by being with another who would not put her down and who did not have another agenda to pursue. She had to get used to trusting an other, what it really meant to trust, and this would involve continued testing.

The second part of validation was then to test out the grounds for such feelings. This was Laura's responsibility and demanded that she look carefully at the anger and the shame and the underlying moral meaning. It was at this point that she began to compare the different moral narratives more closely. The possibility emerged of anger as being reframed in terms of fairness. She had reasons to be angry and she began to tentatively work these through. Against this the ground of shame was becoming less and less easy to justify. She nonetheless clung on to that moral world for some time, not least because of the fear that there was nothing to put in its place and because her 'child' feared that this would lead to final rejection from her mother and ultimately the loss of the self. At these points she did speak of ending life. The continued faithfulness of the counsellor gave her permission to feel and express feelings, so that even the feelings of desolation were seen as acceptable. The strength of Laura's moral world was such that even as she shared suicidal feelings she felt this as an ultimate failure. Again the presence of the counsellor at those points was critical in her facing fully up to this conditional moral world. This also enabled her to still work through the beliefs at the base of these feelings. This stress on cognitive testing is examined more closely below.

Slowly Laura began to articulate a moral agenda of fairness which initially validated her anger:
- It was not fair that she always had to please everyone;
- It was not fair that she should never please herself;
- It was not fair that she should be made to feel shame.

At this stage the development of moral meaning was negative, focusing on the bad effects of the shame injunctions on her life.

## Communication

From the initial attempt to sort out feelings Laura had been able to identify them and begin to recast the moral ground. She was, however, locked into all the texts noted above and many of them continued to discourage her from developing this position. At one point she said, 'Yes, I see the difference and I get excited about it, but it doesn't feel real. I keep expecting to wake up and be back in my prison'.

The continued communication of the feelings then became critically important for three reasons. Firstly, it was important to sustain the underlying feelings of anger. This feeling was a source of energy that would enable Laura to return the shame to its origin. The feeling of exhaustion was very much about the reassertion of the hopelessness associated with the old moral world and needed to be pushed away. Secondly, communication would give the confidence of practice. For Laura, there was the continual fear that anger would give place to loss of control and aggression. She literally needed to practice anger that could both be genuine but also controlled. The counselling process itself gave practice to anger when on one occasion she felt the confidence to confront the counsellor about her being late. Here the juxtaposition of anger and love became very real because it directly affected her relationship with the counsellor. Hence she worked hard at making clear her feelings but avoiding verbally abusing the counsellor. She discovered in the context of a relationship the possibility of righteous anger which did not aim to control or destroy the relationship. This had for her a strong sense of empowerment. Other forms of ritualised anger articulation could be used including physical expression in a safe environment, such as thumping cushions.

Thirdly, the communication of anger needed to be dialogic, with Laura communicating directly with the different relationships and their texts. The sense of unreality would always be sustained if there were texts which sustained the original shame. At one level this involved 'dialogue' with her mother, communicating her feelings as child and adult which she had not been able to offer to her directly. This involved imaginative techniques such as writing a letter to her mother, speaking to the empty chair and so on. All this was a powerful way of wrestling with the authority which her mother represented.

A second key area of dialogue was with the church, the very body which apparently disapproved of the anger. At first, the anger was aimed at the counsellor as a representative of the church. The fact that the counsellor was able to accept the anger and did not reject her showed Laura that there was not a simple response from the church and above all that she could be accepted even if she might disagree with the views of members of the church. This is a critical affective level of moral meaning. It enabled her to begin to find and explore very diverse views about anger and to develop a critique of the different views of anger in the church. This communication increasingly brought her into finding ways of justifying her changing view of moral meaning.

Laura and the counsellor then carefully looked through the various injunctions against anger in the Bible. At first, this was a rather arid exercise in looking at the different texts, with 'the anger of man does not work the righteousness of God' (James 1.20, and 29), ranged against texts such as, 'Be angry but do not sin' (Ephesians 4.26). The clash of texts led Laura to look more closely at what anger was and how it might be viewed in a creative way. All this was preparing the way for the developing of moral meaning which will be examined in the next chapter. It was all part of a wrestling with the church authority which allowed her to see its complexity and that it could never embody perfection, but could begin to point to moral meaning beyond itself.

Behind this was also her relationship with God. Firstly, Laura began to talk about and face up to the God who also shamed her. She saw him first as the angry judging God. There were occasions when she had burst out with anger at this God, expressed in profane language. This made her feel even more intensely ashamed, believing that she in some way offended against the Holy Spirit (Matt. 12: 32), hence, losing hope. The counsellor was able to test this perception and see what the basis of it was. Once more, this view began to erode, once Laura was able to see any idea of anger in God as set within his faithful covenant. Anger is not about failure to reach standards but about love for the other and concern for their well being. None of this took away the importance of accountability for action, but did stand against accountability to standards of perfection. The more these feelings were worked through, the more it became clear to Laura that she was projecting on to God her patterns of thinking. This enabled her to begin to develop an empathic attitude towards God, one which genuinely explored his nature and tested out the moral meaning associated with him.

## Action

In addition to the communication noted above there is the stage of action, which begins to embody the fruits of the dialogue. This takes the person into the practice of shalom and the ways in which justice can be found in the context of love. This is not simply an adjunct but rather a critical part of the development of meaning, and this stage will be examined more closely in the next chapter.

It is important at this stage to underline that the dialogue of affect is not always straightforward. For Laura there was a long period in which the concern for her own pain and anger was taken over by her awareness of the pain of others. She had been conditioned to look out for and respond to the pain of others and ignore her own. Hence, when she began to express her pain to the other she began to look for the discomfort and pain she was causing to them, moving back to her old moral world, feeling their pain rather than hers. This emerged also in the counselling process. Laura suggested that the counsellor must be feeling disappointed and hurt that she had not made more progress. At one level this was a further test of the counsellor's agape, and only once she was reassured of this was she able to move back to working with her own feelings.

## *Thinking it through*

The affective focus, beginning with feelings and moving through to moral ideas, is not then about simply giving the counsellee space to think what they want to think. It is rather about enabling the person to develop an awareness of the self and others and thus develop affective maturity. This in turn enables her to develop moral confidence which is open and part of a continual learning process. As we shall in this next chapter, a critical part of the development of moral confidence is the development of trust in the counsellor and of the moral meaning which is embodied in the relationship.

There is a complementary way of approaching the clarification of values which focuses on the development of cognition - how the counsellee thinks and how she can test that thinking and develop it. The techniques of Cognitive Behavioural Therapy can be used as an alternative to the affective dialogue or alongside it. This approach is very powerful in the way that it enables both the development of meta-cognition and the explicit development of the capacity to critique the perceptions of the self and others in such a way that the self is built up rather than threatened.

Cognitive therapy involves:

1. Focus on how we think. It seeks to enable the person to examine ways of thinking and to develop those ways.
2. Socratic methods. It is based not upon the stereotypic view of the non-directive approach nor on a prescriptive approach but upon the genuine development of dialogue in order to enable the counsellee to discover meaning in her situation. In all this the beliefs which underlie behaviour are examined and viewed as hypotheses, open to testing and developing. Such testing enables the counsellee to see how different thoughts and feeling relate and how they affect practice.

   As P. Gilbert puts it,

   'This involves enabling a person to explore and recognise that the way that they reason about themselves and others is dysfunctional to the extent that they suffer greatly and do not move forward to their goals and aspiration' (Gilbert 1992, 53).

   The whole approach therefore aims to enable dialogue, and the development of rigorous thinking.
3. Focus on learning and discipline. Cognitive methods do not rely on the Freudian idea of catharsis, with the idea that discovery of insight of itself leads to liberation. They recognise that forms of thinking are often deeply embedded and will not simply go away. Hence, there is need to replace those forms with ways of thinking that need to be practised and sustained. This demands the development of personal discipline. Even more importantly it demands the essentially community discipline of dialogue.

Michael Cavanagh suggests seven cognitive stages which are gone through to the development of mature thinking (Cavanagh 1996). These refer not so much to invariant stages of growth as distortions in thinking processes and their opposite. In all cases the immature thinking is usual in childhood and adolescence but can often be fixated in the adult life:

### Egocentric to empathic thinking

The child's and adolescent's 'cognitive universe' often revolves around her. Egocentric cognition in adulthood is not uncommon, leading to drawing conclusions without any supportive data, and selective abstraction - focusing on details out of context. Egocentric thinking often assumes that others must think the same way as the person, or assumes some form of telepathy. People should know how I feel without me having to tell them.

Empathic thinking has a breadth of cognition which enables the person to think beyond the self and be aware of the concerns of others.

### Idealistic and realistic thinking

Children and adolescents often look to the ideal: the ideal parent, grandparent or teacher. The discovery of imperfection in others frequently leads to anger and cynicism. Fixation on idealist thinking means that parents, spouse, children and others are never good enough. As Cavanagh puts it each of these 'take turns being daily sources of frustration' (Cavanagh 1996, 228). Idealists respond negatively, causing the others to respond in a more negative - even less perfect way. An element of this thinking was apparent in Laura as she looked to her brothers and their wives to provide 'perfect' parenting for their children. The more she judged them, the more they lost confidence in parenting skills.

Realistic thinking demands negotiation with reality.

### Superficial thinking to psychological mindedness

Superficial thinking involves overgeneralisation, drawing conclusions on the basis of single events or initial impressions. Whilst initial impressions are important, psychological 'mindedness' involves going beyond the first initial clues of the other, and thus is closely related to empathic thinking.

### Disproportionate to Proportionate thinking

In earlier years appraisals of reality can be disproportionate - minimising or maximising events. In adulthood this can cause a major mismatch in thinking. In a crisis of a child at school, for instance, a father may minimise his son hitting another pupil as something which is natural. The mother may maximise it, seeing him as a potential psychopath. Proportionate thinking looks to balance perception, and is open to the situation, and thus better able to handle any crises.

### Projective to Objective thinking

Projective thinking projects the thinking patterns of the person on to others. Hence, the person believes, 'If I did what she is doing I would be doing it for X reason; therefore she must be doing it for X reason also'. An example of this in an adult relationship is the husband who becomes angry at his wife going out with friends. He believes that she is doing this to make him jealous and thus more attentive. These are in fact his own dynamics, a feeling of rejection from his wife and thoughts of 'teaching her a lesson', and he projects them on to her. Anna had a very similar dynamic in her relationship with her husband. She saw him as working too hard in order to avoid real intimacy with her, reflecting in fact her own thinking and pattern of behaviour towards him. The result was the build up of animosity towards her husband and a self-fulfilling prophecy. Laura also projected her thinking onto her nephew and nieces, seeing them as fearful of their parents, and trying to please them without success.

### Delusional to Reality-Centred Thinking

Delusional thinking in this context is not psychotic but rather thinking which is usual in childhood and problematic in adulthood. This may be exemplified in a marital relationship. A husband may have paranoid thinking, which tends to put on to others responsibility for problems. He is not succeeding in the work-place because of his boss who does not like him. His children do not respect him, mostly because his wife undermines him in front of them. His wife does not understand him and puts pressure on him to be what he is not. His wife may have delusions of grandeur in the sense that she sees her family as exemplifying all things good. Such grandiose thinking obscures her husband's depression and the problems experienced by other members of the family. Reality centred thinking focuses on the difficulty of experience and seeks to take responsibility for these situations.

### False certitude to toleration of ambiguity

Children and adolescents look for global 'certitude', seeing things as black or white. Such dichotomous thinking is unable to see the ambiguity in the other or the self. Hence, Anna saw others as either for or against her.

These different cognitions have several things in common:

a. They impose meaning upon experience. In many cases this involves a fear of that experience, with the cognition and associated belief system seeking to control it rather than to be open and responsive. At its most extreme form this blocks spiritual awareness.

b. They involve automatic thinking. Often the person will experience simply an affect, unaware that there is an underlying automatic thought process going on which leads to that affect.

   This is characterised as : i) the activating event; ii) underlying beliefs or appraisals; iii) consequences in terms of emotions or behaviour. We tend to assume that the activating event causes the consequences, whereas in fact it is the belief which leads to the consequences. A good example of this is minor 'road rage'. A man is hooted from behind by a car trying to pass him on a narrow lane. The consequence is that the driver applies his brakes at critical points to make the driver behind go more slowly. The critical link is the underlying belief, which might range from, 'Cars which overtake me have beaten me. If I am beaten I am of no worth', to 'That driver is rude and it is wrong to give in to rudeness'. Different beliefs will lead to different consequences.

   It is these automatic thoughts and the inference chains that they present which are an important focus of the cognitive work. Along with these are the 'self-other schemata' views of others and how they see oneself, and the basic rules and attitudes which once more are often engrained in the person's thinking. An example of the latter strongly felt by Laura was 'If I do not do well all the time others will not respect me'.

c. Cognition and the development of cognition is intricately related to moral and spiritual development. Each of the distortions noted above in some way interferes with or blocks the basic spirituality such as awareness of others and moral values such as love and justice. As Cavanagh puts it, 'People cannot be more moral or spiritual than their cognitions will allow them to be. Therefore ministers have a vested interest in helping people develop cognitively because developing cognitively also means developing moral and spiritually' (Cavanagh 1996, 235).

   It may be contested that simply to work through criteria for thinking does not lead to a firm moral foundation. However, cognitive therapy is built on basic moral values. Dryden and Ellis, for instance, analyse at some length the principles of unconditional self acceptance (USA), which include:

- Human beings cannot be given a single 'global rating'. This reflects the complexity and uniqueness of any human being, and the impossibility of summing each up under one concept or rating. Low self esteem is often the consequence of such a rating;
- Human beings are essentially fallible. This is something very close to an account of sin.
- All human beings are 'equal in humanity but unequal in their different aspects'.
- USA promotes constructive action not resignation.
- USA is a habit that can be acquired (Ellis and Dryden 1999, 203).

Such values are not worked out systematically and tend to be developed negatively, in response to the distortions noted above. Nonetheless, it is clear that these are fundamental values and not libertarian or liberal, and it is central to successful therapy that they be internalised and developed. It is important to note that addressing such cognitions is not a matter of seeing them as errors to be frowned upon and got out of. Rather, through collaborative activity is the capacity to examine and critique one's own way of thinking developed. It is precisely this which aims to enable the person to take responsibility for her cognitions, and ultimately leads to the most rigorous testing and developing of ethical thinking and practice.

The cognitive approach involves *detection, debate* and *discrimination*. The inference chains, attitudes and schemata should be examined, with each thought taken separately, often ending in an underlying injunction or belief. Each can then be debated, and then the underlying values and how they relate can be examined.

We can begin to see how this all came together in Laura.

## Detection

At one session she came looking agitated. She had begun to work through her anger, but something had clearly caused her to feel bad again. The counsellor commented that she seemed to be unhappy and wondered what may have caused this, what was the *activating event*.

For Laura this was the time that the preacher had focused on the family and mother, noted in the initial case presentation above. She became very distressed in the church. Her feeling of anger at the words of the preacher was equalled by a feeling of pain that she had no real family and that she was there in a church filled with families.

The next stage was to invite Laura to articulate the *underlying beliefs* which were fuelling her response. A clear chain began to appear with the following beliefs emerging:

- It is important to be part of a family. If you are not this makes you different and strange;
- It is important to have a good mother, someone who you can be proud of and celebrate. This belief was fuelled by perfectionist thinking. Mothers should always be good. Faced by a mother who threatened her sense of worth, part of her had to cling on to the hope or myth of a good mother. It was always possible she might change.
- It is important to be loved by my mother. If I am not, then I am unlovable.
- I can only be loved by my mother if I do things that she wants. Here again was perfectionist thinking.
- If I do not do the things that she wants, then I am unworthy and ultimately life would be unbearable. A global evaluation such as this is often at the end of the inference chain and generates the affect which maintains such thinking.

The final stage involves reflection on the feelings, and especially the behaviour that such beliefs lead to. In Laura's case, the belief led her to disturbing feelings which caused her to feel uncomfortable in the church. The result was that she avoided going to most of the church services. This was self defeating behaviour in that the feeling of being marginalised now became a reality. She went to the service where there were few people there and which involved the least creative and positive contact with others - often much older than herself. Further reflection revealed other beliefs which kept this behaviour in place, not least that worth depended on her becoming part of a middle upper middle class organisation, and one which had a strong intellectual bias.

The acceptance of such behaviour as self defeating was in itself part of the uncovering of moral meaning. At its crudest, this placed together side by side the narrative of her present behaviour with a narrative of her imagination as to what did she actually want from being in church. For Laura this was about being able to come to church to be part of the group, to contribute to the community and to feel relaxed. In the light of this she began to chart where she wanted to be, and how she might achieve this. This in itself was beginning to provide values which she could aspire to and which might motivate her for change.

## Debate

All of this provides the starting point for cognitive reflection, and in particular debating of these beliefs. This is where the different criteria for thinking come to the fore, criteria which challenge the counsellee to examine: her rational thought (*logical*); her use of data (*empirical evidence*); and her awareness of reality, not least constraints which cannot be changed (*pragmatic*). For Laura this meant directly asking her what the empirical grounds for beliefs were, taking this all the way down to the core belief. Cognitive work invites the counsellee to take that core belief and see where it takes her, with questions such as : 'What was the worst thing that could happen if you did not please your mother?' She was encouraged to consciously explore the different possibilities, and came up with life as unbearable; banishment from the family; even death. As she analysed these different possibilities herself, she strengthened her adult cognitions against the childhood cognitions and concluded that nothing cataclysmic would happen, and that the power which her mother had over her was based on nothing substantial. This insight was, of course, not the end, and, as we shall see in the next chapter, the counsellee has to get used to thinking this way and living by such cognitions. This meant getting into the habit of new ways of thinking, something which requires discipline and practice as part of the care.

The effect of this was to expand the cognitions which Laura had of the family, to able to see the family as ambiguous. From this perspective she was also able to build up empathic thinking about her mother. Viewing her from a distance she was able to see the way in which her mother was herself subject to major depression and precisely to the automatic thinking which did not allow her to see her child as an other.

This tied in with the pragmatic cognition work. Laura became clear that she could not achieve perfection nor could her mother have been perfect. This, in turn, enabled the loss of her mother to be handled better. She began to go to her mother's grave to tend it and to enter into a dialogue at the grave side. The more that Laura gained distance from her mother and family, the more she was able to see that her mother was not responsible, not to blame, for the cognitions held by Laura. She could certainly be held accountable for her behaviour but Laura did not have to buy in to her mother's shaming.

Only when Laura was able to put to one side the idealised view of her mother, including the hope for someone who would become perfect, was she able to begin effective bereavement.

## Discrimination

Discrimination further helps the counsellee to develop justification for her situation. This involves beginning to distinguish between the fundamental and instrumental values, leading the person to examine values in a rigorous way and to begin to provide reasons for holding them.

Along with this discrimination is the comparison that can now take place between the different competing values. In the light of the dialogue Laura was able to work on the church's narrative about the family and challenge the view that honouring parents means unquestioning obedience in all things. She was encouraged to compare the idea of unquestioning obedience with other values in the New Testament not least the inclusive care which is at the heart of the family ethic (see chapter seven).

In the light of all these developments Laura was able to begin to creatively dialogue with and critique her own thinking and also to begin to critique the thinking of the priest. This was a crucial point of moral development. Prior to this point she viewed the priest as a figure of authority who represented a single moral perspective. It became clear to Laura for the first time that there was no single church position about the family. On the contrary, it was in constant dialogue about the role of the family and a real awareness of the ambiguity of family life. Laura had honestly believed that there was only one view of the family and that one was a failure if this was not achieved. The priest remained important to her but was now someone who could be challenged, along with other narratives and narrators in the church.

## Confrontation

A great deal of this work is also summed up in the idea of confrontation. Confrontation is defined in terms of reflecting back to the counsellee the counsellor's perception of the narrative and its implications. Hence, reality confrontation, for instance invites the counsellee to test her perceptions against reality. This in fact involves reflection on the grounds for any perception. Hence, Laura's perception of her brothers and their wives was tested against the available evidence. This helped Laura to test out the projections of her thinking, and thus of her basic moral position, which were affecting her perception. Once again it helped her to see how basic data collection was affected by judgements based upon her previous moral world. Another form of reality testing is to check out how the different perception will affect practice and what might be possible. Reflection on self-defeating behaviour is also a from of reality testing, inviting the person to see how her behaviour affects her (see Clinebell 1984. Ch. 6). The issue of confrontation will be examined more closely in chapter seven when ethical confrontation and the possibility of moral rebuke will be examined.

## Conclusion

The dialogue continues to develop. Agape enables the counsellee to take responsibility for handling the various 'fissures' and conflicts which emerge as part of the narrative. The clarification of these different 'texts' gives the counsellee chance to examine just what she means and to begin to mean what she says. Lewis Carroll reminds us the two are different, but they point to affective and cognitive narratives which radically affect each other and have to be worked through in order to arrive at some sense of moral meaning which takes into account the spiritual world of the counsellee. An examination of that spiritual world not only looks to conflicting narratives but also to the nature of the demands in the different relationships, and how they are perceived. This is partly a matter of looking at the moral world of the other, but also looking at the particular moral claims of the other on the self. For Laura this involved examination of the moral narrative of her mother and the claims she made upon her. It is precisely at this point that Laura could begin to critique, albeit in a rough and negative way, the narrative of her mother, the very narrative which had provided meaning to her life for over thirty years. This was the time when she worked through the feelings of unfairness about her life. Initially, they were connected to feelings of hopelessness, and her motivation to move forward was affected.

Agape in all this gave her the safety from which she could begin to handle the ambiguity and aporia emerging from the narrative. Of equal importance was the way in which it enabled her to actually see those aporia, and see the possibility of different ways of perceiving the world and finding meaning and value in the world. Shafts of light were emerging, connections in the different narratives which she might be able to put her faith in and perhaps begin to develop meaning from them. Moral meaning was also emerging as something not unique to her, her particular moral perspective, but rather in response to the critical moral dialogue with others. This includes the moral dialogue with the counsellor. As noted in the last chapter, this is initially worked through in the development of and reflection on the contract, and the development of mutual testing. Behind this are often projections of the old moral world onto the counsellor, often in the form of transference, seeing the counsellor as embodying the moral world of the condemning church or the condemning parent. It is precisely the agapeic response of the counsellor which enables the counsellee to view both the other and her moral world differently. This in turn enables the counsellee to acknowledge and examine the moral world which was the basis of her perception, not least the affects which cause her to respond automatically. This enables the counsellee to return those feelings, not least shame, to their origin, and with that to begin to be released from the moral world imposed upon her. That release also involves a letting go of the old moral world and the old hopes of the significant other changing. Alongside the development of the capacity to critique comes the experience of bereavement, something the counsellor has to help the counsellee to articulate and work through.

This in turn enables her to begin to work through to a new moral meaning, one owned by the counsellee and built up in response to her spiritual world. For this to be worked through such moral meaning would have to be made conceptually and somatically explicit, clear in concepts and in responsive action. It is to this stage that we now turn to examine how agape informs that.

### References
A. Campbell, The Gospel of Anger (London: SPCK, 1986).

H. Clinebell, Basic Types of Pastoral Care and Counselling (London; SCM, 1984).

M. Cavanagh, Cognitive Development: Pastoral Implications, Pastoral Psychology, Vol. 44, No. 4, March,1996, 227-236.

A. Ellis and W. Dryden, The Practice of Rational Emotive Behaviour Therapy (London Free Association, 1999).

S. Fleischacker, The Ethics of Culture (Ithaca: Cornell University Press, 1994).

P. Gilbert, Counselling for Depression (London: Sage, 1992).

P. Halmos, The Faith of the Counsellor (London: Constable 1962)

G. Meilander, The Theory and Practice of Virtue (Notre Dame: University of Notre Dame Press, 1984).

L. Raths, M. Harmin, S.B. Simon, Values and Teaching: Working with Values in the Classroom (Columbus, 1978 2nd ed.).

J. Reader, Beyond All Reason (Cardiff: Aureus, 1997).

P. Riceour, 'Ethics and Culture: Habermas and Gademar in Dialogue', Philosophy Today 17: 153- 65.

C. Rogers, Freedom to Learn (Columbus: Merrill, 1983).

C. Tavris, Anger: The Misunderstood Emotion (New York: Simon and Schuster, 1982).

J. van der Ven, Formation of the Moral Self (Eerdmans: Grand Rapids, 1998).

# 6

## Faithful Change: Living in Hope

'The seat of power is in the soul' (R. H. Tawney, Commonplace Book).

'God grant me the serenity to accept the things I cannot change,
the courage to change the things I can,
and the wisdom to know the difference' (A.A. prayer).

## Case

David was a new member of the congregation, referred to the parish priest by his university chaplain. The referral did not indicate any particular problem, just that he needed care. He had done postgraduate work in civil engineering at university, whilst attached to a firm.

Within two months of arriving in the parish he called on the priest with a problem. He had helped to win a prestigious contract for his new firm, but had made calculations for the contract which did not include certain data. David was clearly upset by this, and spoke of sleepless nights, lack of concentration and panic attacks. The priest asked him to explain the importance of the missed calculation and how it came about - through intention or omission. It turned out that the missed calculation was not major, and would not affect the safety of the project. Nonetheless, David remained very tense and disturbed. He felt that he had failed as an engineer. The project work had not achieved the best possible end. More than that, he felt that he had allowed himself to be drawn into what amounted to lying. Once the project had been passed, by a senior engineer who clearly had not checked the figures, then he had to keep the lie up and if anything went wrong then it could come back to him.

Little the priest said could reassure David and he encouraged him to talk about the feelings of guilt and failure. Several things emerged through this narrative.

David had had a very hard time at university. He had become involved with a cult like group which strongly reinforced feelings of guilt that he had. This caused *major stress and a break down, leading to counselling. The counselling had been helpful but he found that underlying anxiety and depression still threatened to disable him whenever significant stress was created.*

*In ensuing sessions with the priest he began to work through the major problem in his life which revolved around his parents. His mother had been ill throughout his life and had relied upon him for help. Her physical illness was often accompanied by depression and because his father had left at an early age David felt that he was responsible for her care. This meant that he put a lot of time and energy into caring for her. He felt responsible for both her physical and emotional health, including any depression. He felt he had to put aside his feelings and in effect learn to lie, giving his mother the reaction he thought she wanted. This was intensified when his mother developed a terminal illness and died in the first year of university.*

*David also felt responsible for his parents' separation, even though this occurred at an early age. This led to ambivalent feelings about his father. He resented him as someone who had let his mother down. He also admired him. He had kept contact with his father, which had become more frequent over the years. He presented as a very attractive personality, with a great interest his son's educational achievements and a concern for his son to a have strong male image. He had a very liberal sexual ethic, with several mistresses over the years. David himself saw it as important to develop a strong physique, and at one point at university pursued a promiscuous life style.*

*His relationship with his father was now taking a more difficult turn as he was in the early stages of Parkinson's disease. He was still able to look after himself, but David felt a major responsibility for him, something not shared by his older brother and sister.*

*The tension from all this had led David to begin to misuse alcohol. He would go on weekend benders and was clearly beginning to depend on alcohol. This was beginning to affect his work and social life.*

*At the same time he was consciously looking at his identity and purpose and, after several sessions with the priest, he expressed a felt vocation to the priesthood. He was unsure about the exact nature of this but at one point had thought about a vocation to monastic orders.*

From the beginning it was clear that David was looking for change - change in the negative attitudes and feelings he had, not least about himself, change in the negative practices and change to a new identity. Such change is at the centre of the pastoral care and counselling process. Different traditions all focus on this in different but complementary ways. Frank Lake looks to the development of integration, including a concern for awareness of reality (Lake 1980). Rogers sees the aim of counselling as the fully functioning person (Rogers 1983). His learning paradigm does not merely assume that the person has not been fully functioning but rather that the aim of personhood is constant learning and development. Paul Halmos focuses on change and healing (Halmos 1964). Baglow sees the development of freedom, something close to the definition of Mendis and Couture, which is liberation from oppressive cultures (Baglow 1996; Couture and Hunter 1995). The classic pastoral theology definition by Clebsch and Jaekle, is of enabling confession and forgiveness - a form of the developmental learning paradigm (Clebsch and Jaekle 1975). The British Association of Counselling sees the aim of counselling as: 'an opportunity for a client to work towards living in a more satisfying and resourceful way' (B.A.C.).

Moral meaning is at the core of such change. At the very least it involves the balancing of change and freedom, so that change is directed by the counsellee. This means that the counsellor can neither manipulate nor leave the counsellee to her own devices. Once change is in progress the counsellee moves into a different terrain. She cannot simply go back to the old country. Though that is familiar, and in some senses secure, it is also a place of pain and despair. In chapters four and five we have seen the counsellee beginning to survey that old country, taking responsibility for the moral world and for the truth of the past. Responsibility was taken, then, for the dialogue which enabled her to analyse and critique values and begin to develop a moral map which showed where she had come from and why she held such moral values. Facing the moral thoughts and feelings enabled the counsellee to return these to their origins and begin think about charting a new map.

It is evident from this that moral identity and meaning are at the heart of real change. Change is neither possible nor significant which does not replace the old values with something else, and something which has been worked out in response to the person's spiritual world. As the person moves into this new world then the careful task of charting a new map begins. Like any exploration, this involves a constant dialogue between the actual experience, what the explorer is in fact faced with, and the meaning which she takes from the experience, the map she begins to develop. The mapping itself also demands dialogue between the person and other maps which might be available - the beginnings of which was noted in the previous chapter.

In this chapter the counsellee moves into that new world and takes responsibility for the practice of change, exploring, establishing a new life, and for finding significant meaning in that life. This involves three major elements, each of which works through in practice sophisticated and complex moral issues, usually confined to the ethics textbooks :

- *Defining and practising responsibility.* How does the person begin to define and put into practice her sense of responsibility for others? This is a natural consequence of increasing spiritual awareness and thus the awareness of others, including their needs and moral demands. In essence, this addresses how the counsellee can begin to love her neighbour.

- *Building right relationships.* Alongside the concern to respond in practice to the needs of others is the need to challenge others where relationships have been broken. This involves the practice of forgiveness, reconciliation, balancing agape and justice. This is the outcome of a transformative ethic.

- *Revisioning spiritual and moral values.* From a position where the person has been either confused, in terms of moral meaning, or has been literally overwhelmed by the moral demands of her life, effective change demands a clear articulation of new moral meaning. For some, this will be the development of life meaning which enables the person to legitimately love her self. The relationship of agape and eros are then worked out in practice and the values made explicit. For others it will mean articulating principles for the first time.

Whilst each of these areas are conceptually distinct they are intimately related and interdependent so that working through responsibility might occur at the same time as the building of right relationships.

Underlying the transformation of practice and principles is the transformation of the person. At the centre of this is the development of the virtues, the strengths which empower and motivate change. The virtues and the dynamic of virtue development will thus be examined, with a focus on the development of faith and hope.

At the heart of this all is the acceptance of change *per se*. For most counsellees change is desirable but also very threatening. Hence, the desire for many to change others and not the self. The key then is to enable change and the acceptance of change which is centred on and directed by the person.

# Redefining and practising responsibility

A natural consequence of increasing spiritual awareness is an increased awareness of the needs of the other, and thus of the moral demand upon the self. It is precisely the moral demand upon the self which the counsellee often cannot handle. The conditional ethic requires that all demands be fulfilled.

As noted in chapter two the negotiation of responsibility is important in breaking through this responsibility overload and in the development of a clear moral identity. J. Finch and J. Mason have been able to show how the negotiation of actual practice was effective at providing shared moral meaning in families which had no ethical rules or even vocabulary (Finch and Mason 1993). The negotiation itself was the means whereby the shared images of individuals within the family were transmitted from one situation to the next. This formed the basis of a moral reputation, such that 'people were being constructed and reconstructed as moral beings' (Finch and Mason 1993, 170). The negotiations which they describe tended to be built on previous work, often decades old, and most often leading to a confirmation or development of the previous practice. Their work points to a critical element of moral reflection which is often not given due weight precisely because formal principles are not always part of the process. These, nonetheless, might easily be drawn from reflection on the practice.

The major problem with this is not the negotiation *per se* but rather that the negotiation, which they describe, did not easily accommodate challenge or change. Hence, in the central case which they use, we see different members of the family being confirmed in their responsibilities, but no development of genuine collaborative practice. One adult child is left to care for their widowed mother, and the other two accept the moral identity of their sibling and refuse to take responsibility for care in the event of him not being able to fulfil it. Hence, the activity described by Finch and Mason actually seems more like consultation, in which there is communication and acceptance of intentions, with no space for the challenge of mutual responsibility.

For David this approach to negotiation could not be satisfactory, partly because there was no previous negotiation to build on and partly because once he began to become aware of his own needs he realised that he could not simply accede to himself taking all responsibility, something his siblings encouraged. He was strongly tempted to do this, taking all responsibility for his father, with the underlying belief that he would please both his father and his siblings. Moreover, the sense of responsibility for his father was made even stronger by the anger he felt at his father's desertion, anger which made him feel ashamed. Equally, he was clear that the issue of responsibility had to be resolved the worse his father became.

As he rehearsed all this with the priest, he expressed anger with his siblings. 'It's hopeless', he said, 'I can't begin to get across to them what my father might need or what I need.' The priest encouraged him to develop this rehearsal, and to focus on the issues of responsibility, and responsibility negotiation which offered the possibility of rewriting his narrative. His role here was not to instruct but rather to help him work out for himself how to achieve these negotiations. Here the priest was helping him to work out his methodology of negotiation. Using a learner centred approach, he invited David to examine his present method of negotiation, analyse it and to think how it might be improved.

David came up with a first step of clarification of the problem and the establishment of need. He recognised that he had not taken time to work this out. Initially, he was very confident about this and locked into his perfectionist side with a whole series of booklets on Parkinson's disease and a list of physical and emotional needs. The priest reflected back the value of collecting data about the problem and asked if there was any more data needed. It was at this point that David began to look at the importance of beginning any negotiation with his father. How did he see his problem? How did he define his need? Was he happy about accepting help and if so would that be from family or from others?

Firstly, David had precisely avoided these kinds of question which would begin to bring him into closer contact with his father, partly because he saw his father as strong and distant. He was fearful of moving into a relationship that would challenge that image through bringing up limitations. Secondly, the moral responsibility he felt for care was always getting in the way of the actual relationship. He simply wanted to please. This got in the way of establishing real contact with his father and checking out what he wanted.

David's method moved 'backwards' to establish a bridge with his father to enable both of them to focus on the condition and what he felt he needed. He was quite aware that this might take some time, not least because any care offered needed to be in response to honest views. It became clear that this meant, regardless of specific actions of care, that he would need to commit time to simply being with his father.

The next step which he outlined was to establish a bridge with his siblings and with all other stake holders. The term stakeholder means anyone who had a concern or the capacity to help in any way. Like the first step this had to involve a sharing of information, including the expressed needs of their father, the limitations which each had in relating to him, and a broad look at shared goals emerging for his care.

The third step was the examination of different methods in fulfilling those goals. Once again, he stressed the importance of focusing on the truth of the different parties' experiences and feelings, and allowing a shared moral meaning and practice to emerge from this. The method was subsequently put into practice and reviewed in the counselling sessions.

His father was a very proud man and did not want his family to be there for his physical needs. The balance between his independence and dependence was discussed, and he accepted that as the illness developed this might lead to a change of mind. They talked over the variety of options for physical care which might be available, initially with someone from the Parkinson's Disease Society. His father made it quite clear that at no time could he accept major physical care from his family. This was not a sign of enmity, but rather pride. Different options for long term care were discussed. In talking over how that care might be realised his father worked through many frustrations and began to speak of his emotional needs and of the importance of knowing his family was there for him.

With clearer information David was strengthened in his moral resolve to start meaningful negotiations with his siblings. This part of the negotiations was relatively swift. Initially, the limitations of the siblings in terms of time, distance etc. were rehearsed, including their reluctance to take responsibility for physical needs. When the needs of their father were discussed they began to see what taking realistic responsibility for his care might involve. This in turn led to a 'contract' - all would see him every month, with the grandchildren. This in turn gave the grounds from which they could begin to challenge each other if this did not happen. They also accepted the principle of a rolling contract that would be reviewed in response to further developments.

In effect David had used precisely the method which he had learned in the relationship with his counsellor - learner centred, enabling articulation of narrative, reflection on purpose and value, and embodiment of goals in practice in response to the needs and claims of the other. This required him to give his father the space he previously had been unable to give to articulate his own needs. David also remarked how important this whole process was for his father. With the separation from his second wife he had lost any real family role, and to have the whole family committed to being there gave him a new sense of identity.

The process of responsibility negotiation overall further enabled David to identify and accept limitations. He began to see limitations not as shameful but as an acceptable part of his life. It also enabled him to develop an explicit sense of moral identity, something he found liberating. He retained some responsibility, but did not have to do everything. Indeed, his moral identity changed from the person who would always take care of things to the co-ordinator who help others to be involved. Moreover, it established a sense of moral self for the first time, something established with and recognised by the other members of his family.

Prior to this dialogue, David was simply driven by a moral purpose focused on conditionality which made constant demands of him, and which had never involved either reflection on purpose or acknowledgement of his work. So much of this moral narrative was kept going with 'hidden' communication. David spoke of the occasion as a teenager when he began to share some of his worries with his mother, as they walked in the street. He vividly recalled how a frown moved across her brow. David was unable to test what this meant but interpreted this immediately as a sign never to share any problems with his mother. This would be too painful for her. True to form he did not share pain with her from then on. Dialogue meant that he could now move to empathic testing of the other.

This, of course, was not possible with his mother, for whom he still felt responsible. He felt a sense of her still demanding and being without any way of finding an answer. Above all he wanted to know if his mother was at peace. He also was concerned to know *where* she was, fearful of her being in a sort of limbo. Two things were needed to work through this sense of responsibility. Firstly, he spoke at length about his mother and the needs that she expressed. He saw her increasingly as an ambiguous figure who was both concerned for him but also fearful of being alone and who, therefore, relied upon him for her sense of well-being. In working through this he began to articulate what he imagined his mother's needs might have been, and see how he could never have fulfilled her hopes of him. He was beginning to gain distance from his mother and work through the grief and guilt that he was still feeling at her death. This was an important affective step but was not sufficient . He also wanted to know that she was being cared for, that someone else had responsibility for her now, so that he could let go. This led to a detailed theological reflection. He was not convinced with the Greek view of the after life, with the idea of God caring for immortal souls. The Hebrew view of the resurrection of the whole person at the end of time did begin to make sense to him. He needed to think of his mother as embodied not a discarnate soul. In this light there was nothing he could do to help her at this moment. At the end of time she would be aware and be there with others. Working through these ideas cognitively gave him permission to let go of his responsibility. In this God was beginning to become one of the care-takers.

The process of negotiation then enabled several things to happen. Firstly, it established need. This involved empathic engagement with the other so that David understood what response was needed. Prior to this exercise he had not really known what his father needed, could not respond and felt guilty. His relationship with his mother had involved trying to answer all her needs. The development of empathy was critical in the establishing of an ethic which is based on the recognition of humanity, sameness, in the other and the self. Once that responsibility is owned in some way then the negotiation of responsibility begins to make sense. Negotiation of responsibility in the light of an empathic relationship keeps the counsellee focused on this question. For those who have taken on too much responsibility, like David, this then allows an understanding of their limitations and the acceptance of the need to share responsibility. For those who have no sense of responsibility towards the other it is still this process of developing empathy for the other which is critical. Secondly, through further dialogue around those needs he was able to focus his own response more effectively, both for himself and for his father. Thirdly, he established for himself for the first time a clear moral identity. Prior to this there was simply a mindless response spurred on by guilt. He did not know clearly what his purpose or identity was. By negotiating with the others 'in public' his moral identity was articulated and confirmed. The result was a confirmation from several people that his contribution was of value. Previously, David had had no sense of the value of his contribution. He simply had to contribute and no one discussed why. This was a critical stage for David in finding meaning and value, effecting a change in perspective and values and providing motivation to maintain the change. David said that he was beginning to feel good about his responsibilities for the first time.

Fourthly, the development of empathy also creates the positive distance which shows that the other is also responsible. Neither David's mother or father had been given the freedom to be responsible for themselves and their own well being. Placing the responsibility for themselves back on to his parents was part of the returning of shame to its origins.

In all this, genuine empathy was experienced not as an individualistic attitude but rather as a social attitude expressed in community and freedom.

Finally, it is important to stress the development of method. Method enables principles and practice to come together. Without working through method David would not have been able to engage with his father either successfully or meaningfully. Method enables the possibility of limited and attainable outcomes, and thus further enables the development of identity and responsibility.

## Building right relationships

Along with the establishment of a response in practice which was clearly of value, which clarified moral identity and which could begin to take the place of the conditional moral identity, there were issues of conflict in relationships which needed to be addressed. This involved the development of right relationships or shalom and with it issues of justice, and forgiveness and reconciliation.

### Justice

David was already looking at justice, in terms of sharing responsibility. At some point doing justice to others had to be practised, especially where there had been offence, abuse or estrangement in a relationship .

David had two concerns for justice, mirroring his concerns for responsibility. The first was his father and facing him with the injustice of his desertion. The second was the increasing anger that David felt about his mother and how she had manipulated him. Both, in different ways, embody the question of the relationship between love and justice. Justice for David demanded that he confront his father with his feelings and with what he had done. At the same time love seemed to demand that he care for and didn't upset this ailing man - someone who looked less and less like a family deserter. For his mother there was a feeling that she had trapped him and ruined the early part of his life, alongside that feeling of responsibility for her.

Once again, it was important that he work his own way through these aporia. The priest was able to help him reflect on this moral dualism, something which arose from David's own concerns. His conclusion was that he wanted to retain the essential elements of both - to be honest with his father and mother *but* not be adversarial. This meant that first David had to work out what his justice goal was. For him it involved an attempt to make sense of the situation, to find out why his father had left. All he had was his mother's perspective about his father. Secondly, he needed to know how his father felt about his actions now. This demanded an attempt to enable his father's narrative and gain empathic understanding. Thirdly he needed to communicate his feelings to his father and share something of how his life had been.

This approach had enabled him to define justice and its goals in relation to his situation and social environment. Far from avoiding the moral agenda this was enabling David to work it through in particular. Later David remarked that though he had read many different books about theology and ethics he had never known what justice was until he had to begin to define it in his situation. The embodiment of justice for David demanded an agapeic and empathic context, leading to confrontation and beginning to find a new relationship with his father.

For his mother the real objective of justice was to make clear to her what he felt and why he had suffered, without harming her. Here, David was concerned to make the articulation of his feelings specific to her. Hence, through forms of imaginative confrontation, such as writing letters to her, or imagining her in an empty chair he was able to articulate confrontation.

Initially then the search for justice involved non-adversarial confrontation, shared reflection on the truth, and identification of offence. This enabled David to condemn the offence without condemning his parents, and led after a time to forgiveness and reconciliation.

For others the particular demands of justice may be very different, not least if there is a concern that any offender may offend again, or because the abuse of power or trust was such that it constituted a criminal offence (Cashman 1993, 79 ff. ). Justice in that situation takes the issue beyond simply a bi-lateral relationship into concerns about other stakeholders. Agape in all this does not preclude recourse to instruments of public justice. It is perfectly possible to remain committed to someone and still be concerned that they face such justice.

Either way, justice and love both accept that the offence should not be forgotten. Articulation of narrative and the reclaiming of memory are the essence of the healing process.

### Forgiveness

Intimately tied in with justice is forgiveness. Indeed, forgiveness and justice are two opposite sides of the coin of agape. Forgiveness, as we have noted in chapter two, is very much based upon the discovery of common humanity. This awareness provides the basis for acceptance even if justice demands that formal action be taken. Forgiveness, in this sense, holds the other accountable for the action without judging the other. L. Smedes notes the danger of dehumanising the other at either of two extremes (Smedes 1998). At one extreme the person can be demonised, seen simply as the enemy, with no awareness of their humanity. At the other extreme there is the danger of not seeing her as being responsible for her actions. This is equally lacking in respect and awareness of the other and her part in the narrative of the person. Once David was able to see his parents as both victims of other narratives, including depression, and also responsible for them, he was able to move into acceptance and forgiveness.

There are two dangers in this movement. Firstly, the proactive approach to forgiveness might be morally aggressive, used as a means of showing moral superiority and not actually engaging the other (Smedes 1998, 346). A second danger is for the counsellor to try to impose the forgiveness. The danger in this is the imposition of the moral meaning and creating further shame when forgiveness is not 'achieved'. Even more profound is the danger of abstract theology putting its shape on practice. A good example of this is the use one writer makes of the Atonement.

Jensen suggests a view of forgiveness in abuse survivors as sacrificial. Based on a view of the Atonement he argues that forgiveness involves exhausting the 'undeserved consequences' of the abuser's wrong doing, so that this will not lead to a perpetuation of damage either to others or to the abuser. The women then 'pays the price' of the abuse in her self (Burns 1996).

As so described Jensen's dynamic of forgiveness presents the worst of all worlds. It places a moral obligation onto the abused to take the weight of forgiveness. It does not enable an expression of justice, and thus does not take the pain of the abused seriously. Nor does this take the abuser seriously, with no addressing of the actions which need to be accounted for.

The dynamic of agape is quite different. Reflective dialogue enables the counsellee to be released from the very dynamic which has oppressed her and which kept in place her pain and anger. The process of affective dialogue, outlined in chapter five enables her to validate her intense feelings of pain and anger and thus accept that she can feel and express them. The anger is then communicated to the counsellor and others. It is precisely in that process that forgiveness is enabled. First, the counsellee begins to see the other as human, the first stage of forgiveness. Secondly, by returning shame to its origin this releases her from the very dynamic which caused her pain, from the oppressive conditionality, which made her feel foolish or worthless. Once this narrative no longer affects the counsellee, then the power of the abuser is gone. The action or attitude which seemed to be unforgivable, which seemed so bad that the victim could not really believe that it had happened, or that the offender could actually be responsible for it, is now seen as no longer having power over her. In that light the victim no longer has to deny the offence or keep it secret. At the other extreme she no longer has to seek revenge.

Forgiveness is part of a process of release, sometimes a slow process. Far from being sacrificial it involves a healing and strengthening of the person enabling her to face the relationships with other. It begins with the openness to the others, sets out the reality, and challenges the other to respond and be responsible. In all this the abuser must both claim forgiveness and respond to the challenge. This brings the process to questions of reconciliation.

### Reconciliation

If, as Smedes observes, the attitude of forgiveness is unconditional, an openness to the other, then reconciliation is firmly conditional. The key condition for such reconciliation is evidence of response from the offender which shows firstly that he has recognised the truth of the offence and genuinely shows a feeling of remorse. Remorse, indeed is an 'affective kind of honesty'.

On the basis of this there can be a negotiation of reconciliation. This emphasises that reconciliation emerges from the particular process. It arises when there has been a testing out of the narrative of both parties and involves a settlement in which the two agree to come together. Reconciliation is 'never complete, never secure, but always fragile' and open to being broken. It may take place at different levels including:
- a return to a previous relationship, e.g. as part of a family;
- a level of friendship which is less intense than the previous one;
- 'cool co-existence' which involves forgiveness but accepts that the relationship should not be reformed.

There may be a forgiveness and a decision to have no contact, precisely because there is no evidence that the person could begin to enter a contract of reconciliation.

Moreover, even if there is an explicit return to the actual relationship, that relationship will be different. Trust will have to be built up around a relationship whose meaning will be different. For David there was no previous position that either his mother or father could return to. Reconciliation involved a new contract of fatherhood, and grandfatherhood. Reconciliation worked very much around the development of roles and the definition of these roles in the family and took on a wider community approach, not simply involving David and his father.

How love and justice relate has been the focus of much discussion (Outka 1972, Woodhead 1992). In the context of counselling it is clear that whilst justice cannot be simply identified with love it is intimately connected to it. Agape involves a commitment to the other which involves remaining true to them. It also demands truthfulness in facing up to the reality of a narrative or relationship. It is in this facing up to reality and responding to it that justice is practised. How it is practised depends upon dialogue with the offender and with other groups in the victim's network of relationships.

Agape then calls the counsellee to respond to the others in her world. It looks to a transformation not simply of the self but of social environment in the development of shalom. In all this judgement is a function of the agapeic relationship. Judgement is not brought to the relationship by counsellor but emerges from dialogue, not least from the ongoing defining and embodiment of justice. At its centre is the growing capacity of the counsellee to critique the narratives of herself and others, and the capacity to respond in a non-judgemental assertive way. Hence, the eschatological dimension, which gives such anxiety to Gordon Graham, is realised in the relationship.

### Living with Reality

Reality is in one sense constantly being made by the ethic of shalom, always searching for the fulfilment of right relationships. However, this has to be carefully balanced. It is all too possible to measure the success of counselling purely in terms of the change *per se* and to attempt to move the counsellee on to forgiveness and reconciliation, with these two seen as normative.

In fact, the person may have to get used to certain things which will not change. This involves limitations in the self, others, the environment and God. David did not become a totally different character. He was still subject to depression, panic feelings, and competitive urges, spurred on by perfectionist shame. Anna was still subject to flashbacks and still was prone to take on too much especially when she was getting tired, and so didn't have the energy to say no. Laura always found the first move that she made was to judge and stereotype.

These were not things which could change overnight and the feelings which are associated with them would still be there. Seeing the feeling of shame or pain as something which can be lived with was for David or Anna in itself a change in that they were no longer being dominated by them. In one sense this is part of the development of a wider spirituality which recognises that therapy and care cannot magic away the suffering and pain which are inherent in life, not least in moments of change. The counsellee gradually begins to develop life meaning in the experience of pain and suffering (Campbell 1995).

The counsellee may well also be faced by others or a social environment which she cannot change. David's mother could not change by definition and so any hopes of this had to be suspended. Anna's father did not even begin to recognise what he had done. Anna's mother never lived up to her expectations and the need was to let go of the things which she had never actually experienced - the hope for a good mother. As noted above this meant time to work through a genuine experience of bereavement.

Not only were certain things not going to change, it was also important to accept where the person could not change others. A key moment for David was accepting that he could not change his father. Part of him wanted to do that, to change him into the stereotypic caring parent. However, only his father could effect that and that only in the light of his own reflection. David had to learn to listen to that narrative and wait for response.

Central for change then is to know what change is possible and what is not, summed up in the AA prayer. This cannot be predetermined but only worked out through dialogue in the context of the situation. An important part of this is establishing achievable objectives, so that the possibility of change can be confirmed in practice. Once more this emphasises the need for negotiation. Continued testing in community establishes what is possible at any time.

This takes into account too the emotional and moral limitations of the counsellee, including facing up to the question of sin. For both David and Anna the idea that they had sinned was anathema. Sin was clearly defined by them in terms of their perfectionist world, i.e. falling short of a standard. They were both very conscious that they had fallen short of that standard and feared that this would question their worth. A great deal of psychic energy was put into not admitting any fault or excluding themselves from the category of sin.

David had to redefine sin in the light of the moral world of his counselling relationship. At one level this was about chipping away at the shame based view of sin, allowing him to see that there was no basis for this. At another level he was able to explore sin in terms of the learning cycle of his life. This arose precisely as he gained empathy for himself. He could begin to see the points where he had got things wrong and see that this did not involve rejection by the counsellor, and could begin to distinguish action from person. This changed his view of confession completely. Up to this point he had tried to use the rite of confession instrumentally, to lift the load of guilt. However, all he did was to bring to confession the 'sins' which he felt were acceptable. Hence, he was never able to genuinely look at himself and share his life with God. This was partly because of the injunction against showing feelings, something magnified in his relationships with God. Confession had become a further way of avoiding disclosure and another attempt at controlling God.

In the context of the counselling contract David was able to see sin in terms of the negative attitudes and behaviour which affected his relationships, causing him to avoid or deny the truth about himself or others. This was focused in the counselling relationship itself when the counsellor helped him to look at his attempts to avoid taking responsibility for reflection and for response. This was simply a further part of the reflective process which invited him to take more responsibility. The reflection on possible responses and method was equally important at this time. These gave David the chance to see that change was possible, that focus on sin was not a condemnation of the person but part of a truthful reflection which enabled learning and responsibility for the self, life meaning and response to others. The connection of all this to the concept of sin was only made after David had begun to work through the process.

Two things were occurring in this process which developed moral meaning and which ultimately enabled the transformative ethic to happen, the change of values and principles, and the development of the virtues.

## Revisioning values and principles

Changes in moral meaning were occurring throughout the dialogue with the counsellor and in the dialogues with David's relational network. However, it was important for him to articulate clearly the moral and spiritual values which were at the base of this change. Kaufman in reflecting on the psychotherapeutic process sees this as explicitly spiritual and central to healing, involving the 'need for meaning in life, for a sense of purpose to what we do, that quest for belonging to something greater than oneself' (Kaufman 1980, 136).

This involves working explicitly through to specific values for several possible reasons. In the case of Anna her moral world of guilt was held in place and confirmed by an explicit set of principles. Any change demanded that she find others to replace them which clearly demonstrated her moral value. For Laura there were principles which had little practical content or testing. She needed to articulate and test the principles she was using. For David there was a confusion about principles which made him feel powerless when faced with guilt about his father and mother. He needed to articulate principles which could give him a strong moral alternative to that guilt.

David's basic moral stance had been sacrificial altruism, always to put the other first. The idea of self-care was alien to him. The development of responsibility and the acceptance of limitations and the development of the awareness of the shame base of the altruistic stance all helped to chip away at the explicit altruism. However, the dynamic of the counselling relationship above all enabled the reworking through the development of mutuality, and thus the acceptance of the needs of the counsellee. Such mutuality was exemplified in the way in which it became safe to test and critique the priest in counselling. The first phase of the relationship involved an attempt by David to please the priest, the power figure who could give him acceptance. Hence, he spent a lot of time on his unsatisfactory experience of work and feelings about vocation to the priesthood and about his work in the local church. As mutuality was established David felt able to challenge the counsellor at points where he disagreed or felt concern. The exchanges worked through to a new phase of dialogue, with David realising that the priest was not 'perfect' and did not require perfection. At the same time the positive accepting response of the counsellor enabled David to reflect on the grounds for his challenge. Where the challenge was based on David's old moral world, projecting old ways of thinking onto him, the priest's response was able to show him that there was no basis to this. This further enabled David to take responsibility for both feelings and thoughts.

This growth in mutuality was exemplified in the way both parties recognised the mutual challenge as being part of the contract. Each was able to call the other back to the contract. In calling each other back the content of that contract itself was revisited and the relationship of the ethical meaning and affective content clarified. The very counselling experience was enabling David to let go of part of his old moral world, and begin to replace it with new purpose. In one respect David was trying on these new values for size. He had to keep discussing them and seeing how they related to the different parts of his life. This led to the explicit formulation of principles. These included the foundation principles of freedom and community and other principles such as mutual responsibility, participation, collaborative service. The development of such principles came directly from attention to the aporia noted above. Once David had begun to articulate the desire to both care for and challenge his father. This ethic, both community and freedom, care and challenge, had to be explored in terms of practice and explicit values.

The explicit articulation of the new narrative of mutuality and self nurture, was tied to practice and David's planning and working out of response to others, and took time to internalise. Often when he moved into doing something for himself he would say, 'I know I shouldn't be thinking about myself', or 'it feels strange to put myself first'. He had to work on the explicit statement and justification of the arguments for this new value in his life and to begin to put into practice and maintain this new mutuality. The counselling process was then able to encourage both habits of reflectivity in which purpose and principles were part of any planning, and habits of practice in which the person was able to hear and respond to the call from her relational network. This has elements of behavioural work, with the counsellor enabling the counsellee to stay focused on self nurture. However, the stress on empathy and the response to the call of the network once more moves beyond the transformation of the individual to the transformation of that network itself.

## Moral and spiritual meaning

The development of moral meaning worked through into the rest of David's life not least in the area of sexuality. This had involved confusion and some polarisation. He enjoyed sexual relationships with women, indeed took great pride in his sexual capacity. This pride was very much in response to his father's hopes for him. At the same time he felt very uneasy about this behaviour because he associated it with his father's promiscuity and with his mother's sense of disapproval. Hence, a polarised view emerged with him either enjoying sex as a pastime at one extreme or avoiding sex completely and believing that he might be called to a life of celibacy. In the light of this sense of vocation he saw Jesus' injunction against adultery in the heart as an injunction against all interest in the opposite sex (Matt. 5: 28).

The development of a sense of mutuality where he did not have to please the other but could explore what was good for him enabled him to critique the two different moral views and work through to a view of sexuality which first distinguished sexuality from the sex act. Sexuality was then valued for what it was, a key part of interpersonal relationships - about the whole person - and the integrity of the self and the other. He began to explore positive sexuality which did not involve sexual relationship or adultery. This meant forming relationships with others which respected and valued their attractiveness but did not seek to use them for personal gratification.

Critical to this development was also the working through of the spiritual dissonance which underlay the moral dissonance. David had been little aware of himself as a whole person and therefore a sexual being. Hence he had dissociated sex from his whole person. Along with this dissociation was then a lack of responsibility for sexuality and its expression. Hence, the polarised moral stance. The reflection on sexuality and the increased awareness of the self led David to see himself as a whole person, with sexuality as a key dimension of his self. With this development of empathy he began to see women as whole persons and thus view relationships with them as valuing and appreciating their sexuality and at the same time taking responsibility for his relationship to them.

These reflections led him to question his relationship to God. David had never been empathically aware of God. He was not a clear, separate other. He was certainly not an other who David could have faith in. He had assented to the idea of faith but faith for him was conditional. God would stand by him if David lived out the sacrificial altruism, and pleased him. Hence, he had never actually experienced a relationship which nurtured faith. He did not know what this faith actually was.

The exploration of mutuality then enabled him to become more empathically aware of himself and of God. This was a genuine spiritual transformation, enabling him to begin to develop trust. At one session he shared this sense of transformation:

'I can see now that I never trusted God. I could never let go. I always had to try and control him, with all things that would please him.'

At the base of this he had begun to understand what faith in God was. Faith in the presence of the other for him. In effect, David had begun to learn to love God.

To David's even greater surprise, it also led to an increased awareness of the physicality of God. This was a creator God who was at home in the material world, and hence delighted in sexuality. Here David was making connections between his greater awareness of sexuality, mutuality and God.

In all this David was not simply exploring the theological images of God. He was rather reflecting on God cognitively, affectively and somatically. This led to complete reassessment of images such as creator, and discovery of new meaning.

## Re-forming the character

At the heart of transformation in counselling is change in the person. Such change is often associated with character development, which has at its centre the development of the virtues. The virtues and character have been a major focus of Christian Ethics from Aquinas through to Hauerwas. As David Tracy notes, there are two problems with the idea of character. Firstly, it tends to assume a grand narrative informing what makes a good character. Secondly, and connected, the character tends to be seen as individualistic, a discrete entity. Tracy, in his writings on virtues, therefore suggests the use of the term soul. This, he argues, picks up the dialogic nature of the self and the idea of the subject-in-progress (Tracy 1996). Even this needs to be extended, though, to take into account a wider spirituality which sees the self in relation to the other, as noted in chapter two.

At the heart of this is the gradual development of agape and empathy, something which as we have seen is enabled at all stages of the counselling relationship, through the articulation of the personal narrative, the reflection on and dialogue with the different narratives and the development of shalom. Along with faith and hope, this forms the three central spiritual virtues, often characterised as the theological virtues.

### Faith

Faith, as we noted in chapter two, is a virtue which embodies unconditional love. The need to discover an other who one can have faith in is critical to well being. Genuine faith is tested at several levels and is not simply a form of magical thinking or unthinking belief. Hence, the whole process of faith development culminates in the capacity to have faith in others and the self, and to share responsibility.

James Fowler notes four elements of the definition of faith:

'(1). the foundational dynamic of trust and loyalty underlying self hood and relationships. In this sense faith is a human universal, a generic quality of human beings;

(2). a wholistic way of knowing and valuing, in which persons shape their relations with self, others and the world in the light of an apprehension of and by transcendence;

(3). the unifying and life directing response of persons, mired helplessly in self alienation or self groundedness to the gift of divine grace.

(4). obedience to revealed truth' (Fowler 1990, 394).

Faith is not simply about relationship to God. It is also essential to the development of the person *per se*.

Fowler notes seven stages in the development of faith ranging from *primal faith* to *universalising faith*. The seeds of trust begin to grow in the first stage which is pre-linguistic, involving a gradual awareness of an environment which is different from the self. The last is a rare stage of faith which has little self reference. Whilst there have been criticisms of Fowler's work, it does give a useful framework charting the development of the capacity to hold together and live with aporia and different moral perspectives, and the capacity to take responsibility for spiritual and moral meaning (Gilligan 1982).

As we shall see in the next chapter development tends to occur at moments of crisis or transition between the stages. It is enabled through person centred agapeic care, where the counsellor offers faithfulness which the counsellee can test and so begin to internalise the meaning.

## Hope

The third spiritual virtue of hope is often not given much space in ethical reflection. However, it is a key virtue in the empowerment for change, and thus repays a more detailed analysis.

For many people the idea of hope is about the giving hope *to* someone and about the ground of that hope. The narrative of hope here is brought to the situation. Two examples of this are theological hope and medical hope. The first of these is often expressed in terms of the resurrection. The resurrection of Christ provides the ground for our hope, for salvation now and in the future. Hence, salvation figures highly in the care of the dying by the church. The medical hope is often expressed in terms of the medical model. Here the hope is placed in the action of an other, the competent doctor or therapist. In each case there is a clear outcome - salvation and health - and faith in the outcome gives us hope. Hope in this sense is future orientated.

Such views have two major dangers. Firstly, the danger of a passive acceptance of the work of the other. Secondly, it does not begin to speak to the affective side. The hope is based upon doctrine, the accepted *idea* that Jesus will save or that the medical model of health will take care of the patient.

However, the virtue of hope is far more complex and finds its ground in the total caring process. At its heart hope is about the capacity to envision and take responsibility for a significant and meaningful future. The experience of hope develops in and through the counselling relationship and language of hope emerges from the dialogue and reflection on that experience. As shall be seen, the development of hope is very much dependant upon other virtues.

### Ground of hope

The primal ground of hope is not in the future but in the present and above all in an other. Many people have a sense of being hope less in themselves. They feel this largely because they have internalised the explicit or implicit judgement of significant others. The ascription hopeless actually means that they have no value, and therefore by definition have no future. Indeed, for many the future simply involves the repetition of patterns of behaviour which always fail to achieve the goal of acceptance (Robinson 1998).

The need here is for the person to feel a significant sense of hope in themselves as themselves, something which can only be supplied by the unconditional acceptance of an other. This is forcefully put across by Henri Nouwen who notes the possibility of hope in a patient even when the patient is close to death, a hope dependant upon the presence of an other and needing no time to generate,

'But when a man says to his fellow man, "I will not let you go. I am going to be here tomorrow waiting for you and I expect you not to disappoint me," then tomorrow is no longer an endless dark tunnel. It becomes flesh and blood in the brother who is waiting and for whom he wants to give life one more chance...

Let us not diminish the power of waiting by saying that a life saving relationship cannot develop in an hour. One eye movement or one handshake can replace years of friendship when a man is in agony. Love not only lasts for ever, it needs only a second to come about' (Nouwen 1994, 67).

### Realistic hope

Hope, as Lester notes, cannot thrive on deceit or untruth (Lester 1995). For David hope was attached to the attempts to please his parents. But it was not a hope based in the parents, but rather a hope based on himself being able to satisfy parents. The whole basis of this was a distortion of the truth and thus a false hope. The generation of hope demands then that the truth be arrived through empathy, with all its ambiguities and limitations. The development of empathy and wisdom thus becomes critical for hope. Wisdom traditionally involves:

*Memoria*, being true to the past;
*Docilitas*, an openness to the present through stillness and listening;
*Solertia*, being open to the future, not least the unexpected.

Through such openness false hope can be identified and released. The acceptance of limitations also involves the development of humility. Humility has often been connected to a lowly sense of self worth, quickly taking on a negative view of the self. In fact, humility is properly charac- terised as the capacity to 'have an accurate opinion of oneself. It is the ability to keep one's talents and accomplishments in perspective..., to have a sense of self acceptance, an understanding of one's imperfections, and to be free from arrogance and low self esteem' (Tangney 2000, 72).

C.R. Snyder suggests that the development of hope as a virtue then depends upon three factors (Snyder 2000) :

- goals;
- pathways;
- agency.

## Goals

The capacity to hope is generated through a sense of morally significant purpose. Such good hope provides meaning which affirms the worth of the person. Hence, hope in those who are dying becomes embodied in concern for right relationships with significant others.

In the light of such purposes, realistic goals need to be set out. Hopefulness develops on goals which can be achieved. Hope may be a major virtue but it needs specific aims for it to be meaningful, aims worked through in dialogue.

## Pathways

Hopeful thinking looks to find ways to the goals. This involves a develop- ment of the imagination to be able to see what ways forward there are. This is enabled through the development of method and through practice, not least the widening of possibilities through negotiation of responsibilities.

It also demands the development of wisdom and empathy. Empathy is important in enabling the person to be aware of the possibilities in others. Wisdom remains open to the future. The use of imagination enables the person to project future narratives and work through the different possibilities, something further facilitated by a clear method of decision making. Snyder notes that hope is associated with the development of multiple pathways (Snyder 2000). Such pathways increase through collaborative work with others, which is enabled through the development of shalom. The development of shalom also enables the practice of the virtue of justice, defined as the capacity for equal concern for the other, and attention to the common good.

## Agency

Hope centres in the experience of the person as subject, capable of determining and achieving the goals she looks to. This is achieved to begin with through the development of the narrative and its related skills. In particular, hope is generated when the person finds she is able to own and take responsibility for the feelings, of shame and fear, which have dominated her life. It is also achieved by the owning of values, the development of one's own method and by the practice which demonstrates capacity in the relationship.

Hope has several dimensions. It is not a discrete virtue but one which is gradually developed along with others. It depends upon several factors including method, reflectivity, process and dialogue. At its base hope depends upon the discovery of faith in the other. Hope embodies the release of control. Control does not need hope but looks to all being worked out before hand. Relationships, however, involve the risk which allows the other to respond.

Several points should be underlined from this review of hope. Firstly, the development of spiritual virtues involves the development of all the others, not least integrity. Secondly, the development of virtues is ongoing. Virtues are never 'complete'. Thirdly, learning the virtues does benefit from conscious reflection, explicitly working out the meaning and value of one's personal qualities. Once again awareness of virtue is often there in the original moral world of the counsellee. For Anna the virtue of self reliance, resilience etc. were very important, as was the attitude of doubt. For David the virtues were in line with the perfectionist shame and the need to get every detail right and be honest. Reflection on such qualities is essential not least in discovering the actual meaning of the prized virtues, seeing how such virtues might be problematic, and becoming aware of new insights into virtue.

Reflection on the virtues can happen naturally in the counselling process as part of any reflection on narrative, inviting the counsellee to think on how she has changed and developed over time, and what qualities are important to her. This focuses on the different aspects of character or spirit, without initially having to articulate and learn set moral vocabulary. Such vocabulary can be developed through reflection on the moral vision and practice. As Meilander rightly reminds us, virtues do not begin to make moral sense without a moral vision which they serve (Meilander 1984).

Reflection on virtues can also be enabled through examining the different virtue narratives, found in the different contexts of the person's life, such as personal professional and public. This may bring up conflicting virtue narratives and thus lead to further reflection. It may point up a lack of narrative in one area and a strong one in another, again leading to further dialogue. Virtues can also be approached from reflection on skills. Hence, reflection on the skills developed at work, an area often explicitly worked through in training, can lead to reflection on related qualities (Carter 1985).

Fourthly, the use of reflection on and development of ones own method is particularly important. It provides a framework for systematic moral reflection and practice, not least through the concern for justice and care. It reinforces integrity through bringing together vision and practice. It provides a framework for holistic learning and the development of related skills.

The virtues then are learned through a complex and rich dialogue which enables reflection, testing, challenge, and practice. The method is in essence person centred, taking seriously the virtues and values of the person, the truth of her spiritual environment, and enabling her to take critical and practical responsibility for both. This involves elements of modelling, testing, practice and habituation. Central to all this is development of disciplines which enable the capacity to reflect to be practised. This will be examined more closely below.

In all this the virtues are not spiritual gifts given by one person to another but rather gifts of the dialogic relationship itself. They emerge from and empower the process which enables the person to see things differently, relate differently, and build up a very different moral world.

## Conclusion

The counselling relationship aims to facilitate transformation. This is not simply adapting to new environments, still less a return to norms, but a genuine learning experience which enables discovery of the self and others and the needs of each, of how those needs can be responded to and of how the other can provide support for the self. Such a change is fundamental not simply to the growth of the person but to the development of moral meaning.

Bridger and Atkinson note of the hermeneutical approach to counselling that this involves the counsellee's 'willingness to accept the ideology of counselling itself' as providing meaning for her (Bridger and Atkinson 1998, 85). This is broadly true of the dynamic outlined. However, the important difference is that moral meaning arises from both the development of critique, through dialogue, noted in the last chapter, and the development of principles which have emerged from reflection upon the *experience* of counselling, and in particular from the development of a new spirituality which depends upon an increased awareness of the self and others, including their needs. In other words it is far more than the acceptance of an ideology. It involves fundamental spiritual change, change in how the world is seen, in values and principles, moving to mutuality responsibility, and change in capacity and response. None of this assumes 'perfect change' but rather change that is significant, involving genuine growth.

The moral meaning builds on agape and its principles. There is in this no need for direction, covert other otherwise, no need to close off avenues as in the Browning approach. On the contrary, such is the strength of the agapeic base that the dynamic is one of opening *up* avenues, of the discovery of moral possibilities. This is only possible in the light of a faithfulness which provides constancy and a truthfulness which allows moral meaning to emerge in practice and through dialogue. Such truthfulness, as we have seen, can include references to the so called 'moral truths' of the church. However, they have no special privilege in the counselling situation. On the contrary, if we are take seriously the importance of the development of self and other critique then these moral truths will be subject to precisely such critique. Indeed they have to be if the counsellee is to develop moral meaning as a genuine agent. This should never cause a Christian moral counsellor to fear because it will involve a dialogic testing of any moral principles in the light of agape, as embodied in the counselling relationship, leading either to an understanding and strengthening of that principle or to the discovery of its misuse.

The core of this counselling is care and ethics which focus on transformation and response. Because they bring the counsellee back always to the moral claim of the self and the other it is in many respects a much tougher approach to ethics than the *a priori* view of Gordon Graham or Browning. It does not shirk the point that if the counsellee is to be true to her self then she has to make moral choices not simply in her life but about the moral meaning which she intends to base her life on. The negative element of that choice is to move away from the conditional moral world. The positive is to begin to move into a moral world which is both unconditional and responsive. The choice remains the counsellee's, the task of the counsellor is to keep before her the alternative, and to embody it in the counselling relationship.

Two things remain to be considered. Firstly the suspicion remains that there may be a time when there should be directive discipline, including the possibility of moral rebuke. This will be examined in the next chapter along with the broader issue of church discipline. The second is the vexed relationship between love and justice. We have seen this in terms of the personal detail but the broader issue will be examined in chapter eight.

### References
P. Avis, Eros and the Sacred (London: SPCK, 1989).

L. Baglow, Contemporary Christian Counselling (Alexandria: E.J. Dwyer, 1996).

B.A.C. Counselling: Some Questions Answered (British Association of Counselling).

F. Bridger and David Atkinson, Counselling in Context (London: Darton, Longman and Todd, 1998).

S. Burns, 'Abuse and forgiveness', Contact, 120, 1996, 8-14.

A. Campbell, Health as Liberation (Cleveland: Pilgrim Press, 1995).

D. Capps, Hope (Minneapolis: Fortress, 1995).

R. Carter, 'A taxonomy of objectives for professional education', Studies in Higher Education, 10(2).:135-149.

H. Cashman, Christianity and Child Sexual Abuse (London: SPCK, 1993).

W. Clebsch and C. Jaekle, Pastoral Care in Historical Perspective (New York: Aronson, 1975).

P. Couture and R. Hunter(eds.)., Pastoral Care and Social Conflict (Nashville: Abingdon, 1995).

J. Finch and J. Mason, Renegotiating Family Responsibilities (London: Routledge, 1993.

J. Fowler, Faith / Belief in R. Hunter (ed.). Dictionary of Pastoral Care and Counselling (Nashville: Abingdon, 1990).

C. Gilligan, In a different voice: psychological theory and womens development (Cambridge: Harvard University Press, 1982).

P. Halmos, The Faith of the Counsellors (London: Constable, 1964).

G. Kaufman, Shame: The Power of Caring (New York: Shenkman, 1980).

F. Lake, The Theology of Pastoral Counselling (Nottingham: Contact, 1980).

A. Lester, Hope in Pastoral Care and Counselling (Louisville: John Knox Press, 1995).

G. Meilander, The Theory and Practice of Virtue (Notre Dame: Notre Dame Press, 1984).

H. Nouwen, The Wounded Healer (London: Darton, Longman and Todd, 1994).

G. Outka, Agape: An Ethical Analysis (Newhaven: Yale University Press, 1972).

S. Robinson, 'Helping the Hopeless', Contact 127, 1998, 3-11.

Carl Rogers, Freedom to Learn (Columbus: Merrill, 1983).

L. Smedes, Stations on the Journey from Forgiveness to Hope in E. Worthington Jr. Dimensions of Forgiveness (Philadelphia: Templeton Foundation, 1998) 341-354.

C. Snyder, 'The past and possible futures of hope', Journal of Social and Clinical Psychology, vol.19, no.1, Spring 2000, 11-28.

J. Tangney, 'Humility: Theoretical perspectives, empirical findings and directions for future research', in Journal of Social and Clinical Psychology, Vol. 19 no. 1, Spring 2000, 70-82.

D. Tracy, Can virtue be taught? Education, virtue and the soul, in J. Astley and C. Crowder (eds.) Theological Perspective and Christian Formation (Grand Rapids: Grace wing, 1996).

D. van Deusen Hunsinger, Theology and Pastoral Counselling (Grand Rapids: Eerdmans, 1995).

L. Woodhead, 'Love and Justice', Studies in Christian Ethics, 5:1, 1992, 44-61.

# 7

## What a Shame

*We shall not cease from exploration*
*And the end of all our exploring*
*Will be to arrive where we started*
*And know the place for the first time*
*(T.S. Eliot, Little Gidding)*

## Case

Denise came to see the lay pastoral counsellor in the parish in a very agitated state. 'I really feel that I am beginning to lose control. It feels as if I am going out of my mind.'

Denise is 35 and had been married for 14 years, with three children. During that time she had been a faithful member of the church - prominent in many groups and on the church council. Most recently, she had developed the pastoral support group for those preparing for marriage and she was still the chair of the group. She took this seriously because the family was a very important value to her. She had joined a national group which supported family life and frequently organised presentations for this at parish and deanery level. Denise also took on some Open University teaching and research related to the family. At the same time she continued to be the centre of her own family, being responsible for the finances and the children.

Her research and work for the family support group led her to reflect on marriage, and faith really for the first time, with all the enthusiasm of someone pursing and directing her own learning. She read widely, and consulted groups in and outside the church. The discussions and the books read led her to begin to question some of the things she had held dear about the family. She began to open up her ideas and feelings to re-examination. At first this was not a problem. Over time, however, she began to feel 'out of touch with myself in the home'.

First, her home life became more pressured. The demands of three growing children, and one elderly ailing parent, were increasing and she found less and less time for herself. The result was that great parts of life were lived on automatic pilot, without any sense of the real value or meaning of what she was doing.

Secondly, she found herself growing apart from her husband. Robert was also active in the church and was spending a lot a time at work to push for promotion. Denise looked for support from him but could find none. She felt her identity was being eroded slowly but surely, along with an increasing sense of guilt that she was failing her family.

Thirdly, her research led to her to question not simply the role of the family and her role in it, but also her faith and how that related to her pressurised life. This too led her to feel ashamed and concerned about her life meaning and purpose.

Fourthly, she formed a friendship with another man. In an attempt to control some of the feelings that were eating away at her she took up aerobics and then marathon running. During the course of this she met a man who had also taken up marathon running in his early forties. Mark was not a Christian. Nonetheless, Denise found a real friendship developing with him. He was a kind and caring man, with experience and confidence and communicated a strong sense of empathy. There was a powerful element of sexuality in the relationship. Sexuality here was distinct from and did not involve sexual relations. It was rather a strong mutual awareness of each other's sexuality. It was a relationship which was great fun and based around their shared interest.

It raised further questions about sexuality in general, both in relation to her faith and to her experience. For her, faith had always seen sexuality as something to be guarded against. Committing adultery 'in her heart' was something she guarded against. In contrast to the strong sense of sexuality she received from this relationship, she and her husband were increasingly unaware of each other sexually.

Until very recently she could not have thought even about forming a friendship with someone of the opposite sex. Now she was enjoying it and actively guarding this increasingly precious part of her life.

Two weeks ago, Mark had asked her if she would like to go run with him in the New York Marathon. This would involve the two of them going together to New York. Without any reflection she had said yes. This was the answer to a dream, the pinnacle of all that training - and New York. Since then she had become anxious and depressed. She thought increasingly about the possibility of being in New York with Mark. He had even talked with her about the hotel in which they would stay (separate rooms) and the things they could do in the evenings in town. At the same time, she began to feel more and more ashamed and sneaky. She dare not tell her husband.

'I just don't know what has been happening to me, and I desperately need to talk this out with someone.'

Denise presented as someone in real crisis, with possible major emotional problems underlying this. However, the pattern of care which I have argued for so far seems inappropriate for her. Here is a problem which at first sight is much more ethically focused.

In chapter four Anna was having problems with her husband and these would have to be addressed, but the underlying psychological problems for her were so profound that it did not make sense to specify her problem simply in ethical terms. Moral meaning had to develop and grow out of the therapeutic relationship. In this situation we have something which involves the danger of making a decision that would go against the church's teaching. Moreover, though Denise had not gone to see the pastor himself she had gone to see the lay pastoral counsellor who is part of the same church and who had been part of the church's education programme, helping to direct the programme on families, including that for newly weds.

This would seem to be an obvious case for a clearer sense of ethical confrontation. In a similar case Hoffman suggested that the pastor should be ready if necessary to respond with moral rebuke - to actually offer a moral judgement and hence to attempt to direct the person to a particular course of action (Hoffman 1979). Clinebell argues for the importance of confrontation, with the minister using 'both the authority of his role and the "rational authority" derived from his competence as an ethical guide' (Clinebell 1983, 142).

Two major issues are raised by the case of Denise. Firstly, how will a strong moral confrontation affect the problems of shame? This will require reflection on healthy shame and its encouragement and an examination of other forms of shame. Secondly, this leads to questions about the moral authority of the pastor or pastoral counsellor and in particular about the relationship of the pastoral care to church discipline and the moral ethos of the church community. Finally, I will note problems associated with shamelessness.

## Shame, guilt and confrontation

Freud and Rogers, in different ways, saw the development of guilt as a principal cause of emotional problems. Freud saw the conscience itself as 'internalised aggression', incorporating the destructiveness of attempts at parental control. Such a negative conscience tends to outweigh the

possibility of a positive one. Underlying this was a negative view of humanity which required constraints to exist in peace. For Rogers it was just such
constraints which created the problems. Behind them were the imperatives
of conditional morality which disabled the person from becoming fully
functional. In different ways then both were concerned to deal with the
negative effects of guilt, exemplified in the toxic shame of Anna. However,
it is a short step from that to seeing guilt *per se* as negative. Hoffman suggests that we can distinguish between the conscious and unconscious levels of the conscience, each of which has a positive and negative aspect. It is
important both to confront the pathological conscience and also to confront the positive conscience, and enable the healthy guilt which can distinguish legitimate moral claims.

On the face of it the case of Denise involves a woman who is going
through a crisis and who is being held back by the healthy positive conscience. For Hoffman this means that ethical factors could be clearly
brought up by the counsellor and that this should even mean that the counsellor should be ready to give a moral rebuke. In the case of Denise such a
rebuke might well be there if she decides to go to New York.

However, simply to assert the possibility of healthy guilt does not mean that
there should the kind of overt moral direction which Hoffmann ultimately
advocates. In recent years the issue of guilt and shame has been researched
more widely. It leads to questions about just how healthy guilt or shame might
be addressed or enabled and also about whether the simple distinction between
two kinds of guilt or shame is tenable (see Fowler 1996, chap.6).

In summing this up, Fowler begins by distinguishing guilt from shame.
Guilt is defined as self judgement which arises from a particular act. Hence,
guilt can distinguish the act from the self and any question of the worth of
the self. One may see guilt as an honest self condemnation based upon
one's view of what makes an act ethically proper or not. Such guilt can easily be addressed by the repentance, apology and some form of restitution.
Shame is rather something which affects one's sense of the whole person.
Hence, as Lewis notes, there is greater bodily awareness in shame, the sense
of the self revealed to the other (Lewis 1971, p. 34), and of the sense of the
failure of the self, leading to embarrassment, humiliation, or disgrace.

Fowler goes on to distinguish a spectrum of shame involving:
Healthy shame;
Toxic shame (see chapter four)
Perfectionist shame;
Shamelessness;

Shame due to enforced minority status;

Healthy shame, perfectionist shame and shamelessness will be examined in this chapter and the shame of enforced minority status in the next.

## Healthy Shame

Schneider distinguishes two aspect of this shame - *discretionary shame* and *disgrace shame*.

Shame as discretion has a long history. It evolved to maintain the bonds in the communities of which the person is a part. It involves tact and sensitivity to others, including respect for the values which are shared in the community or network of relationships. Hence this shame acts as a protector of the self worth in relation to the community. Such shame is anticipatory and enables the person to remain alive to the different ways in which potential actions, situations or relationships might bring the pain of shame. Hence, the Talmud can speak in a positive light of this sense of shame,

'A sense of shame is a lovely sign in a man. Whoever has a sense of shame will not sin so quickly; but whoever has no sense of shame in his visage, his father surely never stood on Mount Sinai' (Nedarim, fol. 20a).

Disgrace shame involves the public awareness of some disconcerting fact or quality. It disrupts and disappoints and so makes the person feel a painful self consciousness. It is not a negative phenomenon not least because as Schneider argues it 'is the immediate awareness that who we are is not who we want to be. It is the emotional price to pay for our encounter with the discrepancy between our ideals and our reality' (Schneider 1990, 1162).

Together, these form healthy shame and provide a protection for the identity of the person. It may be argued that the healthy person does not need this kind of protection, and that protection is really about avoiding change and growth. However, Schneider argues that shame actually protects the process of growth towards integrity. It provides a space for the person to draw back and rehearse the various ways in which the self might relate to practice. Schneider suggests a growth which is not simply about the person disclosing herself but rather also about moments of concealing, precisely because of the sense of shame:

'At heart, human meetings and relations are always simultaneously disclosing and concealing. The sense of shame involves respect for the reality of our separateness and the space that is there between us. Language both discloses and covers in all encounters. The sense of shame implies respect for this depth and resonance of human meeting' (Schneider ibid.).

Such healthy shame emerges through development in childhood and forms the basis of conscience.

It is tempting to see this form of shame as something quite different from the toxic shame previously referred to and as something which can simply be worked through with reference to clear views of morality and ethical meaning. Awareness of healthy shame is only possible in the light of agape. The person cannot begin to understand her shame, feel the sense of something wrong other than in the light of a social environment which enables her to see herself truly and in terms of her relationship to the others and to herself. Van deusen Hunsinger notes this in relationship to Barth's theology, and the view that 'we can finally see and understand our sin only in light of Jesus Christ. Just as we cannot fully appreciate the magnitude of our sin until it is forgiven sin (that is, sin seen in the light of Jesus Christ), so also we cannot know the depths of our true and objective shame unless we know it already to have been taken from us' (van deusen Hunsinger 1995, 198).

Secondly, there is a danger that healthy shame could be characterised in terms of an awareness of the moral norms of the community. By this I mean norms which are not thought through or critically held and which lead to a sense of automatic shame if they are not adhered to.

There is, of course, less and less evidence of such community moral norms. More importantly though adherence to such moral norms cannot be assumed even within small communities. For many people even community norms are not reflected on until there is a crisis and this leads not to a return to what has been held but rather a testing of the values which the person associates with that community. Testing those norms in the light of practical issues and other narratives begins to lead to moral awareness and, with that, to healthy shame. The dynamic is thus not a return to norm but rather a discovery of moral meaning through critical conversation with 'the norm'.

### Denise's narrative

Denise's story seemed to be one which exemplified healthy shame. On the face of it she was having a hard time, including sleepless nights, precisely because she was faced with the possibility of entering an immoral relationship, which could result in the break up of her marriage and negative effects upon her children.

As she reflected on her relational network things became less clear. Her relationship with herself had become more and more confusing. She had lost any sense of meaning.

Reflecting on her family, it became clear that her children were very important to her. Initially she was keen to talk about their success at school and signalled how proud she was of them. The counsellor encouraged her to look below this level of moral meaning which she was trying to present, and talk more about them as people. After a long reflection, she commented on her surprise at how powerful her feelings were for her children, and how she had not often simply thought about them as people.

Reflection on her husband proved even more difficult. She commented on how as she thought about him she found it hard to see his face. To begin to reach out to him she had to think back to the first times together and the marriage ceremony itself. Part of the counsellor's task here was to help her work through projections she was placing on the husband, and begin to develop empathy.

Denise's life with the church had been very important since leaving university. At the beginning there had been the desire to reclaim the student Christian buzz, something both she and her husband were involved in. This had developed as Denise took on more responsibilities in the church and her identity began to be defined in terms of the church community. She had seen members come and go, fall in and fall out of the community, and she became determined to provide an example of faithfulness - to be there for the community whatever.

That identity and faithfulness was now being questioned through both her relationship with Mark, providing a very different identity outside the church, and by her research into family life.

The narrative then was already showing a number of conflicts emerging in the values which her different relationships represented, leading to a dialogue which might begin to clarify those values and the underlying issues.

In one sense this was calling her back to the several different covenants to which she had committed herself. However, the conflicts which were emerging showed that she would have to begin to reassess those covenants and any contracts which had developed from them. This would involve an attempt both to see what values those relationships were built upon and to see what claims those relationships now had upon her.

This was crucially a learning situation to examine her pastoral and moral world and why that meaning was not holding together.

In working through the different dialogues two major factors emerged. Firstly, it became clear that there was a key conflict between a perfectionist shame and the narrative of mutuality which Mark had brought into her life. Secondly, Denise was going through an important time of transition between what Fowler sees as stages of faith. Both of these conflicts demanded that the counsellor use the person centred approach outlined in the previous chapters.

## Perfectionist shame

As Fowler notes, the different 'categories of shame' are really a spectrum. We are all somewhere on this spectrum. For Denise, perfectionist shame was very much behind her narrative. This involved seeking to gain approval and worth through the highest achievement, with shame arising over failure to achieve. Fowler writes,

'In perfectionist shame as in all distortion shame experiences ... there is a significant measure of suppression of access to the place of truth in the heart and soul of the ones who bear it. In order to gain the approval and affirmation of the people the young child most depends upon, he focuses attention upon meeting the program, values and behaviours they require. This approval, so indispensable to the child's sense of worth, comes at great cost. The child pays the price for their approval and esteem in neglect of his own evaluation of experiences and his developing sense of inner guidance and desire' (Fowler 1996, 114).

Much so called burnout in later years is caused by this life script of achievement which is set down by family and often social groups such as school. The script is often formed in earliest years, with parents who are uncertain of how to interact with the child, thus relying on rules and procedure and missing a sense of the presence and needs of the child. The result is a failure in a sense of trust in the child's relation with the parent and the need to prove herself acceptable through meeting the standards set by the parent.

For Denise this script was reinforced by the academic pressure leading to a sense of failure in her getting a good 2:1 at University. It was also reinforced by the church, not least in her perception of the need to maintain the very best family - which included high achieving children. Hence, her first concern in reflecting on her children had not been them but rather the achievement which they represented, not least of her as a parent. Even her roles in the church were fuelled by the need to make her mark on the matter of family theology. There was also a strong sense of this perfectionism in her marathon running. She had to keep up a high performance and wanted to achieve in New York.

At various points in the sessions Denise began to express anger at the counsellor when he enabled her reflection on the family, partly because she felt shame at the though that she had failed the family. She recognised that she and her husband were drifting apart and that the friendship with Mark might create a permanent rift. She felt that she was responsible for the possible break down and not achieving the best possible success for her family. At one point she protested that the counsellor was making her feel so ashamed, viewing him as the root of the shame, and extension of the church's judgement.

With careful reflection he was able to help her see the way in which shame had grown and those who had reinforced this shame, and begin to work her way towards returning that shame to its origins.

Ironically, at the same time as she experienced the perfectionist shame, she was aware that her relationship with Mark had already begun to eat away at this shame. He brought a sense of humour to his relationship with Denise which was able to gently tease her about the perfectionist script and cut away at its effects. She did not feel ashamed with him and didn't worry about any sense of failure. She was expressing the desire to please herself with him and not simply others. However, the reflection with Mark had been in a social vacuum. She felt safe to explore this side of her life both because of him and because it was away from the part of her life which still seemed to demand so much of her. The result was that she was beginning to face up to the effects of the script, something which demanded changing her relationship with parents, church and family, including her parents.

The counsellor was able to help Denise explore both her relationship with Mark and the part that perfectionist shame played in her life. This led to further awareness of conflict, not least a sense of anger at Mark that he should be causing her to question her secure life meaning. She spoke of being torn in two and losing any sense of integrity, but being unable to go back to where she was. It became clear that Denise was experiencing a period of transition.

### Transition

As Bridges has noted of important times of transition, these involve:
- disengagement;
- disidenification;
- disenchantment;
- disorientation (Bridges 1980).

Extreme experiences of the first of these include death or divorce. For Denise there was a strong sense that almost quietly she had been disengaging from her husband. They spent less time together, with a less focused life together. He had become more and more distant.

This had further led her to begin to break away from relationships - not least in the church which had up to that point been the ones which defined her. Giving up the chair of the family support group especially was an important move.

Disidentification was experienced in the ways in which she no longer 'felt like herself'. As she left roles or changed her view of roles she lost what had been seen as essential markers of her identity. Without these markers she was struggling to find herself.

Disenchantment was there throughout the whole process. The family for instance was no longer seen as a critical value to be fought for, as she re-examined it. Even her view of God was beginning to change in a scary way. God for her was very much a cognitive and conditional character, who reinforced the sense of perfectionism. Now he was appearing more human and more open, but with that she feared a loss of commitment. With disenchantment came a sense of loss and confusion.

Denise was simply losing her sense of direction. Bridges writes of entering the 'neutral zone'. This is experienced precisely as a time 'out of ordinary time'. As Kegan notes, there is a real sense that the person is out of their mind - out of the life meaning that is familiar to them (Kegan 1982). Fowler notes that transitions seen in terms of faith, in it broadest sense, have the quality of the 'dark night of the soul'.

The core part of Denise's transition was from a script which others had set, often unconsciously, and which she had accepted as from them, to one which she would control and which would involve meaning and value for which she had taken responsibility. This is well summed up in terms of a movement between Fowler's stages of faith.

Denise broadly inhabited the fourth of these stages - *individuative/reflective* faith. This is one involving a deepening of self-awareness and the taking of responsibility for values which are integrated into an ideology. Identity is still very much found in the larger group. Those in this stage tend to be drawn to unambiguous teachings - especially in religious faith. At the same time, such persons are 'often unaware of the sharp limits of their empathy and their abilities to construct and identify with the interior feelings and processes of others' (Fowler 1996, 64). There tends to be a confidence in their thinking. Hence, Denise was very clear about her role and very confident in the whole theology family approach. Without attention to the unconscious processes which attend such faith it is easy for emotional burn-out to occur, with the person concentrating on managing the self and its boundaries.

This was very much the case with Denise. She had had a clear sense of identity and purpose, with several different relationships contributing towards this. This was built around communities with tight boundaries. However, Denise had little awareness of the people who formed those relationships. Moreover, she had experienced overload with the work on Open University and the family, and became more aware of the ambiguities not simply in the cognitive realm but also the experiential realm. This was the beginning of a mature sense of empathy which involved awareness of the cognitive, affective and somatic self, with a move from a largely cognitive way of thinking to a more profound awareness of feelings and of the physical environment.

Denise was then very much in between *Individuative /Reflective faith* and *Conjunctive faith*. Conjunctive faith involves a recognition that truth has to be approached from many different perspectives. This faith holds the tensions between the different perspectives, refusing to collapse them into any one. As Fowler notes, such faith comes to terms with paradoxes and ambiguities. It has an 'epistemological humility' which clearly accepts that it cannot simply find truth through analysis of data or symbols, and thus remains open to both.

Denise found herself thoroughly between these faiths. She was developing empathy and yet very much blocked in her perception of her husband. Indeed, her husband had become in many ways the object of some of her projections. Typical of the perfectionist shame development she was angry at her husband, seeing him as a major source of her problems, and as representing the source of shame in the perfectionist sense. She had expressed anger to him in different ways - through sarcasm and through withdrawing love. She had not however, begun to own that anger and to look at the seat of that anger, or begun to articulate that anger and reach some kind of conclusion. Hence, she was up to this point unable to share with him.

She had begun to see the possibility of what Fowler refers to as healthy narcissism of mid-life, a sense of self care (Fowler 1996, 64). But this was still wrapped up in the world, with no connections made to family or church. She was also taking more responsibility for thinking and the integration of thought, and affective and cognitive dialogues were being played out.

All told the balance sheet was fruitfully ambiguous. It involved a great deal of growth, and a real step towards a new way of relating and thinking. It also involved some anger and blockages which threatened to subvert the whole response if they were not brought through to be part of the whole.

## Response

To simply stress the 'moral agenda' from the perspective of norms and values would have done two things - reinforced the perfectionist shame, and prevented her from making the transition. Transition, as Poling notes, demands a holding environment, the development of new meaning and hope and the letting go of the old, giving rise to a sense of bereavement (Poling 1991, 113). To do that it was important to give her the space and power to gain confidence in her new found spirituality and autonomy of thinking, and also to allow her to explore more fully the new perspectives on moral meaning which had to replace the old perfectionist approach and explore the healthy shame which was still very apparent in various ways. It is precisely the reflection 'in community' that would enable her to effect the transition but still retain her identity. Fowler refers to one person in transition who puts it this way:

' "There is an identity beneath all the belief systems that have dissolved...There is something undeniably 'me' present, constituted by the pain as well as the denial of the pain. And the revisioning generates assurance of this identity at the very same time as it threatens it" ' (Fowler 1996, 118).

The very reflectivity generates the knowledge of the self. The presence of the other demonstrates hope and continuity for the self. None of this necessarily takes the pain of the experience away, but rather enables meaning to be found in that experience. In examining this the counsellor was enabling Denise to develop further her identity.

- Truth work then enabled Denise to examine her feelings and begin to see how she perceived her husband and where the feelings about her husband were coming from. It enabled her to get her feelings for Mark into perspective. She could see how important he had been, and yet her attraction to him was partly simply the discovery of somatic awareness which she had kept so well controlled in the past, partly as a result of her own family narrative. The counsellor helped her to articulate that narrative and to begin to critique it.

- The faith, value work and clarification then led to the Denise's reflection on her faith and the church's view of the family. This gradually began to highlight various things. Firstly, her view of God was being radically challenged. He had been a very demanding God who expected her to strive for perfection. He was also a God who demanded careful control of sexuality, which for her had meant a negative view of the body and sexual fulfilment. The counsellor helped Denise to focus on the conflict emerging between that view of

God and the narrative of Mark. The resulting dialogue began to bring together the strong affective and somatic elements of her relationship with Mark into her faith world, rather than seeing them as hermetically sealed off. In turn this caused her to think and feel through her view of God. The result was the beginnings of a radical change in her view of God, as someone who accepted her for herself and who rejoiced in the material and physical. None of this meant a shift to permissive morals but rather a broadening in her spiritual awareness.

Secondly, she began to reflect on the family. 'I used to think that the family was all important, a central value in itself, the end to which I worked. Then I began to see that the family was not an end in itself.' It was only important in so far as it actually embodied something of real love, only important in so far as it reached out, embodying inclusivity.

This growing awareness of the inclusive family had set up a tension with the felt need to succeed as parent and wife, and Denise needed to reflect through the Christian view of the family. She and the pastoral counsellor reflected on the family not as an end in itself but as a means to the end of broader values - not least community and freedom. Hence, the family is subordinate to higher commitment (ref. Mark 3: 31 -5, Luke 14: 26).

Far from providing a simple call back to the value of family and marriage, this helped Denise to begin to review what marriage was about and what it meant to bring life to the family. It helped her move away from the perfectionist view of the family and thus of holding together at all costs to a view of her family and how it might embody Christian spirituality. This enabled her to critique her husband's approach and also be open to a critique of her approach to family life.

Thirdly, Denise began to reflect on her position in the church and the response of the church. Increasingly, she felt that there was a difference between how the other members of the church felt about marriage and family. She saw them as being quite legalistic and with a concern for family as a primary value. Hence, she was very concerned about how they would respond - fearing the reassertion of negative shame. The counsellor encouraged her to check this perception out. Was it true that all felt the same? Had she listened to the different narratives of the family in the church? Did she know of many members who were divorced etc.? Further reflection led Denise to conclude that she did not know what most of them felt or believed about the family. She had been projecting on to the church, as also on to God, her perfectionist shame. This meant that whatever she decided to do she would have to think and pray things through with the people who she knew in the community.

- Denise reflected on the question of responsibility and dependency. She noted the pattern of family life and the way in which she ended up without space and felt that the family depended upon her. She felt unable to let go of the family, yet also felt that she wanted to be free from them. The counsellor helped to her to rehearse the negotiation of responsibility within the family, with each of the members, further enabling the development of moral identity.
- Finally, she began to look at the embodiment of her moral meaning. The conclusion was clear - that she was growing, that this was good, and that the next stage of the growth had to be to integrate her empathy and broader spiritual awareness into her family life. If she felt that way she then had to both reinforce the growing awareness and also to test out the right relationships, including identifying the moral claims of her relational network. This was a real development in integrity for her. She wanted a both/and ethic; to grasp and retain the increased awareness and work through shalom.

Hence, she decided to do several things:

1. To go to New York, but that this should include her husband and children on the trip. In her previous marathon her husband had been too busy, and the children weren't able to come. She had been affirmed in that experience, but felt guilty that she was gratifying herself. This time she wanted the family to be there together and to affirm her and each other. Luckily there turned out to be no constraints. This was a good start in bringing the family together and for Denise to begin to articulate her needs to them.

2. To work with Bob. Denise realised she would have to re-negotiate the 'contract' of her marriage. It meant that she had to begin to assert her idea and feelings and begin to enable dialogue. At first, she felt that this might need the help of Relate. In fact, as they talked more constructively about different aspects of the family life, so they began to develop the contract themselves. This meant restarting their relationship from a very different place, and working through the important values.

This also meant working through the secrecy with which she had surrounded her relationship with Mark. This was something which had been kept in place partly by her affect shame and her group dependant view of faith.

3. To face the children. They too needed to be challenged to take responsibility within the family. Denise's approach to family life had meant that

they were not fully participants in family life. Things had been done for them and they had not had to take responsibility. As part of the new deal they began to participate and take responsibility.

4. To face the church members, including the pastor. Denise had a view of the pastor as someone who saw it as his task to provide moral guidance and that he would be affronted to have this failure before him. She needed to approach him and work through where he was and assert her view of a theological narrative that was rich and varied. She felt that he needed to know that she was not buying in to an off the peg view of marriage and that the kind of honesty and integrity that were being developed might need his help.

5. To face Mark. Denise had to let go of several narratives, not least the female perfection one. She also had to let go of the unformed narratives which had been gathering around Mark. She had valued his openness and the sense of affect atunement he brought to her life, and it was important to be clear about that. It was also important to fully articulate the narrative around Mark and as she did this two things emerged. Firstly, part of her view of Mark involved magical thinking, the possibility that he would take her away from all the problems which were piling up, he would take her through all this without pain. This showed that she had not really begun to work to an empathic view of Mark. Denise was only able to come to this conclusion through articulating her hope and fears surrounding Mark. Secondly, this led her to a testing of Mark's narrative, and a dialogue with him which clarified just where each was coming from. From that dialogue it was clear that whilst each was giving good support to the other neither had really thought through the implications of their friendship, thus allowing boundaries to be re-negotiated.

None of this meant that she would necessarily stay in the marriage. It did mean that she took seriously and worked through the basic implications of her commitment. There was real growth and the formation of new contract in all of relationships enabling her to move to a new ethic which both took on the greater spiritual awareness and also looked to the development of shalom.

In the context of this growth the idea of moral rebuke grows less clear.

## Counselling, Care and Discipline

Lurking behind the counsellor is the wider church community, and with that many questions about continuity and integrity. How can the pastor or anyone involved in the education of the ethical meaning in the church not raise and expound the very principles which she proclaims in the pulpit? Where is the integrity if the pastor simply allows the person to think what they want? This raises questions about community discipline and the moral role of the pastor or pastoral counsellor.

## Discipline

Stephen Pattison notes how the past two decades have seen a backlash against the so called permissive approach to counselling and care (Pattison 1988, Chap 4). This has involved a number of concerns, mostly around purpose and identity. Church communities have been decreasing in size and increasingly relying upon more committed core members. Such 'remnant' churches are no longer simply the repository of general civic virtues but are increasingly distinctive from wider society.

At the centre of the church is a growing awareness of discipleship based upon an awareness of its distinctive aims and mission. Such discipleship demands discipline. In Henry Nouwen's words,

'Discipline and discipleship cannot be separated. Without discipline discipleship is little more than hero worship or fadism; without discipleship discipline easily becomes a form of emulation or self assertion...They strengthen and deepen each other' (Nouwen *et al.* 1984, 90).

In the concern for clear Christian identity there are dangers. Firstly, amongst some writers there is the assumption that such identity is based upon clear norms and values and that the role of discipline is to maintain these. Hence, Browning writes,

'Discipline is first of all a matter of deeply implanting within the character of a people the basic norms, patterns, values and sensibilities that govern the culture of the group' (Browning 1976, 59). Such a view of community seems to assume that the particular norms, values and practices are already clear and that the tasks of the community is simply to transmit these to the members. The very term 'implant' also suggests a passive community which will act as the soil for these norms. As we have seen this ignores the importance of reflection and dialogue in developing the broad moral meaning into the particular moral rules and procedures.

Secondly, there is the danger of using discipline as simply a means for the maintenance of community. In this sense discipline can be used to maintain the boundaries of community and define identity in negative terms over against the wider community. This has the danger of polarising the Christian identity and not being able to see the sameness as well as the difference with other communities. Moreover, it runs the danger of losing the inclusivity of the community when boundary maintenance takes priority.

Thirdly, there is the danger of discipline not arising from the core relationships, but seen as something quite separate.

The final danger is of discipline becoming a means of judgement and control. The calls for the pastor or counsellor to have integrity between the pulpit and pastoral care are often built upon moral panic which wants to maintain moral control within the church and which sees this control as essential to identity. At the base of this is a fear of loss of identity. Such a fear in turn leads to a polarised view of the situation. The community has to be controlled, with clear values that all adhere to, and the individual pastoral work is too liberal, with no real moral substance.

In the light of an agapeic analysis this is seen to be a false picture. The practice of agapeic counselling involves clear discipline in terms of:

Building the interpersonal bridge;

Establishing the contract;

Clarifying values;

Identifying and negotiation of responsibilities;

Embodying plans in the light of constraints and possibilities.

This discipline is:

Person centred, calling individuals to take responsibility for their own learning and development;

Relation / spiritual centred, calling for an awareness of others. At the centre of this is God;

Morally centred, calling for a response to others, taking responsibility for others;

Practice centred, enabling practice and the regular reflection on practice.

This is a far more powerful discipline than simply that of guidance about moral principles - not least because it focuses upon the reflection on the truth of any situation and relationship and on the responsibility of the person to respond to that truth.

Far from being the opposite of the community, this is the basis of Christian approach to community, a community built upon:

- Ensuring that the community takes responsibility for reflection on and articulation of its narrative. The annual church planning weekend is not just about keeping the church 'maintained' but about revisiting the spirituality and purpose of the church, and how the church in all its aspects reflects (or not) the community God calls us to. This process also begins to establish the particular expectations of the community and to build relationships between the members.

- Articulating the community narrative beyond the group. As noted in chapter three such articulation is critical in clarifying meaning and developing community identity.
- The articulation of the narrative to God in prayer and in worship. The whole gamut of theses dialogues is contained in worship, including:
  Articulating and reflection on the gospel narrative;
  Value clarification;
  Reflection on different stakeholders in the wider community, not least through prayer;
  Openness to future possibility and collaborative strategies.

In all this, discipline is basically about keeping the community relation centred, and focusing on mutual responsibility and response. Jean Vanier notes the importance of each person feeling that they are responsible for the whole community. 'Each person in a community' writes Vanier 'is responsible for its fidelity - not just its head.' He recalls the words of the mother abbess of the sisters of Rueil spoken to each new sister,

'Receive this cross. It is a sign that you belong to God at the heart of your community. From now on the community is yours. And you are responsible, with us, for its fidelity' (Vanier 1979, 38).

The opposite of this is the dynamic, highlighted by Wesley Carr, of projecting responsibility on to the figure of the pastor (Carr 1989). The pastor then becomes the convenient figure of blame if things go wrong.

The development of mutual responsibility requires both a framework of expectation which will undergird practice and also the space which allows for reflection and the development of spiritual awareness in and outside the group. It is a positive view of discipline and brings together self and group discipline (Oden 1984; Duffy 1983). Pattison extols a similar positive view arguing that it brings together care and control. The term control, however, is problematic. Its logic is that of power used to maintain order. The logic of agape is quite the reverse, of order emerging through dialogue, reflective process and collaborative activity - focused once more on the central values of freedom, community and equality. Neither integrity nor shalom can be imposed.

In this light there need be no incongruity between the way in which the Christian community develops its positive discipline and the way in which the counsellee develops hers. There is no need to bracket principles and values just for the care relationship.

## Moral Rebuke

A number of writers are happy to support this positive non judgmental approach and still wish to have for extreme moments the possibility of moral rebuke, or 'hot seat confrontation'. If all else fails, there should be the possibility of confronting the person with a moral judgement on her behaviour (Hoffman 1979). Underwood argues that there will be a grace in judgement. The communication of moral judgement can actually enable the person to see what she is doing.

However, when we try to pin these ideas down things become less clear. When would a moral rebuke actually be called for? Hoffman suggests that in case of a wife deserting her family he was prepared to use such a rebuke. In the end he informs us that he did not have to. Moral rebuke thinking then seems to be focusing on the kind of extreme cases so beloved by ethicists of yore. But what is a reasonable case for this thundering rebuke? What are the criteria for administering it and what might it actually involve? Is it a matter of warning against the effects of the consequences of certain behaviour? Is it a clear statement that the person or action in question is immoral? The implication is that moral rebuke is not to judge but to bring the person to her senses. In which case the rebuke is being used instrumentally rather than just as moral judgement in its own right.

Such a use of moral rebuke has two dangers. Firstly, it is not clear that a moral rebuke would actually help the person to reflect more clearly and carefully about their moral decision. It is far more likely to focus on negative shame, and thus to take away from responsibility for moral thinking. The pedagogy of the agapeic process does precisely this, always challenging the person to think again and look beyond their perception of the situation. Secondly, the rebuke may be an instrument of control, to stop the person doing something. Not only does this go against the dynamic of agape, it also assumes an *a priori* moral meaning, and that this meaning is being presented by a responsible person.

If, however, the aim is to enable the person look at consequences then it is hard to see how moral rebuke is the most effective way of doing this. This falls under the very clear reflective confrontation which enables the person to work at the different options in the light of the moral dialogue which has been progressing throughout the counselling relationship. This is a confrontation which has far more power than the moral rebuke. Firstly, it emerges from the contract. As such it calls the person back to the moral meaning which has been developed. Secondly, it confronts the person with the call to integrity. There is nowhere to hide and no way of denying the truth as it emerges about the past, present and future, in the light of empathic reflection. Thirdly, it leads to a reflection which is far more than simply examining the consequences of actions. For Denise there was reflection on all possible options, including the negative effects of divorce on the children, but also the negative effects of staying as things were. Perhaps more importantly the agapeic approach looks at these in the light of shalom - a radically different perspective which focuses on the ways in which justice and peace can be effectively created.

### Pastor or counsellor

Several writers, as noted in chapter one, feel that it is important to distinguish the roles of pastor and counsellor. At least this could then allow the pastor to retain a role which includes moral authority. However, even this distinction causes difficulties. Firstly, in the attempt to make the roles different I noted in chapter one that the result was the build up of a false dichotomy. Counselling was caricatured to make it appear not simply value neutral but valueless, ignoring its complexities and the clear concern for value. Secondly, if we accept the paradigm of agape in pastoral care and ethics, there is nothing to suggest that the basic dynamic shared by pastor and counsellor, and for that matter spiritual director should not be the same. It is the same concern for the freedom and the formation of moral meaning in dialogue. The difference would be the context or intention of the particular relationship. The counsellor begins from the crisis experienced by the counsellee and forms a contract of care. The spiritual director begins from the desire to build up life meaning or spiritual discipline, and from this moves into the process of nurturing empathy. This in turn will lock into the historic narrative of the church. A different kind of contract will then be made. When it comes to the pastor, it is perhaps not clear where she might begin, partly mirroring a lack of clarity about the definition of pastor. It can be said, however, that the pastor will be in the role of offering some kind of leadership and thus will be someone who has been given authority by the church. Precisely because of that authority role the pastor needs to take even greater care as to how she uses the power she has or the power she is perceived to have. The need to make a contract of care from the outset becomes critical in a relationship which has such an imbalance of power that it engenders feelings of shame, a dynamic which applies to counsellors and even more to pastors. Scheff and Ratzinger write of the double burden of shame in caring situations where the person reveals inner most secrets often to a stranger. Where any interpretation is involved there is moral judgement implied, exposing the person's flaws, deficiencies and failures before an other (Scheff and Ratzinger 1991, p. 135). The therapist/carer, moreover, is one who does not reveal such a level of her thoughts and who is seen as the wise and balanced one over against the weak and dependant other (Thompson 1996, 315). Whilst the pastor may be more familiar to the person, the problem of the power imbalance remains. Like the therapist the pastor will inevitably reawaken a sense of shame and often this will be one of shame about shame.

Of equal importance is the shame also there for the pastor or counsellor. For the counsellor there is the shame involved in the counsellee resisting improvement (Thompson 1996, 316). The competence of the therapist is then called into question. For the pastor there is the possibility of even more profound shame, with the expectations that her community might have of her and her own felt need to ensure that the person does live according to the ethical code of the community.

Firstly, this demands a careful response from the pastor that will enable the person to move that shame. The dynamic is about developing mutuality and enabling the person to learn. Secondly, the pastor herself has to be aware of her own shame factors and how the relationships affect her. Simply because she has been placed in a position of authority does not mean that her response will not be distorted by shame. It is precisely the agapeic dynamic which will enable the pastor's own position to be tested, leading to a degree of mutuality. Moral meaning will once more emerge through the relationship.

The counsellor will doubtless share the moral views of the church. For Christian counsellees these will be of concern. They are part of their life meaning, implicitly or explicitly, and of will naturally be part of the reflective process. However, such data is not especially privileged, and has no particular authority apart from the relationship. The counselling relationship handles all meaning, moral and spiritual in a way which enables both awareness of the meaning, and what lies behind, and the capacity to handle that meaning critically, to test it. It is essential that such data be thought and felt through in a critical fashion. To attempt to assert the 'moral authority' of the counsellor or pastor in such a way as to view him as central keeper of community moral meaning is precisely to discourage critical dialogue. Such critical dialogue in fact establishes a relational authority, based above all on trust and not on 'right ideas'.

Precisely the same dynamic applies to the non Christian counsellees. They too can be counselled in a way which enables the development of critical thinking and feeling. Within that relationship this will also lead to a review of spiritual meaning, life meaning as distinct from religious meaning. This in turn may lead to cognitive reflection on the narratives which the counsellor holds. Once more such narratives are open to critical reflection. Within that dynamic, they have the freedom then to explore the spiritual meaning embodied by the pastoral counsellor and possibly discover more about and respond to God.

## Shamelessness

### Case

*A 15 year old boy, John, who had been going to church services in a housing estate church plant for several months was found taking money from the collection. The pastor did not want to bring in the police and said that he would not if the John went on a regular basis for six months to the pastoral counsellor.*

*It emerged that he was being brought up in an abusive family and that he did not see anything wrong in stealing. He tried to justify this. At first he argued that he had no real income and thus was forced to turn to this. Then he argued that this was the moral norm on the estate. If you left your beer down on the table for a minute it was gone. It was almost a matter of honour that it should go.*

*When the counsellor began to quiz him about how he could justify this John came up with a number of statements to justify the action. No-one would miss the money. It didn't actually belong to people but to an organisation and there was no real deprivation involved. His need was greater. If he didn't get cigarettes he would not be able to survive another night with his mother. He was doing it for others.*

Here was surely a good example of how one should move beyond the basic person centred approach and begin to be morally directive. The child had had no guidance and not even a basic sense of moral meaning. The resulting shamelessness grew out of early family relationships. Fowler notes the lack of parental mirroring which gives the growing child a sense of the self. This mirroring involves an 'affective tuning' in which the child is assured of the presence of the parent there just for her. In effect, this gets her used to the presence of the concerned other and helps her to experience empathy, the fact that the other can understand and accept her. This acts as the basis of developing empathic feeling in the child herself. When such lack of affective tuning is combined with abuse or neglect the lack of empathy can be combined with a strong anger. As Fowler puts it,

'Such children can develop hardened hearts; they can lack *conscience* (*con*, meaning "with"; *scientia* meaning "ways of knowing"; *conscience*, a "feeling or knowing with others"). In its hardened and extreme forms we are speaking here of the sociopathic personality. This is the person who so lacks empathy and compassion, who has such measureless rage that he can injure or destroy others with little feelings of remorse, guilt or shame' (Fowler 1996, 127).

Shamelessness then is a failure to engage the discretionary and disgrace shame - both based upon the empathic awareness of others. Whereas the perfectionist shame attempted to make up for that lack by the trying to elicit positive response from the other through high achievement, shamelessness either leads to a listless conformity, or a distortion of power, tending to see others as means not ends to taking power. The attempt to bring out the moral agenda with such people is not easy.

Nonetheless, even though there was little conventional morality there, the boy did try to justify himself. There was a rudimentary form of moral identity even if it simply was one which was looking to put himself in a good light. He clearly did want to be seen as having a moral reason for doing what he did. John then already had some sense of moral reputation, and this was possible to build on and develop.

For others there is the real danger of mimicking the moral agenda. The sociopath may try to manipulate and work on the guilt of the counsellor, play the moral game well, trying to provide the values wanted, not simply to please the other but rather to gain power in some way.

The critical thing for the counsellor therefore was to work hard building up of the conscience, not least through empathic awareness of the others in his life. Over a long time this involved John becoming used to the faithfulness of the counsellor. It is precisely this bridge which forms the basis of a long term build up of spiritual meaning and moral meaning. A core part of this relationship was reality testing - for instance, confronting John with the self defeating nature of his reality-denying nature. The consequences of raiding the collection could be the loss of the only community which has given him respite. The ultimate consequences of such behaviour might be the loss of liberty. The more he looked at such consequences, the more the counsellor enabled him to focus on what was important to him. This was critical because much of the culture in which he operated saw the idea of holding values as a sign of weakness. The counsellor also helped him to focus on the ways in which his values contrasted with his irresponsible behaviour. This helped him to begin to take responsibility for criticising his own moral views. 'Oh I know that in the end it doesn't achieve anything, but sometimes I just think I have to'. This helped the counsellee, through cognitive techniques, to focus on the underlying beliefs which made him feel obliged to steal, using cognitive techniques. Several conflicting values emerged which provided rich ground for dialogue, including independence, a strong sense of fairness, and a concern for security, something which was often translated into money.

Money made him feel more secure - though not for long. It meant that he could buy cigarettes and be acceptable - one of the group. The counsellor tested out the reality of this security. It did not last long and did not feel good. All this enabled John to chip away at the beliefs which had held his world together.

The counsellor was then able to help John explore alternative ways of finding and feeling self worth. This involved the giving of responsibility to him, enabling him to participate in community in such a way that he was genuinely needed and appreciated. Clinebell notes that simply to accept someone whatever he did - permissiveness - tends to make the counsellee feel that the counsellor is actually indifferent to them, something which further hurts the lack of self esteem (Clinebell 1983, chap 6). The counsellor then looked to enable the development of community and of a role which was prized and which would be the basis of learning a new moral meaning. Part of this was to set targets which would be achievable and which would raise self esteem. For John that included working on academic achievement, starting with GCSEs. This did two things. It firstly enabled him to build up the analytic / cognitive, reflective side of his spirituality. Secondly, he began to find himself moving into a cultural narrative very different from his home community. The resulting value conflict enabled further reflection and the development of self-critique.

None of this is to underestimate the difficulty faced by a sociopath. It is to say that moral meaning for one who is shameless will only develop significantly with the development of empathy and this in turn demands inclusion and participation in community.

## Conclusions

The case for moral intervention in pastoral care and counselling has not been made. Moral reflection and the development of moral meaning emerges directly from a relationship based upon agape. The hottest of hot seat confrontations is one which is based upon the common understanding of that relationship. This calls the person back to the relationship, and clearly points out places where the other is not responding with integrity, such as not taking responsibility. That is the whole point of reflective confrontation, that the self deception and self defeating behaviour is revealed. That is not moral rebuke or moral direction. Dialogue is at the core, especially with the development of spiritual meaning. This dialogue calls the person back to the relationship enabling her to discover meaning in the contract or the interactions, perhaps reminding the person what she had committed herself to, perhaps realising this for the first time.

### References
W. Bridges, Transitions: Making Sense of Lifes Changes (Reading Mass: Addison-Wesley, 1980).

D. Browning, The Moral Context of Pastoral Care (Philadelphia: Westminster, 1976).

W. Carr, The Pastor as Theologian (London: SPCK, 1989).

H. Clinebell, Basic Types of Pastoral Care or Counselling (London: SCM, 1983).

R. Duffy, A Roman Catholic Theology of Pastoral Care (Philadelphia: Fortress, 1983).

J. Fowler, Faithful Change (Nashville Abingdon, 1996).

J. Hoffman, Ethical Confrontation in Counseling (Chicago: Chicago University Press, 1979).

R. Kegan, The Evolving Self: Problem and Process in Human Development (Cambridge Mass: Harvard University Press, 1982).

H. Lewis, Shame and guilt in neurosis (New York: International Universities Press, 1971).

H. Nouwen, D. McNeill, and D. Morrison, Compassion (London: Darton, Longman and Todd, 1984).

T. Oden, Care of Souls in the Classic Tradition, (Philadelphia: Fortress, 1984).

S. Pattison. A Critique of Pastoral Care (London: SCM, 1988).

J. Poling, The Abuse of Power (Nashville: Abingdon, 1991).

C. Schneider, Shame R.Hunter (ed.) Dictionary of Pastoral Care and Counselling (Nashville: Abingdon, 1990). 1160-1163.

T. Scheff and S. Ratzinger, Emotions and violence: Shame and rage in destructive conflicts (Lexington Mass: Lexington Books, 1991).

J. Thompson Jr., 'Shame in Pastoral Psychotherapy', Pastoral Psychology, Vol. 44, No. 5, 1996, 311-320.

R. Underwood, Empathy and Confrontation in Pastoral Care (Philadelphia: Fortress, 1985).

J. Vanier, Community and Growth (London: Darton, Longman and Todd, 1979).

D. van deusen Hunsinger, Theology and Pastoral Counselling (Grand Rapids: Eerdmans, 1995).

# 8

## Counselling and Justice: The Rust on the Razor

James Fowler's final level of shame, often ignored in pastoral care, is that arising from 'enforced minority status'. He refers to Maya Angelou's autobiographical novel *I Know Why The Caged Bird Sings* and to one scene where Angelou, the schoolgirl, has to recite a poem before the Colored Methodist Episcopal Church on Easter Sunday. As she struggles with remembering the poem her thoughts turn to her dress:

*'The dress I wore was lavender taffeta, and each time I breathed it rustled, and now that I was sucking in air to breath out shame it sounded like crepe paper on the back of hearses.*

*As I'd watched Momma put ruffles on the hem and cute little tucks around the waist, I knew that once I put it on I'd look like a movie star (It was silk and that made up for the awful colour.). I was going to look like one of those sweet little white girls who were everybody's dream of what was right with the world. Hanging softly over the black Singer sewing machine, it looked like magic, and when people saw me wearing it they were going to run up to me and say, "Marguerite [sometimes it was 'dear Marguerite'], forgive us, please, we did not know who you were", and I would answer generously, "No, you couldn't have known. Of course I forgive you".*

*Just thinking about it made me go round with angel's dust sprinkled over my face for days. But Easter's early morning sun had shown the dress to be a plain ugly cut-down from a white woman's once-was-purple throwaway. It was old lady long too, but it did not hide my skinny legs, which had been greased with Blue Seal Vaseline and powdered with the Arkansas red clay. The age-faded color made my skin look dirty like mud, and everyone in church was looking at my skinny legs.*

*Wouldn't they be surprised when one day I woke up out of my black ugly dream, and my real hair, which was long and blond, would take the place of the kinky mass that Momma wouldn't let me straighten? My light blue eyes were going to hypnotize*

*them after all the things they said about "my daddy must have been a Chinaman"*
*(I thought they meant made out of china, like a cup) because my eyes were so small*
*and squinty. Then they would understand why I had never picked up a Southern*
*accent, or spoke the common slang, and why I had to be forced to eat pig's tails and*
*snouts. Because I was really white and because a cruel fairy stepmother, who was*
*understandably jealous of my beauty, had turned me into a to big Negro girl, with*
*nappy black hair, broad feet and a space between her teeth that would hold a num-*
*ber two pencil* (Fowler 1996, p. 121).

This scene superbly illustrates the juxtaposition and mutual reinforcement of different kinds of shame. There is the shame associated with
adolescence. The physicality of this is underlined in Angelou's last line,
where she is ill at ease with her body. This sense of vulnerability has echoes
of the Genesis story where Adam and Eve are suddenly aware of their bod-
ies, are ashamed and need to hide them.

However, alongside this innocent shame, Angelou was vulnerable to
shame which was ascribed to her, shame which was to do with class, race
and possibly gender. Angelou graphically sums this up:

'If growing up is painful for the Southern Black girl, being aware of the
displacement is the rust on the razor that threatens the throat. It is an
unnecessary insult' (Fowler 1996).

In fact, the shame which Angelou experiences is that of negative difference. Her ethnic roots do not provide a background and narrative of which
she can be proud. Instead, she yearns for a different narrative summed up in
the images of the pretty white girls, images which promise inclusion and
power. It is part of a complex experience. At one level this may be reinforced
and made more acute by other experiences of shame, such as toxic or perfectionist shame. At another level the shame is reinforced by a series of public
stimuli - ranging from the media images of what is 'cool' to the specific structures of power which seek to marginalize groups - formally or informally.

Several writers stress the importance of not simply seeing the pastoral
domains in the individualistic or curative sense (Graham 1992, Pattison
1988, Poling 1993, Selby 1983, Couture and Hunter 1995). There is a need
to add to the individual or therapeutic model of care social perspectives and
action which enable social and economic justice, equality and anti-discrim-
inatory practices. Care of persons also demands care of attention to the
world and the social environment in which they live. Such care will critique
both the power structures themselves and the underlying values which
maintain them (Tawney 1972, 46).

In one sense this view is unexceptionable. The impetus of agape is towards shalom, hence the idea of pastoral care which does not take justice into account is odd. Nonetheless, major questions are raised about the balance between love and justice and how this is worked through in pastoral care and counselling. To focus purely on the individual as Halmos, for instance does, thus excluding the political from pastoral care, denies the spirituality of the person and how they are affected by and in turn affect their network of relationships and meaning (Halmos 1964). To focus purely on the issue of justice and liberation from oppressive culture and values can take away from individual responsibility not least for addressing and clarifying values. Moreover, the oppressed person in many cases espouses values which are contrary to the narrative of justice and liberation. A good example of this is those who experience poverty. On the face of it they clearly experience economic oppression. However, the associated stigma of poverty is such that many do not see themselves as one of the poor (Forrester and Skene 1988, p. 25ff). Rather do they identify poverty with fecklessness and espouse an ethic of self-reliance, independence, and honour marked by a reluctance to take, or to be seen taking, charity. It is important not to underestimate such ethical identity, and the associated strength of feeling.

This is not simply a matter of the person uncritically accepting the values of the prevailing socio-political ethos. It involves a complex dialogue between different narratives, affective, cognitive and social, which might express group solidarity as much as individual identity. Often all the narratives and the resulting dynamics are uncritically accepted. Hence, simply to change social organisation is not enough. Liberation demands enabling the person or group to reflect on and critique all the different narratives in the situation.

Three short cases will be reviewed to examine the complex relationships between justice and care in the counselling context. I will conclude with a reflection on justice, prophecy and truth in contemporary society and the relationship of this to counselling. The cases involve:

1. Justice in the work place, and work values.
2. Justice and homosexuality. Some would argue that this is a matter of justice, in which the church at pastoral and ethical level should stand out against the oppression of homosexuals. Others argue for the primacy of ethical standards.
3. Justice and abortion. Once more the liberationists argue for freedom from the oppression of grand narratives.

## Workplace justice

*Geoff came to the his vicar suffering from work based stress. Geoff was aged 55 and had been under pressure at work for some years as head of his section. New management had led to a change in operations. The new head of department was putting him under further pressure. She increased targets, took away several staff from his section, and introduced more stringent quality control. At the same time, she subjected him to gruelling interviews trying to persuade him to take early retirement. Anyone over 50 was being targeted, but he as head of section felt particularly vulnerable. The stress was affecting his family life and now was beginning to affect his work functioning. He was losing concentration and having to stay later at work. In turn this caused him to lose his temper with colleagues and deadlines were not being met. The response of his department head to this was to put more pressure on. He felt that she was trying to oust him, that this amounted to harassment. Geoff was anxious and depressed and felt he was losing his sense of identity and life meaning.*

Three narrative strands began to emerge in the counselling. Firstly, Geoff suffered from perfectionist shame. As an administrator in a large public service organisation he took tremendous pride in meeting the deadlines and in the matters of fine detail being worked out. Not to finish it was a sign of failure. In the work context this developed into a strong form of the Protestant Work Ethic (PWE), with great stress on the need for resilience, self reliance and achievement (Furnham 1990).

Closely allied to this was a sense of vocation and identity connected to the public service ethos. He had internalised the values of a public service organisation and was proud to provide the support necessary for its functioning. He valued the tradition of this organisation and the sense of community and collaboration. His sense of life purpose was more in this area than with his family.

The third narrative was that being imposed on him by the new management. This was about customer care, quality control and maximising value. The ethos of this was task rather than person centred and the operation had a degree of transparency which Geoff was not used to. Such values were becoming part of the culture of the organisation as a whole and were clearly reinforcing his perfectionist shame.

In addition the fact that his head was a woman was very disturbing. She was attractive and younger than he. Previous heads had been older and authority had been easy to accept. Indeed, power relationships had been understood without any need to negotiate or set out expectations.

Further reflection showed:

1. Geoff had internalised the values of the institution's tradition with its stress on community. These values felt safe and purposeful. He also felt a part of that community along with a sense of status and position. He had also internalised the PWE, something which reinforced and was reinforced by the perfectionist shame. In a real sense it was this which held together his position in the organisation.

When he began to reflect he noted how the work practices had changed but that the previous regime had not been free from pressure. In fact stress had become institutionalised. His department and section were given responsibilities that it was almost impossible to achieve. The result was that the organisation took advantage of the good nature of such as Geoff. He would work, along with his staff, for several weeks, seven days a week and 12 hours a day, to meet deadlines. At first, he sought to justify this in terms of his moral world. 'It was worth it in the end if we knew that all was being done well, and somehow you knew you were being valued'. Further reflection, however, revealed that the dynamic was exploiting not simply the good nature but the perfectionist shame. Moreover, as Geoff went on it became clear that he had been very much part of the whole dynamic. Just as the management had put intense pressure on him so he placed intense pressure on his section members to try to hit the deadlines to please the management. He noted the high turn over of staff in his section and also the high sickness rate. Invited to reflect further on this, he became increasingly uncomfortable and began to articulate a sense of unease about the way in which he had been treating his colleagues. In effect, he had colluded in a form of emotional abuse. He had accepted the abuse from his superiors as they played on his 'good nature' and in turn had abused his work force. Like the dynamic of abuse in families, this also built up a wall of secrecy around the section. No-one in the department dare articulate their distress, and so the problem was suppressed.

For Geoff this was a major moment in becoming aware of his own moral world and how it affected others and led to a major reassessment of his views of justice.

2. The arrival of the new head did two things. Firstly, it disturbed his sense of order generally, not least introducing the questions of sexuality and gender. He found it hard to work with someone in authority who he found so attractive. He also found it hard to accept the authority of a woman. This caused great tension for him. Secondly, the new management approaches were very

hard to handle. The openness to quality control was perceived by him as constant criticism. 'I am always being told that I do not meet my targets'. His conclusion was that they did not want him there, that he had no value. The priest helped him to test out these perceptions. What emerged was not a sense of the management being 'after him' or questioning his worth but something more impersonal, a sense that they did not really care about persons in particular. At the same time he could begin to see some important reasons for the management style, not least the need to react to economic problems outside the organisation. The management style then was in an impersonal way placing even more stress on a man who already had grown used to immense stress as a way of life, and as part of proving his value.

Thirdly, though the question of injustice was beginning to be clarified into many different strands, the priest encouraged Geoff to begin to articulate practice and process which were unacceptable, which could be viewed as unjust or harassment. He was able to keep a diary and log occasions when unacceptable pressure was applied, either through an implied threat to his job, or through interviews from his head which disempowered him in some way. In effect, Geoff was working through in practice his view of what constituted injustice. This was facilitated by the dialogue between the different narratives and the careful reflective testing of the priest.

3. Geoff then spent some time beginning to think through how he might respond. Initially, he had been very angry and wanted to blame his head for everything and to simply bring her to justice. He began, however, from much further back by reassessing his value and working on the shame. In working this through he developed a far more balanced view of justice, as relational, and began to reflect on the options of how this could be achieved. These ranged from 'facing up to reality', and accepting that he could do nothing and so looking for the best and most lucrative way out of the firm. Another was to begin to see how he might change and how he might influence his work environment to change.

The first of these involved developing Geoff's personal power in facing up to his head of department. The sense of powerlessness he felt in meetings with her had running beneath it anger and resentment. He explored this anger and was encouraged to express it in the counselling sessions. The articulation helped him to recognise the underlying dynamics and to accept that they were part of the relationship. It also helped him to focus on his role and the particular aspects of their relationship, and how they worked, which would need to be re-negotiated. This would mean confronting her with examples of ageism. An important part of this process was the development of assertiveness skills.

A second way was to examine collaborative power and how this might effect change. One obvious way of moving into this was through union or harassment counsellor work. Neither was very acceptable to Geoff, partly due to the perfectionist shame, not least the shame of admitting that a women was 'harassing' him. Such services were also a very different world from the work traditions he was used to. Another approach to collaboration was to begin to change the way his section operated. There was to be a review of the department in the near future. He feared this was a way of getting rid of him. However, in the light of his reflection on justice, he began to explore the possibilities of using this as an opportunity for change which would enable him to listen more closely to his section members, to include them in the process of management, and to develop work practices which would value the members and not abuse their goodwill. In a real sense, this involved a process in the work place of forgiveness and reconciliation. The initial work done before the review was such that Geoff began to see very real hope for a meaningful last 10 years in the job.

Equally important in the developing of these workplace values and practice was the fact that he began to see how his Christian faith fitted in with his work. Prior to this, work and faith were totally different worlds. There was very little life meaning in the practice of either world. Now his spirituality began to find meaning in both together.

The development of integrity and shalom in the section and between the section and the head did take place and had the effect of showing management that he, Geoff, could manage and meet the targets effectively. However, the concern for relational justice did not end there. Geoff felt that there was greater need to work on the culture of the firm as a whole. This meant him looking at wider collaboration with human resources and the union representatives to look at work organisation that could effectively empower the work force. This led to a review of whistle-blowing policy. Whistle-blowing tends to be seen as adversarial, involving disloyalty to the corporation. Greater transparency and trust between different levels of management enable an approach which is based more on mutual learning (Armstrong *et al.*, 1999, 53-58).

## Homosexuality

*Jean came to see her work place chaplain 'to talk about' her sexuality. She was clearly uncomfortable articulating these thoughts, but even more uncomfortable in her church. She was an evangelical Christian, who valued her tradition and did not want to simply turn her back on it - 'It is a matter of integrity'. At the same time she was feeling angry and increasingly marginalised by her fellow Christians. She was always aware of the heterosexual frame of reference they operated in. Those who she told of her orientation respected her and then simply assumed that she would be celibate. She resented this and wanted to engage them in dialogue but did not feel right in making this an issue of justice.*

*Nonetheless, things became more difficult with evidence of homophobia when the youth work co-ordinator asked her to stand down as a youth leader. The co-ordinator had learned of her orientation and said that though she had every confidence in her, the church members would find it hard to have a homosexual in a position that might influence young people. She did not know how to face that without becoming very angry, and so spoiling any attempt to bring together her Christian practice and sexual orientation. She was left confused and powerless, neither aware of where the sin was in her orientation nor how to handle her relationships in the church.*

Jean began to work through her relationship network and how it affected her view of value and truth:

1. *The family.* The family for her had been a place of great security. One of three children, she developed a conditional script which demanded high achievement in all things especially academic work. This had developed into a form of perfectionist shame.

When she revealed her orientation to her parents she had been given great cognitive support, but their body language had shown a sense of shock. Jean did not take this further with them but felt intense pain at a physical and emotional level. Her brother died several years earlier and her elder sister showed no signs of marrying or having family. She believed that she was the only hope of her parents for a grandchild, something they had often spoken of. The sense of failure, being unable to please her parents was palpable. The counsellor enabled Jean to work on this conditional ethic. Homosexuality for her at this affective level had become associated with failure and shame.

At the same time, the concern for perfect performance had put great stress on intellectual work and away from affective awareness. Hence, Jean had a degree of affective shame. A great deal of the feeling of marginalisation and confusion came from this narrative.

2. *The church.* Most of Jean's friends were part of the church and she had grown with them over her years at university to see the good life as involving

family. This was partly a reinforcement of the perfectionist shame that she felt within the family but also something about the stage of her faith. At this point she was very much in Fowler's fourth stage of faith, finding her faith identity in relation to group norms (Fowler 1996). She felt secure and accepted in a church which had sorted out its ethical and theological views.

Jean was now moving into a time of transition, seeing the security being eroded by attitudes towards her sexuality and beginning to see major 'fault lines' emerge in her faith. This feeling of being 'in between' made her sense of vulnerability increase, further needing the 'holding environment' of a pastoral counsellor to work through the transition.

Jean had to begin to address and challenge the conditional moral world of her relationships with her family and then move into reflection on the moral world of her church community. This involved looking at the nature of the community and the important security it gave to her. This did not mean, however, that she would have to agree with all the views of the community. At this point she began to see the different perspectives even within the evangelical church.

Jean was at great pains to reflect empathically on the different viewpoints, noting the fear and frustration which underlay them. She understood the frustration behind the Christian gay lobby and the sense of alienation, but did not see this as a good basis for articulating justice. She examined the pro-gay arguments in the light of agape and was happy with a theology of friendship which could begin to affirm the possibility of a life long relationship. The issue for her was about finding a fulfilling friendship rather than about justice or rights. The principle of gradualism for her was important, allowing others to come to terms with their fears. She was also clear that there was a danger in identifying sexuality too closely with human identity as a whole. Yes, this is a part of the person and yes, there is a real sense in which the person should affirm their sexuality, in its broadest sense. However, this is only part of what it is to be a person and the central value is about relationships. Because of this she was happy about the possibility of a celibate life style as there was no obvious partner. The issue would only be clarified when she was faced by love for an other.

Facing the more conservative narratives, Jean was happy to see the homosexual as different. There was sameness in the sense of a concern for a shared covenant ethic of long term love in partnership. However, the homosexual relationship was different and could not be seen as the same as heterosexual marriage.

She understood the intense fear of some heterosexuals, not simply about the question of difference but also in terms of normalising the homosexual relationship, not least through wedding services. Jean was happy about the idea of blessing a friendship, thus elevating a very important relationship which the church has tended to devalue. She was less happy about imitating wedding services, and trying to erase any difference.

Jean then concluded that she was happy holding together some moral insights which were often seen as contradictory. Fascinatingly, she felt great sympathy with the Anglican Bishops' document 'Issues in Human Sexuality', so often pilloried as contradictory, happy to hold on to a natural law approach which accepted heterosexuality as part of God's purpose in creation and to also to the affirmation of life long single sex partnership.

In holding on to this ambiguity, she was acknowledging the ethical complexity of the issue and taking seriously the ambiguity at its heart which cannot be resolved. She felt that this was an important contribution that she could make to the community, without having to leave. She was clear that this would tend to be a provisional ethical viewpoint, not least because she did not want to cause offence to others in the church.

As she reflected on the question of justice in building shalom, she also became clear that she would have to confront her community, not least about her expulsion from the youth team. Up to this point, she had not been able to stand up against this because her different underlying ethical narratives led to confusion. Now, she was in a position to confront. First, this involved a request for clarification from the person in question. The clarification was not convincing and Jean was able to challenge several of the assumptions made in it. The youth leader was still not convinced and Jean suggested that they talk it over with the pastor. This led, secondly, to a series of conversations which enabled the church leadership to overcome fears and doubts and so to clarify the issue for all in the church, and to bring Jean back on the team. This had involved reflective confrontation of the perceptions of the church, not least the belief that a homosexual might 'influence' young people. It also enabled the church to reflect on their policies and on how they treated homosexuals. The result was an important step forward ensuring that no one would be excluded from church groups unless there was evidence of harm or danger to others. Hence, this was an important step in the community taking responsibility for justice in its midst. The whole process also enabled Jean to define what justice was for her in practice.

# Abortion counselling

*Mary, a first year student and the daughter of a church warden in her home church, came to see her university chaplain. She could not speak with her church minister because she felt that he was too close, and she saw the chaplain as not representing the institution of the church. She revealed that a week before she had been confirmed pregnant. The father was a man with whom she had been in relationship since the first year of the sixth form, and she was drawing towards the end of her first year at university, with exams not far away. Her boyfriend was at another university and had told her recently that he wanted to review their relationship. Mary was doing languages and had to make a decision within the next few days as to where she would go for her year abroad.*

*She had been thinking about some placement with the EEC as her hope was to go into top flight interpretation work.*

*Faced by all of these factors and the need to make up her mind quickly, Mary looked shocked and depressed. 'Whichever way I turn I am lost'.*

The chaplain realised the importance of speed and began to help Mary to articulate her narrative and identify the underlying values:

*Family.* All her family, but especially her father, saw her as the great hope of the family, not least because Mary's brother had never achieved in academia or in his career. Clarification of this showed a strong perfectionist shame. Not to achieve success at university or in her career would be a failure to her father. Showing affection or sharing feelings was also not encouraged, and from this emerged general disapproval of Mary's boyfriends. Her present one was seen as a bad influence and not the kind of person who would help her to pursue success. The consequence was that Mary felt that she had never quite got things right for her parents, and that they always were a little ashamed of her.

*Church.* Mary had been a church-goer up until university. At this point she began to strongly argue against the views of the church. This had included strong ethical argument which was pro-choice. To her surprise she found that now she was pregnant she felt very guilty. She began to speak in the language of punishment as if this were a judgement for moving away from the church and from her parents. This all reinforced her perfectionist shame.

*Career.* Career was very much her means of pleasing her parents. The possibility that she could lose this made her feel panicky. At the same time the career plans that she mapped out did give a strong feeling of purpose and worth.

*Partner.* Mary's partner had seemed the answer to her prayers. What attracted her to him was that he was non-confrontational. He never set down an agenda that she had to live up to and seemed to value her for herself. The two could have fun in an unaffected way that was not possible in her family. She saw him as a saviour and learned from him the capacity to share feelings. He was, however, not responsible and she found herself increasingly caring for him - mothering him. Faced by the pregnancy he had simply walked away to 'try to get my head round this'.

*Medical narrative.* Mary had not been helped by the medical process that she had been through. Her doctor saw this as a matter of fact case where abortion was indicated. He did not begin to help her address the feelings. Mary had asked about counselling but he had not referred her. He inferred that counselling was only necessary if the patient felt upset.

This may not be a typical medical response. It did however sum up the dangers of the medical model of health, that of medical intervention as the solution to problems. As Harrison notes, this can reinforce a patriarchal medical system and take away the autonomy of the patient, or at the least discourage real reflection, or the development of decision making process (Harrison 1987).

The core of Mary's problem was precisely that she was faced by too many narratives all of which were trying to control her and she had no clear sense of how to judge between them or to find a moral meaning which would really allow her to feel integrity and also allow the development of right relationships with all involved. Working through these relationships she began to see hope emerging:

a. She realised how much of her values were about pleasing her parents and accepted that she would have to do some longer term work to begin to move away from that ethic to one that she was responsible for. She had been moving into that transition at a cognitive level but her emotions were still locked in to the conditional ethic. This meant rebuilding her relationship with her parents on a different footing.

b. Mary realised that her reliance upon her boyfriend had been a response to the lack of emotional nurture in her family. Parental disapproval had made her firmer in her resolution to stay with him and she had fantasised about marrying him and having a family. She felt that she had used him to work through some of her problems and that, accepting though he was, he could not challenge her or begin to take responsibility for any crisis. The right thing she felt was to effect closure of that relationship.

c. As Mary focused on her relationship with the foetus she found it hard to develop any empathy for it. The only imaginative projection to the future had been for a moment when she first heard the result, when she pictured herself and her boyfriend happily married with child. Reflecting on this, she felt that she may have allowed this to happened in an attempt to push him into commitment and so resolve all her problems. The foetus for her was a thing without reality and without integrity, something which she felt was being used as a means to an end - an end, moreover, based on self deception. She was also faced with a rising sense of fear, about her own capacity to care for a child. The chaplain helped to test the reality of this and what resources there might be available if the child were kept.

d. At this point she began to reflect more deeply on the demands of the church and how this was relating to the other narratives. As her perfectionist narrative moved into dialogue with the church narrative, it became clear that the bad feeling about abortion was based more in the shame about failure than in any values she had worked through. Beginning to return the shame narrative to its origins was therefore very important in the move towards making a decision about abortion. Importantly, once she began to do this it did not automatically mean that the she would choose against abortion. The effect was to enable her to critique the affective and cognitive moral narratives and so enable her to focus on and develop her own moral meaning.

In reflecting on the church narratives, this also enabled her to see how many different ones there were in the church. In a relatively short space of time, she was able to look at the development of the different narratives. It became clear, for instance, that the there were two strands running throughout church history, one holding that the foetus was the moral equivalent to the child it would become, one seeing it as of a different moral order (Neuger 1995, 126). Importantly early church law canon law suggested that whilst abortion was not approved, it was not murder. This applied to the unanimated foetus. Animation or ensoulment took place at 40 days for the male and 80 for the female. As the gender of the foetus was not obvious until about the fourth month then all could be claimed to be female, thus allowing abortion which was not murder until 80 days (Whitney 1991, 43). Such reflection helped her to begin to see the moral ambiguity in abortion. Yes, it was a serious matter but not equivalent to murder. All of this led Mary to see the issue not in polarised terms such as rights versus duties or life versus murder.

Mary's decision then to abort the foetus was not taken lightly. It was also not the end point of the pastoral process. Just as the choice to keep the foetus would have demanded support, so abortion involved the chaplain continuing to offer counselling. This provided the supportive environment for her to carry forward the development of life meaning and establish the change in relationships. It included a letting go of the foetus and a service helping her to express awareness and repentance for the whole situation.

Justice in all this was not simply a matter of asserting rights, of Mary or her foetus. It was far more a question of enabling her to reflect and work through the particular moral demands of her situation. Faced by many competing narratives the danger was precisely that she did not have the freedom to decide (Harrison 1987).

## Conclusions

These three cases have several factors in common. Firstly, they demonstrate that the situation is invariably more complex than simply the need to liberate people from the 'dynamics of racism, classism and sexism' (Neuger 199, 137). The power of any of these is not unidimensional but rather feeds off and maintains a deeper level of shame, something which emerges from the interaction between the narratives of home, peer group, school, work and so on. The very power of dynamics of racism and so on is lessened if the other shame dynamics are dealt with. It is significant that the stress on liberation focuses on the systemic, the corporate and the cognitive. Changes at these levels are important but they precisely do not engage the affective dimension of person or the need for the person to take responsibility in her relation to any major narrative. Moreover, whilst a narrative of subversion which critiques the negative narratives is important, it can never be truly effective without empathy. It is empathy for the self and the other which enables a full awareness of the interpersonal dynamics, and of the whole situation.

Secondly, it follows that there are no quick answers. The 'issues' of homosexuality and abortion are too dense and complex for simple judgements, and there is need to come to terms with ambiguity. Simple appeal to consequences is not satisfactory any more than simple appeal to principles. We can never know the consequences. The fears of homosexuals influencing individuals or culture, for instance, have no basis in evidence.

Thirdly, these cases confirm that there is no objective moral truth that we can appeal to. The gradualism of moral theology claims that there is a dialogue between subjective and objective (Gula 1997). The term objective assumes that there is some fixed truth that is not dependant upon perception, and the things which affect perception. However, I cannot know the other, including any situation, in an 'objective' way, apart from my own feelings, ideas and physicality, and the life meaning which I have generated from them, and apart from the perspectives of others. More than that, to know the other demands empathy, enabling the revelation of the other and a relationship of mutual discovery. In the same way, I cannot know moral truth apart from an awareness of the values of others and their life meaning. That awareness will continuously test and refine my life meaning, developing an awareness of shared meaning and meaning which is particular to the situation or the person.

Each side in the moral justice debates tends to want to see their view as universal. But the challenge of agape and empathy is to see the ambiguity at the heart of any issue of justice and to live with that creatively. It is true that a homosexual relationship can express real covenant love (Anglican Bishops 1996). It also true that homosexuality is different from heterosexuality and the evidence points strongly to procreative sexuality as central to created order. Accepting both truths demands that they are held together in an ethical response which embodies both.

This forces us to an ethic which is about shalom and about the embodiment of justice. The moral field itself is transformed. We are no longer doing battle over a single issue, but rather trying to relate to the whole social network, enabling all to be involved in change and in ethical response. The meaning of justice is worked out in practice, leading ultimately to a change in structures and the values which underlie them. Justice in this sense is defined by agape (Tillich 1954), and as Riceour argues 'justice is the efficacious, institutional and social realisation of love' (Bonino 1983, 114). Whilst the institutions of justice, with their concerns for rights etc., can never fully embody such love this means that Christians can never serve simply under the banner of love and not justice, as Woodhead would argue (Woodhead 1992, 61). Not only does the impetus to shalom demand that justice is sought in right relationships, agape also gives Christians a particular view of justice and its meaning which should be proclaimed as part of the dialogue on the practice of justice. A sign of such justice is that it looks to set up process and structure which enable all concerned to reflect on and wrestle with the meaning and practice of justice. Justice then remains critical at personal and societal levels.

# Prophecy

It remains tempting to make a strong distinction between prophecy and pastoral care and counselling. Prophecy in this model is about standing out for truth and against injustice. Pastoral care is about enabling the person to come to their own mind. Without the prophecy, it is argued, we will lose moral meaning in society, something just as important as respect for the freedom of the counsellee. Such prophecy is also about standing out for the oppressed, the ones who have no power to stand for themselves, and as such it has involves advocacy and may be adversarial.

Such a view of prophecy in the 21st century is fatally flawed. Firstly, it ignores the competing prophets, even within the church. As Cardinal Winning seeks to protect the foetus, so Beverly Harrison seeks to protect the woman - with both parties seen as oppressed. The reality at that level is once more pluralistic, and the attempt to see one of these views as universal is to fly in the face of that. Secondly, the adversarial prophetic model has an epistemological arrogance which presumes a clear vision of all aspects of the situation. As noted above, it is very difficult in pastoral care to discover the truth about a situation without personal reflection and dialogue with others. The same is true of prophecy on a national or international scale. The prophets, in their urge to protect can easily lead to a constant debate simply about the status of the evidence. A good example of this is the Nestle baby milk substitute case. There, data gathering has been dogged for over twenty five years by the inability of the different groups to work together. The value of the data collected then becomes corrupted. As the pastoral model shows, data collection is most effective when collaborative, and when the different parties are open to the possibilities of the data.

Thirdly, prophecy is most effective when the different parties recognise similar or complementary values. The adversarial model of prophecy is such that the values of the other are doubted or ignored. The dynamic tends to be one of demonisation. There is in this dynamic a form of 'moral panic'. The prophetic group must do all it can to save the victim. If there is a victim then there must be someone who is responsible. The responsible group is most often perceived as the most powerful, such as government, church or multinational. Hence, so the logic goes, the responsible group must be controlled and brought to book. Such a group inevitably is seen as having no values, or at best values which go against the safety of the victim.

A fourth problem with the adversarial model of prophecy is the inability to move to a recognition of and negotiation of responsibility. Because the data and the values are seen in polarised terms, responsibility is seen to be that of the power group. This can lead to ignoring the responsibilities of other stakeholders and thus the possibilities of empowering them in a creative response which builds up relational justice. With a collaborative model of prophecy the aim is to empower all who are involved to take part in all levels of ethical reflection, from data gathering, to value clarification, to responsibility negotiation, to response. All involved then take on the mantle of prophecy, contributing to moral meaning through the development of shalom (Robinson 1994).

Adversarial prophecy has many of the marks of moral panic. Each tends to focus on single issues and be concerned for rapid results. Each tends to demonize and find someone to blame rather than spend time in reflection. Each assumes an objectivity in moral truth and justice and fears the loss of moral meaning and with that either anarchy or take over by power groups. Collaborative prophecy seeks to widen the reflection and empower the prophets, something which builds up moral confidence along with moral meaning, shared and developed around practical response.

## Summing Up

This book began with Julia Buckroyd asserting the incompatibility of freedom and moral meaning in pastoral counselling. Such a view only makes sense if we accept a view of Christian Ethics which is *a priori* and a view of the church which is one of asserting such an ethic through discipline and teaching. I have suggested that it is impossible to view Christian ethics in this way. Based in the moral imperative of agape, it is concerned about an ethic which begins with recognition of the humanity of the other and from that accepts responsibility for her. Such responsibility is the starting point of ethical thinking, and the practical content of that thinking is not pre-determined. On the contrary, agape demands that the individual be her own moral interpreter, working through how she responds to the other. Such a response is not about individual effort but rather a social response, with the individual as part of a mutually responsible community. Hence, the moral agent has to look both to the other and to his community in working this through. This view of Christian Ethics suggests an ethic of outcomes or fruits, involving transformation of the person, the community and the other as each is faced with the call and claim of the other. At the core of this ethic is the impetus to integrity and shalom, stressing the unconditional value of the person, and the value of her contribution to that shalom. This links together personal value and moral meaning. The ethical process embodies the content, which stresses a dynamic community of principles including equality, in the sense of mutuality, inclusive community, and freedom. Such principles have profound meaning and yet can only find their full meaning in practice and through reflection on practice, just as the common humanity of the other can only be recognised in awareness of the particular. This means finding meaning through dialogue with and participation in communities.

In the light of this, freedom is not incompatible with Christian ethics but rather central to it. This is not freedom in a limited sense of autonomy, either freedom of choice or freedom from coercion, but something far richer and complex:

- Freedom from the tyranny of shame and sin. As Jean Vanier notes, this is a freedom based in truth which means that the person no longer has to expend energy on the protection of the false self, and is no longer dominated by narrative of shame (Vanier 1999, 120ff.). Central to such freedom is the development of empathy and the capacity to transcend the self.
- Freedom based in the truth of the situation enables the person to accept what is, the reality of the situation which cannot be changed. This is the freedom to live with ambiguities, and not having to resolve them, the freedom to be the self in spite of the pain and suffering which might be still there. It is a freedom which does not demand some magical lifting of pain or magical cure.
- Freedom to belong. Many who approach counselling feel they are consigned to the margins of community. They do not feel they have permission to belong. Agape brings the freedom to trust, to know that you belong.
- Freedom to be responsible for the self and others. Such responsibility is virtually impossible if it is seen only as an individualistic thing. Being part of a community means mutual responsibility and thus that possibility that the demands and claims of others can be recognised, appreciated and responded to. This freedom is essentially social.
- Freedom to work out purpose and make meaning. This dynamic involves the articulation of the personal narrative, the development of the capacity to value and critique that narrative, an explicit and positive letting go the old moral world, whether its meaning was explicit or

implicit, and creating and recreating moral meaning, through critical reflection on narratives and through practice.

- Freedom to create. The moral response is not simply to 'a problem' but rather to the relational network. Through collaborative response to the network the capacity to create and develop shalom becomes possible.

Such a freedom is in essence a moral freedom in and through which moral meaning is tested, practised, affirmed and developed.

If the first part of the process enabled the awareness of reality which is given, and provided the basis for change, this final part looks to the generating of possibilities and the creation of reality. This is a freedom which can begin to make a difference. If the first part was beginning to handle the aporia which are part of life and cannot be resolved, this final freedom enables aporia which exist because of sin and shame to be resolved. Such resolution involves both a critique of the old narrative and the development of a new ethical narrative. This involves an explicit letting go of the old narrative. The process itself further creates and deepens moral meaning. It is a process which reveals more surprises because it means as the collaborative work moves forward so the other discloses his or herself even more through the action.

- Freedom to be. Central to such freedom is the development of the virtues. Trust enables the development of the narrative, empathy the development of truth and hope the development of imagination and different possibilities.
- Freedom to learn. Awareness of limitations and possibilities, the development of the capacity to accept and critique all enable the person to learn and so to change. With this is the freedom to take risks, not least the risk of disclosing the self, the risk of trusting an other, and the risk of being faithful to the other, waiting for her response.

At the heart of such freedom is grace. This is not grace as a 'semi-material, infused substance' (Schwobel 2000, 278). It is rather the free gift of agape. The fact that the gift is genuinely free means that there is no attempt to control. At the same time, the gift has to be accepted freely, with no attempt on the part of the donee to control. This means that counselling or any pastoral care cannot assume that change will occur or attempt to manipulate change. It can only offer the care and enable the challenge. Assessing outcomes then becomes a matter of dialogue, not least in the negotiation of responsibilities.

The idea of grace extends to gracefulness, the image of the person who is co-ordinated, integrating cognitive, affective, somatic and social. Grace enables and emerges from the agapeic relationship, with timing and awareness arising from empathy.

Enabling this grace full change, this constant creation and recreation of moral meaning is what Vanier refers to as the 'accompanier' (Vanier 1999, 128). There is need for an other or more than one other, who can enable the person to lock into the transcendence which is known through the development of empathy. Part of the image here is of the companion who joins the person for some part of their spiritual and moral journey, helping her to make that journey. Equally interesting is the image of the accompanist. The accompanist provides the support for the singer to express her narrative. It is not simply the repetition of notes. Rather does the accompanist enter real dialogue with the singer, echoing phrases of the song, providing harmonies which deepen the meaning of the song, and together with the singer creating the affective and cognitive meaning of those words. It is this dialogue and reflection which enables change which maintains the continuity of personal identity and the development of meaning.

Ultimately God acts as such an accompanist, enabling us to create spiritual and moral meaning. The Incarnation, with the death and resurrection of Jesus embodies the faithfulness and truthfulness of God. The Trinity, embodies the mutual responsibility and responsiveness of community, enabling creative response. All this ends in a view of eschatology which is grounded in truthfulness and faithfulness, leading to judgement which is a function of the relationship, arising out of increased awareness of the truth.

At the heart of this is an ethical stance which starts from the position of forgiveness, and thus one which offers ultimate freedom, challenging all ethical narrative to go beyond the simply rational and find meaning which will always transcend the human horizon. In the light of that, all moral meaning in an ethically pluralistic world, including attempts to systematise or codify ethics, is inadequate. Agape requires that they be taken seriously and also seriously challenged. Testing ethical meaning in practice and against the ethical imperative and experience of agape lies at the heart of the counselling relationship.

### References
J. Armstrong, R. Dixon and S. Robinson, The Decision Makers: Ethics and Engineers (London: Thomas Telford, 1999).
J. Bonino, Towards a Christian Political Ethics (London: SCM, 1983).

P. Couture and R. Hunter, Pastoral Care and Social Conflict (Nashville: Abingdon, 1995).

L.K. Graham, Care of Persons, Care of Worlds (Nashville: Abingdon, 1992).

D. Forrester and D. Skene (eds.) Just Sharing (London: Epworth, 1988).

J. Fowler. Faithful Change (Nashville: Abingdon, 1996).

A. Furnham, The Protestant Work Ethic (London: Routledge, 1990).

R. Gula, Moral Discernment (New York: Paulist Press, 1997).

P. Halmos, The Faith of the Counsellors (London: Constable, 1964).

B. W. Harrison, Theology and Morality of Procreative Choice, in S. Lammers and A. Verhey, On Moral Medicine (Grand Rapids: Eerdmans, 1987). 422-33.

C. Neuger, 'The Challenge of Abortion', in P. Couture and R. Hunter (eds.), Pastoral Care and Social Conflict (Nashville: Abingdon, 1995), 125-140.

S. Pattison, A Critique of Pastoral Care (London: SCM, 1988).

J. Poling, The Abuse of Power (Nashville: Abingdon, 1993).

S. Robinson, 'Modern Business Ethics and Prophecy', Crucible, Oct-Dec1994, 189-203.

P. Selby, Liberating God (London: SPCK, 1983).

C. Schwobel, Grace, in A. Hastings (ed.). Oxford Companion to Christian Thought (Oxford; Oxford University Press, 2000). 276-278.

R. H. Tawney, The Commonplace Book, ed. J. Winter and D. Joslin (Cambridge; Cambridge University Press, 1972).

P. Tillich, Love, Power and Justice (Oxford: Oxford University Press, 1954).

J. Vanier, Becoming Human (London: Darton, Longman and Todd, 1999).

C. Whitney, Whose Life? (New York: William Morrow, 1991).

L. Woodhead, 'Love and Justice', Studies in Christian Ethics, 5:1 (1992), 44-61.

### Report
Anglican Bishops, Issues in Human Sexuality (Church House 1996).

# Index